Triumphant Death

Wesleyan and Methodist Explorations

EDITORS
Daniel Castelo
Robert W. Wall

DESCRIPTION

The *Wesleyan and Methodist Explorations* series will offer some of the best Methodist Wesleyan scholarship for the church and academy by drawing from active participants in the international guilds of Methodist scholarship (Oxford Institute of Methodist Studies, Wesleyan Theological Society, American Academy of Religion—Methodist Studies Section, and others).

There is an urgent need within Wesleyan Methodist scholarship for constructive theological work that will advance the field into interdisciplinary and creative directions. The potential for the series is vast as it will seek to establish possible future directions for the field.

Another key concern of this series will be to tap the emerging field of theological interpretation of Scripture located in and for particular ecclesial traditions. Theological interpretation offers insight to historical study, especially the reception of Scripture and its effects within the Methodist church, as well as exploring the epistemic gains to particular biblical texts and themes. Theological interpretation offers insight into the holy ends of these gains for the life of the church in worship, instruction, mission, and personal devotions for a people called Methodist.

The series will seek out great monographs, while also considering superior and adapted doctoral dissertations and well-conceived and tightly focused edited volumes.

EDITORIAL BOARD

Carla Works	Hal Knight III
Karen Winslow	Priscilla Pope-Levison
Sangwoo Kim	Sharon Grant
Matt Sigler	Frederick L. Ware
Ashley Dreff	Dennis Dickerson

Triumphant Death

Grace, Holiness, and Death in the Theology of John Wesley

Christine L. Johnson

CASCADE *Books* • Eugene, Oregon

TRIUMPHANT DEATH
Grace, Holiness, and Death in the Theology of John Wesley

Welseyan and Methodist Explorations

Copyright © 2025 Christine L. Johnson. All rights reserved. Except for brief quotations in critical publications or reviews, no part of this book may be reproduced in any manner without prior written permission from the publisher. Write: Permissions, Wipf and Stock Publishers, 199 W. 8th Ave., Suite 3, Eugene, OR 97401.

Cascade Books
An Imprint of Wipf and Stock Publishers
199 W. 8th Ave., Suite 3
Eugene, OR 97401

www.wipfandstock.com

PAPERBACK ISBN: 979-8-3852-3888-0
HARDCOVER ISBN: 979-8-3852-3889-7
EBOOK ISBN: 979-8-3852-3890-3

Cataloguing-in-Publication data:

Names: Johnson, Christine L., author.

Title: Triumphant death : grace, holiness, and death in the theology of John Wesley / Christine L. Johnson.

Description: Eugene, OR : Cascade Books, 2025 | Series: Wesleyan and Methodist Explorations | Includes bibliographical references.

Identifiers: ISBN 979-8-3852-3888-0 (paperback) | ISBN 979-8-3852-3889-7 (hardcover) | ISBN 979-8-3852-3890-3 (ebook)

Subjects: LCSH: Wesley, John, 1703–1791. | Death—Religious aspects—Christianity. | Theology, Doctrinal.

Classification: BX8495.W5 .J65 2025 (paperback) | BX8495.W5 (ebook)

VERSION NUMBER 100225

To my family for their unfailing love and support.

CONTENTS

Acknowledgments | xi

Abbreviations | xiii

Introduction | xv

Chapter 1   **Death in Eighteenth-Century England: John Wesley's Historical Context | 1**
Introduction | 1
Death in Eighteenth-Century England | 2
High Risk Populations | 4
Post-Reformation Attitudes Toward Death | 5
Ars Moriendi: Origins of the Tradition | 7
The Nature of English *Ars Moriendi* Literature | 9
Jeremy Taylor and the *Ars Moriendi* | 11
Dying and Holy Living | 12
Deathbed Temptations and Virtues | 14
Wesley's Sin of Fear | 16
Faith Overcoming Fear | 19
Conclusion | 23

Chapter 2   **Death: The Distortion of God's Design for Humankind | 24**
Introduction | 24
Creation: The Context for Understanding Death | 25
The *Imago Dei*: The Life of the Soul | 26
Natural Image | 28
Political Image | 29
Moral Image | 30
The Fall: Sin as the Harbinger of Death in All its Forms | 31

        Spiritual Death: The "Life of God" Lost | 32
        Original Sin: Spiritual Death Passed Down to the Human
           Race | 34
        Three Dimensions of Death and Depravity | 37
        Physical Death | 39
        The Mystery of Death | 40
        Sin: The Ongoing Cause of Physical Death | 41
        Death as Punishment | 44
        The Soul's Existence After Physical Death | 46
        Eternal Death: Total Separation from God | 50
        Conclusion | 52

Chapter 3   **Grace, Regeneration, and a Good Death | 54**
        Introduction | 54
        Sola Fide and Salvation | 55
        Free Grace | 56
        Free Grace and Cooperant Grace | 58
        Prevenient Grace as Free Grace | 59
        Prevenient Grace and Universal Redemption | 61
        Prevenient Grace, Universal Redemption, and Infant
           Mortality | 63
        Free Grace and the New Birth | 65
        Justifying Grace as Free Grace | 67
        Regenerating Grace as Free Grace | 69
        Instantaneous Conversion: A Fruit of Free Grace | 70
        Free Grace and the Holy Dying Tradition | 71
        Justification in the Holy Dying Tradition | 73
        Wesley in Contrast with His Contemporaries | 74
        Free Grace and the Gallows | 77
        Faith in the Face of Execution | 81
        Assurance in the Face of Death | 83
        Conclusion | 85

Chapter 4   **Progressive Sanctification: The Mortification
        of the Sinful Nature | 87**
        Introduction | 87
        The Remaining Sinful Nature | 88
        Progressive Sanctification | 91
        Progressive Sanctification and the Metaphor of Death | 93

Living the Dying Life | 94
Mortification of Self-Will | 96
Mortification of Worldly Desires | 97
The Process of Sanctification as Preparation for Physical
   Death | 99
Physical Death as a Motivation for Mortification | 100
Freedom from the Fear of Death | 102
Fears Inconsistent with Sanctifying Grace | 103
Fear That May Coincide with Sanctifying Grace | 105
Degrees of Assurance | 106
Conclusion | 107

Chapter 5   Entire Sanctification and Death | 108
Introduction | 108
Christian Perfection as the Highest Degree of Love | 109
Christian Perfection as Death to the Sinful Nature | 111
Christian Perfection Properly Explained | 115
The Body Is Not Sinful | 117
Physical Death Does Not Sanctify | 118
Christian Perfection as a Work of Free Grace | 123
Christian Perfection Instantaneously Given | 124
Believers Cannot Die Without Christian Perfection | 125
The Instantaneous Aspect as a Guard Against
   Complacency | 127
The Instantaneous as a Guard Against Works
   Righteousness | 129
Suffering Does Not Sanctify | 130
Christian Perfection as Happiness | 134
Happy Death | 136
Full Assurance | 137
Full Assurance and Fear of Death | 139
Desire for Death | 140
Christian Perfection and Children | 142
Conclusion | 143

**Chapter 6   Triumphant Death: The Culmination
of a Sanctified Life | 145**
Introduction | 145
Missional Purpose of the Deathbed Accounts | 146

      Analysis of Deathbed Accounts in the Arminian
         Magazine | 148
      Deathbed Genre | 151
      Methodist Pattern of Death | 151
      Acceptance of the Dying Role | 153
      Authority of the Deathbed Role | 155
      Examination of the Dying Person | 157
      How Do You Find Your Soul? | 158
      Are You Afraid to Die? | 159
      Are You Happy? | 160
      Are You Willing (Or Do You Desire) to Die? | 161
      Deathbed Examination and Christian Perfection | 163
      Triumph Over Death and Sin | 164
      Triumph over Pain | 167
      Triumph over Satan | 168
      Deathbed Testimony—A Gift to the Community | 170
      Deathbed Testimony—A Final Testament to Christian
         Perfection | 173
      John Wesley's Death—A Testimony to Holiness | 176

Conclusion | 180

Appendix   Death Accounts in the *Arminian Magazine* 1778 to February 1791 | 183

Bibliography | 195

ACKNOWLEDGMENTS

I would like to thank Asbury Theological Seminary for granting me the sabbatical leave to complete my manuscript as well as my colleagues at Asbury Theological Seminary for the encouragement and interest they took in this project. A special expression of gratitude belongs to Dr. Kenneth J. Collins and Dr. David Rainey (of Nazarene Theological College) for their guidance, stimulating conversation, and careful critique of my thought and writing. Their enthusiastic support of my work was invaluable. I also wish to thank Elizabeth Fink, a ThM student at Asbury Theological Seminary, for her assistance with reference material. Finally, I want to thank my family (Carl, Beth, Sue, Cindy, and Caiden) for their unwavering support.

ABBREVIATIONS

AM John Wesley, ed. *The Arminian Magazine.* vols. 1–14. London: Printed for the Editor, January 1778–February 1791.

(*BE*) Frank Baker, ed. *The Bicentennial Edition of the Works of John Wesley.* Nashville Abingdon, 1975-.

ENNT John Wesley. *Explanatory Notes Upon the New Testament.* Repr. London: The Epworth Press, 1954.

ENOT John Wesley. *Explanatory Notes Upon the Old Testament.* 3 vols. Repr. Salem: Schmul, 1975.

(Jackson) Thomas Jackson, ed *The Works of John Wesley.* 14 vols. Repr. Grand Rapids: Baker, 2007.

INTRODUCTION

THE MOTIF OF DEATH is an important theme in John Wesley's theology since it played a significant role in his journey of faith and consistently appeared in key places throughout his writings. At every major point along Wesley's *ordo salutis*—from the Fall, the new birth, the process of sanctification, and the work of Christian perfection—he addressed death in some manner. One of Wesley's main theological concerns was humanity's grace-enabled potential to overcome sin in this lifetime. Since he considered human death a direct result of sin, the places in his theology that addressed sin in its various forms often intersected with his understanding of death and the dying process. Wesley's perception of death was multifaceted; he defined death in three different senses: spiritual, physical and eternal.[1] Therefore, it should come as no surprise that he engaged death on a variety of levels. Death for Wesley was not simply the end of a life; it was a metaphor for spiritual realities, a tool to encourage holy living, and an opportunity to prove both the graciousness of God and the truthfulness of Wesley's teachings. In some ways, Wesley's view of the Christian life could be seen as triumph over sin and consequently death. Thus, a proper understanding of Wesley's variegated reflections on death is essential to appreciate fully his theology.

This book proposes that death was not only an important theme in Wesley's theology but that a comprehensive knowledge of his approach to death is essential to a full-orbed understanding of Wesley's overall conception of holiness and what it meant to be rightly related to God. Wesley utilized death to illustrate and support his crucial doctrines of free grace, the new birth, progressive sanctification and Christian perfection. This work seeks to identify the major intersections between death and these key doctrines and to explore the ramifications of Wesley's views. For example,

---

1. Wesley, *Doctrine of Original Sin, Part II* (BE), 12:220.

it was Wesley's reinterpretation of justifying and regenerating grace that caused him to stress the immediacy of salvation and thus transformed his ministry to the dying. What follows is a thorough investigation of Wesley's various observations on death which provides a window to his more well-known theological commitments.

This text consists of six chapters. Chapter 1 places Wesley within his historical context and explores death in eighteenth-century England. It brings to light the *ars moriendi* tradition, which was a fading, but vital, influence on the early modern English approach to death. This chapter demonstrates that Wesley was both positively and negatively influenced by Jeremy Taylor's works, *The Rule and Exercises of Holy Living* and *The Rule and Exercises of Holy Dying*.

Chapters 2 through 5 examine Wesley's notions of death in conjunction with his overarching theological commitments. Chapter 2 defines death in Wesley's terms and describes each aspect of Wesley's threefold view of death (spiritual, physical and eternal). Chapter 3 considers death in light of Wesley's understanding of free grace, preventing grace, justifying grace, and regenerating grace. This chapter proposes that Wesley's appropriation of free grace and his reinterpretation of justifying grace not only set him at odds with the holy dying tradition and his Calvinist counterparts, but it also opened the doors to his dynamic ministry among the dying—especially among condemned malefactors. Chapter 4 considers death in the context of co-operant, sanctifying grace and explores Wesley's understanding of progressive sanctification. Wesley considered freedom from the fear of death a vital aspect of the Christian experience; therefore, he proposed that the fear of death receded as one increased in holiness of heart and life. Chapter 5 focuses on Wesley's doctrine of Christian perfection. Wesley viewed death itself as emblematic of Christian perfection since the motif of death in his theology represents the instantiation of entire sanctification with the concurrent demise of the carnal nature. This imagery, combined with Wesley's insistence that believers must be entirely sanctified before the moment of death, inextricably linked his theology of death with his doctrine of perfection.

The sixth chapter examines how Wesley utilized the dying experiences of early Methodists to substantiate his theological beliefs. Wesley was convinced that entirely sanctifying grace empowered those perfected in love to confront their own physical death with sure confidence and trust in God. Therefore, he carefully selected accounts of believers whose dying experiences bore witness to this belief for publication in the *Arminian Magazine*. Chapter 6 is an examination of these accounts along with Wesley's own deathbed experience.

Considering that Wesley's emphasis on death, especially as it relates to his theology of holiness, has been largely overlooked, this book contributes a new perspective to the area of Wesley studies and Methodism.

Chapter 1

DEATH IN EIGHTEENTH-CENTURY ENGLAND
John Wesley's Historical Context

Introduction

"Death meets us every where, and is procured by every instrument, and in all chances, and enters in at many doors...."[1] This statement in the opening pages of Jeremy Taylor's *The Rules and Exercises of Holy Dying* succinctly captured the reality of death in eighteenth-century England. Without the advantages of modern medicine, life was precarious for everyone, but the motif of death played an especially significant role in the life of John Wesley. Indeed, even his name was a reminder of the uncertainty of life since he was the third son in his family to be christened "John." His two predecessors, for whom John was a namesake, had died in infancy, and all the hopes and dreams for his deceased brothers rested upon his shoulders.[2] This was not atypical since, like most of the eighteenth-century population, he was born into a family that lost nearly half of its children to death. What *was* notable was John's escape from a fiery death when he was only five years old. Wesley's father had already given him up for dead when the young boy was snatched from the second story window of the burning rectory. This

---

1. Taylor, *Rule and Exercises of Holy Dying*, 7.
2. See Anthony J. Headley's helpful description of how the death of the two earlier sons shaped the surviving John Wesley's life. Headley, *Family Crucible*, 46–47.

close encounter with death shaped Wesley's self-understanding and caused his mother to treat him with special favor.[3] It also earned him the life-long moniker, "a brand plucked out of the burning" (a reference to Amos 4:11 and Zech 3:2). Later in life, Wesley once again had a brush with death on a stormy sea en route to Georgia which exposed his deep-seated angst over the prospect of dying. He was drawn to literature which provided a wholistic Christian approach to death such as Jeremy Taylor's *The Rule and Exercises of Holy Dying*, but it did not ameliorate his fears. His experiences, combined with his terror of death, caused Wesley to embark on a spiritual quest to obtain a degree of faith which addressed his fears.

Death in Eighteenth-Century England

While Wesley's personal history undoubtedly shaped his attitude toward death, he was by no means alone in his aversion to death and his search to find a solution to his anxiety. Life was uncertain in eighteenth-century England, and many of his contemporaries were equally frightened at the seemingly capricious nature of death. Death was an ever-present part of life until the rise of modern medicine. Not only were the plagues still fresh in England's collective memory, but the most common illnesses or minor injuries could just as easily culminate in death as in a cure due to infection and the lack of effective medications.

There were, of course, medical regimens available for the sick. In fact, Wesley published his own volume of medical treatments called *Primitive Physick*, but these treatments were crude by today's standards and often largely ineffective. "Bleeding" and popular folk remedies were among the most common therapies. Unfortunately, some of the remedies for illness were more likely to kill than cure.[4] The eighteenth century witnessed advances in medical science such as the development of a smallpox vaccine. However, a pervading skepticism over the actual abilities of those in the medical profession abounded, and many people were reticent to accept the new treatments. Roy Porter suggested that one of the worst things an

---

3. After the fire, Susanna Wesley recorded, "And I do intend to be more particularly careful of the soul of this child that thou has so mercifully provided for than ever I have been, that I may do my endeavour to instill into his mind the principles of thy true religion and virtue." Wesley, *Susanna Wesley*, 235.

4. Mary Dobson noted that many remedies contained ingredients such as urine, dog feces, earthworms, and rotten eggs. Dobson, *Contours of Death and Disease*, 263.

eighteenth-century patient could do was summon the doctor, and witticisms such as "a young doctor fattens the churchyard" or "a physician is more dangerous than the disease" flourished during Wesley's time.[5] Wesley, himself, questioned physicians who "play with the lives or health of men to enlarge their own gain. Who purposely lengthen the pain or disease which they are able to remove speedily. Who protract the cure of their patient's body in order to plunder his substance."[6] With lingering mistrust for new medical developments and so few viable options for the critically ill, death remained a constant threat.

Unlike today, the dying were not isolated from general society. Rather, in most cases the sick and dying were cared for in their own homes, and it was the duty of friends and family to gather around the sickbed to pay their respects. Even after death, the bodies of loved ones were kept close at hand by being buried in the local churchyard or sometimes under the floor of the church itself.[7] One might expect that the constant exposure to death would ameliorate its terrors, but because death often appeared to be random and unforeseeable, it remained a frightening prospect. Ralph Houlbrooke in his book, *Death, Religion and the Family in England 1480–1750*, noted, "Sharp and irregular oscillations in mortality perhaps contributed to anxiety about death through their scale and unpredictability."[8] There was simply no telling when or where death would strike.

Mary Dobson recorded the demographic effects, epidemiological events, and psychological fears that death had on the early modern English population. Her study provided a fascinating record of the bewilderment felt by the common person who was forced to face the daily dread of infection, disease, and death. She noted, "We can scarcely begin to sense the pain and suffering, the fear and panic, the obsession and frustration, as individuals and their families fell victim to these persistent and mysterious scourges. Every person in this era was vulnerable to, and beset by, a host of maladies that were ever present...."[9] Dobson's research revealed over two hundred causes of death listed in entries from six parish registers, which

---

5. Porter, "Death and the Doctors in Georgian England," 77.
6. Wesley, *Use of Money* (BE), 2:272.
7. Anglican churches were required by law to provide a place of burial for all parish members except for the unbaptized and suicides; although, even these were typically provided a plot in an unconsecrated portion of the church property. Morgan, "Burial Question in Leeds," 95.
8. Houlbrooke, *Death, Religion and the Family in England*, 6.
9. Dobson, *Contours of Death and Disease in Early Modern England*, 285.

chronicled the seventeenth and eighteenth centuries. Infectious diseases were especially feared because of the way the deceased were treated. The bodies of those who died of communicable illnesses were rarely allowed in the church, and the corpses were often buried at night in their own fields.

High Risk Populations

Mortality rates across all populations were appallingly high. The average life expectancy at birth in Wesley's day was about thirty-five years of age if the infant mortality rate was included.[10] In addition to the already dismal mortality rate, Houlbrooke noted that between 1540 and 1750 there were eleven crisis years in which the death rate rose at least 30 percent above the average trend. The years 1727 to 1730 and 1741 to 1742 held some of the worst mortality rates since the 1600s due to diseases such as smallpox, whooping-cough, and "putrid fever," and the average life expectancy dropped to an astounding 27.88 in 1731.[11] Furthermore, while not included within the crisis years, 1719 and 1720 also touted a 20 percent increase in the average morality rate due to an outbreak of fever and smallpox.[12] With such bleak prospects for survival, it is little wonder that death produced anxiety in eighteenth-century society. It is also unsurprising that Wesley first sought out Jeremy Taylor's works, *The Rule and Exercises of Holy Living* and *The Rule and Exercises of Holy Dying*, during the uncertainty of the 1720s.

While life was uncertain for everyone, there were certain populations which were affected by death and disease more severely than others. Lucinda Beier observed, "Infants, young children, child-bearing women, and the elderly inhabited a kind of no-man's-land between life and death. Indeed, these groups were so at risk that mere mention of the age group or category itself was sufficient explanation of the cause of death."[13] Furthermore, environmental conditions contributed to higher mortality rates; thus, those living in low-lying areas, fens, and marshes were consistently more vulnerable to certain illnesses.[14] Certain trades such as work in quarries, seafarers,

---

10. Rack, *Reasonable Enthusiast*, 8.
11. Houlbrooke, *Death, Religion and the Family in England*, 6–7.
12. Dobson, *Contours of Death and Disease in Early Modern England*, 426.
13. Beier, "Good Deaths in Seventeenth-Century England," 44.
14. Houlbrooke, *Death, Religion and the Family in England*, 14. Lincolnshire, the county of Wesley's birth, was a notorious marshland before Charles I arranged for the

millers, metalworkers, and miners were also attended by high rates of mortality due to the hazards of their professions. As is true for any era, the poor were especially at risk due to malnutrition and the unsanitary conditions of workhouses and slums. For sickly infants born into poverty, the chances of survival were almost hopeless. Jonas Hanway, an eighteenth-century philanthropist, revealed the unfortunate condition of children in workhouse sick wards. In 1765, Hanway observed that at London's St. Clement Danes workhouse there was only one nurse for twenty-three sick children. By January 1766, eighteen of the twenty-three children were dead, two had been discharged, and a mere three remained alive. Workhouses in other parishes had no better statistics. The united parishes of St. Andrew and St. George, Holborn, received seventy-eight children into the workhouse sick ward during 1765; by 1766, only fourteen of the seventy-eight children remained alive.[15]

Post-Reformation Attitudes Toward Death

The English Reformation had a resounding impact on the eighteenth-century approach to death and dying. Prior to the Reformation, the Catholic Church wielded significant sway over its members. This was partially due to the Church's sovereignty over a person's eternal destiny which included the power to translate souls from purgatory into heaven or hell. Henry Rack noted that Catholicism's "elaborate network of last rites offered the penitent the assurance of the church's well-tried means for easing the soul's passage to the next world."[16] Consolation was fostered by the knowledge that even if one was not ushered directly into heaven an individual's time in purgatory could be minimized through the prayers of family, friends, and masses offered by the church. With the rejection of purgatory, this comfort was removed; only two realms existed after death and neither sphere could be altered by any type of ritual or supplication.

Dutch engineer, Vermuyden, to drain the land. For more about Lincolnshire's marshland, see Willingham Franklin Rawnsley's work *Highways and Byways in Lincolnshire*.

15. In addition to the above cited examples, Hanway reported that of the forty-eight children received at the St. Luke Middlesex workhouse in 1764 "for nurture" thirty-seven died. St. George's workhouse in Middlesex fared no better; of the nineteen children admitted in 1765, sixteen died. Pugh, *Remarkable Occurrences in the Life of Jonas Hanway*, 145.

16. Rack, "Evangelical Endings," 43.

Protestants were afraid that belief in purgatory lulled people into a sense of false security about their eternal fate and undermined the necessity of repentance and holy living in the here and now. Prayers or ritual ceremonies for the dead were deemed superstitious at best and pernicious at worst. Jeremy Taylor cautioned against the harm of espousing the doctrine of purgatory in the following terms:

> But to dream of a punishment temporal when all his time is done, and to think of Repentance when the time of Grace is past, are great Errors, the one in Philosophy, and both in Divinity, and are a huge folly in their pretence and infinite danger if they are believed; being a certain destruction of the necessity of holy living when men dare trust them, and live at the rate of such Doctrines.[17]

After the Reformation, some Protestants remained wary of anything that smacked of Catholic ritual. Wesley himself was accused of "popery" because he published an ancient prayer for the faithfully departed.[18] David Cressy noted that some radical Reformers such as Thomas Cartwright even frowned upon funeral sermons since they insinuated prayers for the dead.[19] These extreme attitudes did not dominate the Church of England; however, many Reformers believed that their Catholic counterparts lavished more care upon individuals *after* death than before their passing when it actually had the potential to alter the fate of their souls. This perspective caused disdain for Catholic practices such as minning day as was markedly noticeable in the following observation dating from 1590:

> All the day and night after the burial they use to have excessive ringing for the dead, as also at the twelve months day after, which

---

17. Introduction to Taylor, *Rule and Exercises of Holy Dying*, para. 8.

18. Dr. George Lavington, Bishop of Exeter, published two installments of *The Enthusiasm of Methodist and Papists Compar'd* in which the bishop accused Wesley of popery. One reason for the accusation was that Wesley published an ancient (albeit heavily edited) prayer from St. Mark's Liturgy for the faithful departed. Wesley argued that it was pointless to pray *for* the dead in the hope of changing their eternal state; however, he had no qualms about prayers such as those from the Burial Service in the *Book of Common Prayer* which expressed a desire to attain the consummation of bliss in the resurrection along with those already dead in Christ. He wrote, "Yea, and whenever I say 'Thy Kingdom come'; for I mean both the kingdom of grace and glory. In this kind of general prayer therefore, for the faithful departed, I conceive myself to be clearly justified both by the earliest antiquity, by the Church of England, and by the Lord's Prayer." Wesley, *A Second Letter to the Author of The Enthusiasm of Methodists, etc.*" (BE), 11:423. For a detailed defense on Wesley's behalf, see Carrier, "Wesley's Views on Prayers for the Dead," 123–25.

19. Cressy, *Birth, Marriage, and Death*, 411.

they call a minning day. All which time of ringing, their use is to have their private devotions at home for the soul of the dead. But while the party lieth sick, they will never require to have the bell knolled, no, not at the point of death; whereby the people should be stirred up to prayer in due time; neither will any almost at that time desire to have the minister to come to him for comfort and instruction.[20]

The danger did not lie in the rituals or ceremonies themselves; rather, the peril resided in the underlying belief that one's destiny could be altered after death. With the rise of Protestantism, all spiritual preparation had to occur *before* death which framed the deathbed as the final checkpoint to secure the fate of one's soul.

Thus, the deathbed took on increased significance since a person's destiny hung in the balance; to die unprepared meant almost certain eternal damnation.[21] Those, like Wesley, who were spiritually sensitive, grappled daily with an awful awareness of impending death. In fact, Charles Goodwin asserted it was this general fear of death and eternal punishment which accounted for the success of the eighteenth-century Methodist revival since most conversions were motivated by fear of death, judgment, and hell.[22]

Ars Moriendi: Origins of the Tradition

Throughout the ages, the church had always offered some sort of resolution to the bleak prospect of one's physical demise, separation from loved ones, and divine judgment.[23] "Death was the Terror," Porter observed. "But

---

20. Cressy, *Birth, Marriage, and Death*, 401. Cressy quoted here from F. R. Raines (ed.), *A Description of the State, Civil and Ecclesiastical, of the County of Lancaster, about the year 1590* (Chetham Society; Manchester, 1875), 5–7.

21. Since purgatory was no longer a theological option, some may have softened their view of God's judgment. Wesley was not among those who moderated their stance, but Houlbrooke noted that with the dawn of the age of reason, "horror and pain in death and the hereafter came to seem increasingly hard to reconcile with the compassion of a benevolent Creator, while confidence in the powers of science gave rise to new hopes that the incidence of death might be reduced and life prolonged." Houlbrooke, *Death, Church, and Family in England*, 25.

22. Goodwin, "Terrors of the Thunderstorm," 101. David Dunn Wilson made a similar argument in his study of eighteenth-century Methodism. Wilson, *Many Waters Cannot Quench*.

23. Houlbrooke noted that, "Religious beliefs offer by no means the only key to late medieval and early modern attitudes toward death, but certainly the most obviously

it would be silly to assume that this perception of Death's Sting, understood within a faith vibrant with providentialism and eschatology, produced mass hysteria . . . ."[24] It would also be naïve to assume that the Anglican Church disconnected from this lively tradition or rejected all Roman Catholic responses to death. One of the most prevailing deathbed aids within the history of the church was the *ars moriendi* tradition. The *ars moriendi* or "art of dying" was a body of literature which provided guidance for the dying and for their caregivers. It consisted of exhortations, questions, prayers, and prescribed actions which assisted individuals through the dying process and led them to a good death. As a literary tradition, the *ars moriendi* cannot be traced back any further than the early fifteenth century. However, Donald Duclow observed that the church already had a well-established ritual for the dying by the 1400s since catechisms and handbooks to assist parish priests in their ministry to the dying had been crafted by the fourteenth century.[25] The *ars moriendi* simply consolidated these practices into a precise written format.

In its earliest form, the *ars moriendi* existed in two, anonymously written, relatively short Latin works: a brief piece entitled *Ars moriendi* which contained eleven woodcut illustrations and a longer piece called *Tractatus artis bene moriendi*. Both works were similar in content, and the Protestant English Church quickly adapted the *ars moriendi* for its own use. By the mid-1400s, there were English manuscript translations of the *Tractatus artis bene moriendi*. The earliest printed English version, *The Arte & Crafte to Know Well to Dye*, was translated from French into English by William Caxton in 1490.[26] Written over the course of nearly two centuries, the English *ars moriendi* literature represented the theological diversity within the Church of England; however, Atkinson pointed out that there were several commonalities among English *ars* literature which are worth noting.[27] 1)

---

important and readily accessible one. A high proportion of the written evidence that survives is set in a religious framework." Houlbrooke, *Death, Religion and the Family in England*, 2.

24. Porter, "Death and the Doctors in Georgian England," 80–81.

25. According to Duclow, it is likely that a short essay entitled *De arte moriendi* by Jean Gerson, chancellor of the University of Paris, was the basis of the *ars moriendi*. Gerson presented his essay to the Council of Constance (1414 to 1418), and the anonymous *Ars moriendi* was probably drawn from his essay and spread throughout the networks of the Dominicans and Franciscans. Duclow, "Ars Moriendi," 37.

26. Atkinson, *English ars moriendi*, xiii.

27. For example, some English *ars moriendi* literature was strongly Calvinist in

Because of the Protestant emphasis on the role of the individual conscience, English works tended to use moral principles as a guide to navigate the deathbed rather than the Catholic tendency to emphasize conformity to specific instructions especially in terms of ritual and liturgy. 2) Protestant *ars moriendi* literature also deemphasized the deathbed sacraments (which were essential to the Catholic tradition) as well as the deathbed temptations which were so prominent in the earlier Catholic translations. 3) Most English writers devoted the largest portions of their works to preparing for death through living a good Christian life. 4) The Protestant *ars moriendi* aimed at awakening the sinner to death, judgment, heaven and hell but tended to focus on heaven as a reward rather than judgment and hell.[28] Thus, the overarching purpose for the English *ars moriendi* was to offer guidance to the dying which was consistent with its own Protestant commitments and traditions.

The Nature of English *Ars Moriendi* Literature

It is best to examine William Caxton's *The Arte & Crafte to Know Well to Dye* to discover the essence of the English *ars moriendi* since Caxton's work revealed the basic structure of the written *ars* tradition upon which later authors built. Caxton clearly stated the purpose of the *ars moriendi* in his opening lines. He bemoaned the fact that there were few people who properly advised others of their end, "and therfore, hath this present treatyse be made ... for to teche euery man wel to deye, whilys he hath vnderstandyng, helthe, and rayson."[29] The author conceded that physical death was a fearful thing; therefore, time should be spent in arming the soul for the life to come and preparing to die well.

The Arte & Crafte was divided into six sections which were meant to help a person successfully navigate through the valley of the shadow

---

nature while other pieces fit within the Arminian tradition. Thomas Becon's *Sycke Mans Salue* (1561) was strongly Calvinist (see Introduction, xviii–xix). A more balanced work was William Perkins's *A Salve for Sicke Man* (1595), which recognized the role of human agency in preparing for eternity while also keeping in view that "it is not in the power of man to repent when he himselfe will. When God will he may . . . . Christ saith that many shall seeke to enter into heauen, & shall not bee able. But why so? Because they seek when it is too late . . . ." Perkins, *Salve for a Sicke Man* (1595), 137. Jeremy Taylor's *Rule and Exercises of Holy Dying* (1651) was more representative of the Arminian view.

28. See Atkinson, *English ars moriendi*, xxii–xxiii for a full discussion of these themes.
29. Caxton, "Art and Craft to Know Well to Die," 21.

of death. The first section was a commendation of death. Caxton admitted that death was a terrible prospect for unrepentant sinners, but for the Christian and the contrite sinner, death was the entrance into joy and glory. Therefore, death was not to be dreaded. "For well to deye is gladly to deye. And to con [learn to] deye is to haue in all tymes his herte redy and appareyled to thynges heuenly & supernall, and that . . . when the deth shall come . . . that he be founde redy, and that he receyue it wyth out ony contradiccyon, but also ioyusly . . . ."[30]

The second section dealt with the "temptacyons that the person hath at thoure of the deth."[31] The *ars moriendi* tradition viewed the deathbed as a time of extreme trial and temptation. Therefore, one of the longest sections of Caxton's work examined the following five common temptations: 1) the temptation of unbelief against faith, 2) the temptation to despair versus hope in the mercy and forgiveness of God, 3) the temptation of impatience as opposed to longsuffering due to one's love for God, 4) the temptation of spiritual pride set against humility, and 5) temptation to avarice or occupation with family or things versus detachment. In other words, inordinate love for family or possessions caused the dying to be unwilling to depart from this life; thus, complete commitment to God required a readiness to relinquish all that one held dear.

The third through fifth sections combined an interrogation of the dying person along with spiritual instructions and a remembrance of Christ's suffering. Questions such as, "Byleueste thou that thou mayste not be saued, but by the deth of our Lord Jhesu Cryste and by his passion?" or "Byleuest thou alle the pryncypall artycles of the faith of holy chirch, & alle the holy scripture in alle thynges, and thexposicion of the catholyke and all holy doctors of our moder holy chirche?" were put to the dying person.[32] The questions were followed by directions for resigning the soul to God along with Scripture and prayers designed to be repeated by the dying person. The last section included instructions and prayers mainly for those who assisted at the deathbed. If the dying person could no longer speak, it fell upon the onlookers to commend their loved one's soul to God. Caxton recommended the following prayer:

> Ryght dere brother or suster, I commaunde the to God almighty, and commytte the to hym, of whom thou art creature to the ende

---

30. Caxton, "Art and Craft to Know Well to Die," 22.
31. Caxton, "Art and Craft to Know Well to Die," 22
32. Caxton, "Art and Craft to Know Well to Die," 26.

whan, by thy deth, thou shalt haue payd the duty of nature humanyne, thou mayste retorne to thy maker, whiche of the slime of the erthe formed the. Thy soule yssue and goo oute of thy body whan it shall please God.[33]

In its most basic format, the *ars moriendi* was meant to alleviate the fear of death and help the dying and their families overcome the trial of the deathbed through Christian faith. "Nothing in life confirms one's sense of aloneness and alienation from God more than death," Atkinson observed. "What the *ars moriendi* does is provide a way of overcoming this alienation so that one recovers the security and comfort of knowing one is complete in one's relationship with God."[34]

Jeremy Taylor and the *Ars Moriendi*

The *ars moriendi* had a resounding impact upon Christians from the fifteenth to the eighteenth centuries.[35] By Wesley's day, *ars moriendi* literature was favored devotional reading because these writings not only offered solid instruction for Christian living but also gave the dying hope for the next life. There is no evidence to prove that Wesley read the *ars moriendi* in its original Latin or even Caxton's early translation from French, but Richard Bell in his article, "Our People Die Well," surmised that it is likely Wesley read one of the thirteen copies of the original *ars moriendi* which circulated in the Oxford libraries during his time.[36] What can be said with certainty is that the *ars moriendi* was mediated to Wesley through Jeremy Taylor's *The Rule and Exercise of Holy Dying*, and this work was one of the most influential pieces of literature on Wesley's early spiritual formation.

---

33. Caxton, "Art and Craft to Know Well to Die," 34.

34. Atkinson, *English ars moriendi*, xxv.

35. Christopher Vogt proposed that the *ars moriendi* tradition was deeply significant because: 1) It was read in both Catholic and Protestant countries; thus, it was applicable to all Christians regardless of denominational attachments. 2) Some of the most prominent theologians of the time authored *ars moriendi* literature. 3) Ars moriendi literature influenced not only theological ideology but also actual practice in terms of death and dying. 4) The tradition placed dying within the context of the whole Christian life. Vogt, *Patience, Compassion, Hope*, 16–17.

36. Bell did not indicate exactly what he meant by the "original" *ars moriendi*, but perhaps he was referring to one of the Latin versions. Bell, "Our People Die Well," 214–15.

The Rule and Exercise of Holy Dying has been described as the "artistic zenith of the *ars* tradition."[37] Besides its poetic and literary appeal, Atkinson credited Taylor with writing a work "that integrates the best of the *ars* tradition, be it Catholic or Protestant."[38] Unlike the earliest works which were mainly focused on the deathbed, Taylor placed a great deal of emphasis on holy living in preparation for death.[39] In the introduction, Taylor observed, "It is a great art to die well, and to be learn'd by Men in health, by them . . . whose understanding and acts of reason are not abated with fear or pains: and as the greatest part of Death is passed by the preceding years of our Life, so also in those years are the greatest preparations to it."[40] The first two chapters of his five chapter book focused on the brevity of life and the necessity to prepare for death "by the general provisions of holiness, and a pious life. . . ."[41] For Taylor, dying well entailed a lifetime spent in cultivating the holy virtues and graces of the Christian faith. Unlike Caxton's work which encouraged contrite sinners to seek forgiveness upon the deathbed and extended the hope of a good passing, Taylor offered little optimism to those who had not practiced a godly life. Taylor insisted, "A resolving to repent upon our Death-bed, is the greatest mockery of God . . . for therefore he threaten'd us with Hell if we did not, and he promised Heaven if we did live a holy life: and a late Repentance promises Heaven to us upon other conditions ev'n when we lived wickedly."[42]

Dying and Holy Living

For Taylor and other Caroline Divines, the entrance to heaven required more than justification by faith alone. It also required a life engaged in the works of holiness. Bishop George Bull remarked, "Justification signifies that love of God, by which He embraces those already leading a holy life and determines them to be worthy of the reward of eternal life through

---

37. Atkinson, *English ars moriendi*, xxiii.

38. Atkinson, *English ars moriendi*, xxiv. It was virtually the last English work published in the *ars moriendi* tradition.

39. Taylor's *Rule and Exercises of Holy Living* (1650) stood as the counterpart to *Rule and Exercises of Holy Dying*.

40. Introduction to Taylor, *Rule and Exercises of Holy Dying*, para. 3.

41. Taylor, *Rule and Exercises of Holy Dying*, 38–39.

42. Taylor, *Rule and Exercises of Holy Dying*, 146.

Christ."[43] Without the mark of holy living, a person was not justified and was, therefore, unfit to stand before God after death. In a sense, Taylor viewed holy living as a reversal of death itself since he defined death not as a cessation of the physical body but rather as a state introduced through the sin of humankind.

> Then Death began; that is, the Man began to die by a natural diminution, and aptness to disease and misery. His first state was and should have been (so long as it lasted) a happy duration; his second was a daily and miserable change: and this was the dying properly... Change or separation of soul and body, is but accidental to Death; Death may be with or without either: but the formality, the curse and the sting of Death, that is, misery, sorrow, fear, diminution, defect, anguish, dishonour, and whatsoever is miserable and afflictive in nature, that is Death. Death is not an action, but a whole state and condition; and this was first brought in upon us by the offence of one man.[44]

Death, properly speaking, was the separation from God brought about by the effects of sin. The only way to combat the state of death and its insidious effects was reconciliation with the Creator which was achieved through faith in Christ's atonement, the work of repentance, and the dedication of a holy life.

Those who would embark upon the journey of holy living and reverse this state of death required a great measure of self-discipline and thorough self-examination. In the second chapter of *Holy Dying* Taylor warned, "He that desires to die well and happily, above all things must be careful that he do not live a soft, a delicate and a voluptuous life; but a life severe, holy, and under the discipline of the Cross, under the conduct of prudence and observation, a life of warfare and sober counsels, labour and watchfulness."[45] To ensure that one's life was in order, Taylor encouraged his readers to daily examine themselves every evening before they slept. Sleeping was for Taylor a "little image of Death."[46] Thus, preparation for the evening's rest by giving an account of one's actions was a way to continually practice and prepare for the final slumber of death. To be sure, a holy life which concluded in a holy death was much more than discipline, self-examination,

---

43. Bull, *Harmonia Apostolica*, 7.
44. Taylor, *Rule and Exercises of Holy Dying*, 60–61.
45. Taylor, *Rule and Exercises of Holy Dying*, 41.
46. Taylor, *Rule and Exercises of Holy Dying*, 43.

and obedience. Taylor believed that true holiness sprang forth from a believer's love for God. He observed that all the "wise Christians" in history were so enamored with God they were willing to die for their love of God; "the Apostles, and millions of the Martyrs did die for him: And although it be harder to live in his love than to die for it, yet all the good People that ever gave their names to Christ did for his love endure the crucifying of their Lusts, the mortification of their Appetites . . . "[47]

Deathbed Temptations and Virtues

Even though Taylor believed that most of the preparation for death should occur before the deathbed, he did not neglect to address those who were facing imminent death. The third chapter of his work was written to help the dying face the two temptations common to sickness. The first temptation was impatience or peevishness during the agonies of death. Taylor encouraged the dying to think of their suffering not as meaningless pain but as "the last opportunity that ever God will give thee to exercise any virtue, to do him any service, or thy self any advantage."[48] Furthermore Taylor reminded his readers that God chastens every child he loves, and if this chastening came in the form of suffering and death, it was not to be rejected. He wrote, "And if this be the effect of the design of God's love to thee, let it be occasion of thy love to him: and remember, that the truth of love is hardly known, but by somewhat that put us to pain. Use this as a punishment for thy sins; and so God intends it most commonly . . . . If . . . thou submittest to it, thou approvest of the Divine Judgment."[49]

The second temptation was the fear of death. Taylor asserted, "He that is afraid of Death, I mean, with a violent and transporting Fear, with a Fear apt to discompose his duty or his patience, that Man either loves this World too much or dares not trust God for the next."[50] The foremost remedy for fear was Christian fortitude. Taylor noted that believers were commanded to be willing to die for Christ; therefore, "as he that does his duty, needs not fear death, so neither shall he; the parts of his duty, are parts of his security."[51] If further courage was needed, then Taylor recommended

---

47. Taylor, *Rule and Exercises of Holy Dying*, 153.
48. Taylor, *Rule and Exercises of Holy Dying*, 78.
49. Taylor, *Rule and Exercises of Holy Dying*, 78.
50. Taylor, *Rule and Exercises of Holy Dying*, 109–10.
51. Taylor, *Rule and Exercises of Holy Dying*, 104.

prayer, belief in a better life to come, and the duty of resignation. Whatever the remedy, love, not fear, must be the motivating characteristic of the heart when the time of death was near since those who feared rather than loved God had the "passions of a Servant" and not "the affections of a Son."[52]

In the fourth chapter, Taylor encouraged the practice of deathbed virtues and provided the dying with prayers for each type of necessary grace. To die well, the person must practice patience, faith, charity, and repentance. It should be noted that the repentance Taylor spoke of was not the initial repentance of a sinner turning from sin, but contrition or a "general or universal sorrow for the sins not only since the last communion or absolution, but of thy whole life; for all Sins, known and unknown . . . ."[53] For Taylor, the best way to approach death was with a humble and repentant attitude. He believed that Christians could face death with confidence and that believers had many reasons not to despair. However, the Caroline Divine also asserted,

> A true penitent must all the days of his life pray for pardon, and never think the work completed until he dies . . . And whether God hath forgiven us or no, we know not, and how far we know not; and all that we have done is not of sufficient worth to obtain pardon: therefore still pray, and still be sorrowful for ever having done it . . . then those beginnings of pardon which are working all the way, will at last be perfected in the day of the Lord.[54]

There was always an element of uncertainty; therefore, the believer must practice the graces of holiness until the point of death.

Taylor's concluding chapter was dedicated to the instruction of those who ministered to the dying. It was a fitting end since the whole of his treatise was pastoral in nature and demonstrated deep concern for the spiritual well-being of both the living and the dying. He recognized that life was short; therefore, both the living and the dying were best served by keeping eternity in view. "God hath given to man a short time here upon Earth, and yet upon this short time Eternity depends . . ." Taylor had earlier cautioned.[55] Those who were heedless of God's holy commands ran the risk of coming to the end of their lives with the burden of an evil conscience,

---

52. Taylor, *Rule and Exercises of Holy Dying*, 152. Wesley also associated "faith of a servant" with fear and the "faith of son" with love.

53. Taylor, *Rule and Exercises of Holy Dying*, 150.

54. Taylor, *Rule and Exercises of Holy Dying*, 276.

55. Taylor, *Rule and Exercises of Holy Dying*, 4.

and there was little that could be done for them. In contrast, those who lived lives of holy obedience were like fruit ripe for picking. "Such a man must die when he ought to die, and be like ripe and pleasant fruit falling from a fair tree, and gather'd into baskets for the Planter's use. He that hath done all his business . . . can never die too soon, nor live too long."[56] True to his conviction that a holy death was not possible without a holy life, Taylor ended his work with an appeal to live in such a way that death could always be welcomed. "It remains, that we who are alive should so live, and by the Actions of Religion attend to the coming of the day of the Lord, that we neither be surprized nor leave our duties imperfect, nor our sins uncancel'd, nor our persons unreconcil'd, nor God unappeased . . . ."[57]

Wesley's Sin of Fear

Wesley's connection between holiness and freedom from the fear of death was directly related to his introduction to Jeremy Taylor's treatises on the topic. Wesley recalled, "In 1725 I met with Bishop Taylor's *Rules of Holy Living and Dying*. I was struck particularly with the chapter upon Intention, and felt a fixed intention to *give myself up to God*."[58] In the introduction to *A Plain Account of Christian Perfection*, Wesley once again specifically named Jeremy Taylor, Thomas à Kempis, and William Law with awakening his heart to the necessity for "simplicity of intention," "purity of affection," and the "absolute impossibility of being half a Christian."[59] So strong was the impact of Taylor's writings that after reading his works Wesley immediately determined to "dedicate all my life to God, all my thoughts, and words, and actions; being thoroughly convinced, there was no medium; but that every part of my life (not some only) must either be a sacrifice to God, or myself, that is in effect, to the devil."[60] Wesley's realization that holiness was the *telos* of religion blossomed at the same time he grappled with his terror of dying. Because he accepted Taylor's thesis that anyone who truly loved and

---

56. Taylor, *Rule and Exercises of Holy Dying*, 24.
57. Taylor, *Rule and Exercises of Holy Dying*, 259.
58. Wesley, *Letters of the Rev. John Wesley*, 4:298. Taylor was not the only theologian to influence Wesley's thinking on this topic since it was Thomas à Kempis who bestowed upon Wesley the understanding of inward holiness and William Law who conferred the necessity of both inward and outward obedience to the moral law.
59. Wesley, *Plain Account of Christian Perfection* (BE), 13:136–37.
60. Wesley, *Plain Account of Christian Perfection* (BE), 13:136.

trusted God would not fear death, Wesley's quest for holiness was hindered by his overwhelming anxiety regarding death. Wesley quickly correlated his fear of death with his lack of purity and a deficiency in his love for God.[61]

Between the years 1725 and 1738, Wesley's desire to live a life of holiness was tainted by his failure to live above the bondage of sin and the fear of death. It was noted earlier that the years 1727 to 1730 held some of the worst mortality rates since the 1600s which meant that Wesley's anxieties were likely a constant concern. The death of his close friend Robin Griffiths (1727) provided a window into Wesley's angst. Griffiths's sudden demise left Wesley shaken to the core. Wesley Chambers noted, "The death of Robin Griffiths in particular made him acutely aware of the shortness of life which imperiled the process of sanctification and therefore of readiness to appear before God in judgement."[62] Griffiths's death also revealed to Wesley the discrepancy between his theological ideals and Wesley's actual spiritual condition. In a letter to his mother, written nearly two months after Griffiths passing, Wesley observed:

> I never gave more reason to suspect my doctrine did not agree with my practice; for a sickness and pain in my stomach, attended with a violent looseness, which seized me the day he was buried, altered me so much in three days, and made me look so pale and thin, that those who saw me could not but observe it.[63]

Despite his reliance on Taylor's advice and his own resolve to lead a holy life, the prospect of death continued to haunt Wesley for the next decade. Nowhere were his uncertainties more prominently displayed than during his travels to Georgia in 1736. The rough seas and unexpected weather highlighted Wesley's fears and lack of heart purity. During one storm on the voyage to Georgia, Wesley recorded the following sentiment: "About eleven I lay down in the great cabin, and in a short time fell asleep, though very uncertain whether I should wake alive, and much ashamed of my unwillingness to die. O how pure in heart must he be who would

---

61. There are many examples of this connection in Wesley's journal entries. In Georgia, Wesley was frightened by a violent thunderstorm and wrote, "This voice of God, too, told me I was not fit to die; since I was afraid rather than desirous of it! O when shall I wish to be dissolved and to be with Christ? When I love him with all my heart." Wesley, *Journal* July 10, 1736 (BE), 18:165. See similar sentiments recorded on December 28, 1737 (BE), 18:207; January 8, 1738 (BE), 18:208–9; January 24, 1738 (BE), 18:211 and January 29, 1738 (BE), 18:213.

62. Chambers, "John Wesley and Death," 152.

63. Wesley, *Letters* March 19, 1727 (BE), 25:214.

rejoice to appear Before God at a moment's warning!"⁶⁴ Less than a week later, another storm buffeted the small ship. This time, Wesley observed the Germans who "calmly sung on" while the English screamed with terror. Amazed, Wesley questioned, "Was you not afraid? . . . Were not your women and children afraid?"⁶⁵ Wesley's heart must have condemned him when even children showed more fortitude than he felt. After arriving safely in Georgia, his "sin of fear" continued to haunt him as evidenced in his account of a young woman's demise. His shock at her sudden passing and his distress over the loss of one who was just entering the bloom of life was almost palpable. That same evening a powerful thunderstorm shook Wesley to the core. He wrote, "This voice of God, too, told me I was not fit to die; since I was afraid, rather than desirous of it! O when shall I wish to be dissolved and to be with Christ? When I love him with all my heart."⁶⁶ Wesley clearly recognized that his love for God should be able to dispel the terror of death, and his inability to conquer his fear led him to cry in despair:

> I went to America, to convert the Indians; but Oh! who shall convert me? Who, what is he that will deliver me from this evil heart of unbelief? I have a fair summer religion. I can talk well; nay, and believe myself, while no danger is near: But let death look me in the face, and my spirit is troubled. Nor can I say, "To die is gain!" I have a sin of fear, that when I've spun My last thread, I shall perish on the shore!⁶⁷

Chambers noted, "His head told him his faith should overcome his fear of death; his emotional reactions revealed the poverty of his faith and his unreadiness to die. How to overcome this fear of death—and the ensuing experiences of the soul—was Wesley's major problem."⁶⁸

To add to Wesley's difficulties, not only was the fear of death an existential dilemma that he desired to resolve for himself, but the presence of death hung like a foreboding cloud over the population which held Wesley's

---

64. Wesley, *Journal* January 17, 1736 (BE), 18:141.

65. Wesley, *Journal* January 25, 1736 (BE), 18:143.

66. Wesley, *Journal* July 10, 1736 (BE), 18:165. Richard Baxter recorded a similar sentiment in his reflections upon death. He exclaimed, "O that I could be as willing as reason convinces me I ought to be! Could I love God as much as I know I ought to love him, then I should desire to depart and to be with Christ, as much as I know I ought to desire it." Baxter, *Dying Thoughts*, 52.

67. Wesley, *Journal* January 24, 1738 (BE), 18:211.

68. Chambers, "John Wesley and Death," 153.

greatest pastoral attention—the poor and laboring classes. Furthermore, as an Anglican clergyman, the young minister bore a heavy responsibility to care for the dying. Rack noted, "In a lightly governed society lacking most official social services, the clergy were the expected sources of education, charity, even medical care, as well as being among the natural leaders and guide of village communities."[69] Thus, the clergy's responsibility for caring for the sick and tending to end of life issues were much greater than they are today.[70] Wesley did not take this responsibility lightly. Randy Maddox noted that by the seventeenth century the basic study of medicine had been incorporated into the training of those preparing to become Anglican clergy, and Wesley devoted much time to fervently study the latest medical handbooks.[71] While the hope of the minister was to cure the sick, the reality was that many people were beyond any medical ministrations the clergyman could offer, and it became the minister's task to prepare the person for death. Beier noted, "Indeed, the duty of the priest or minister of instructing believers in how to die was secondary only to instructing them in how to live."[72] The problem Wesley faced was how to help others when he could not overcome his own anxieties regarding death.

Faith Overcoming Fear

Taylor exposed Wesley's "sin of fear," but the Caroline Divine also provided the solution. All that was necessary to dispel the fear of death was the inculcation of the Christian virtues; in other words, holiness was the key to overcoming Wesley's problem. Looking back upon this period of his life, Wesley recalled being bent on achieving a holy heart. He resolved to "alter

---

69. Rack, *Reasonable Enthusiast*, 10.

70. Even after it became commonplace to summon a physician to the sickbed before the clergy, the doctor withdrew when it became evident that the person was beyond recovery. The deathbed was left to the care of the minister. Beier noted, "Indeed, conventionally the minister took the place of the healer when death approached, and he was welcomed as the physician's equal or superior in the sick-room." Beier, "Good Deaths in Seventeenth-Century England," 56.

71. Maddox, "John Wesley on Holistic Health and Healing," 5. Maddox observed that Wesley read George Cheyne's *Essay of Health and Long Life* shortly after it was published in 1724. Cheyne's writing on the connection between emotional, spiritual and physical health greatly affected Wesley's thinking on such matters. Like Wesley, Cheyne believed that the love of God was the solution to the misery of both body and soul.

72. Beier, "Good Deaths in Seventeenth-Century England," 47.

the whole form of my conversation and to set in earnest upon *a new life* .... I watched against all sins, whether in word or deed. I began to aim at and pray for inward holiness."[73] However, Wesley soon found that his resolve to be holy was void of any real power. His terror of death on the sea and his disabling fear at the death of his friends were constant reminders of the failure to achieve the type of holiness and love of God for which he longed. Wesley admitted that during his whole time in Savannah he was only "beating the air."[74] "I was still 'under the law,' not 'under grace,'" Wesley recalled. "For I was only 'striving with,' not 'freed from sin.' Neither had I 'the witness of the Spirit with my spirit.' And indeed could not; for I 'sought it not by faith, but (as it were) by the works of the law.'"[75]

Taylor had properly pointed Wesley in the direction of holiness, but he had failed to equip Wesley with the means to receive a holy heart. For Taylor, justification and the resulting acceptance with God was not based upon faith alone. "A man is not justified by faith alone, that is, by faith which hath not in it charity and obedience," Taylor stated. Rather, Taylor proposed, "our sins indeed are potentially pardoned" when one looks to Christ's death in the fight against sin, but "we must partake of Christ's resurrection before this justification can be actual; when we are 'dead to sin, and are risen again unto righteousness' ... then we are truly, effectively, and indeed justified, till then we are not."[76] Cannon observed that for the Caroline Divine "the means of its achievement [justification] are within man's power, and the deciding factor is the moral quality of man's own deeds. Why is man pardoned and freed from guilt? Because he deserves to be pardoned. He has merited the sentence of innocence."[77] Therefore, a believer's successful performance of good works and attainment of righteousness was essential to receiving pardon. "If faith does not make you charitable and holy, talk no more of justification by it, for you shall never see the glorious face of God," Taylor declared.[78] Under such teaching, Wesley's "sin of fear" along with his failure to achieve lasting holiness caused his own heart to condemn him.

---

73. Wesley, *Journal* May 24, 1738 (BE), 18:244.

74. Wesley, *Journal* May 24, 1738 (BE), 18:246.

75. Wesley, *Journal* May 24, 1738 (BE), 18:247.

76. Taylor, "*Fides Formata*," 8:292–93. Taylor essentially blurred the distinction between justification and regeneration.

77. Cannon, *Theology of John Wesley*, 38.

78. Taylor, "*Fides Formata*," 8:290.

Taylor also determined that those who had sinned after their baptism were relegated to a state of uncertainty. To be sure, Taylor believed that repentant Christians could face death with confidence and had good reason not to despair, but he also declared that believers could not be assured of God's pardon until the day of the Lord.[79] Wesley chaffed under Taylor's assertion that believers could never be certain of their standing with God. In a letter written to his mother regarding Taylor's views, Wesley voiced his complaints:

> the Holy Ghost confers on us the graces we pray for, and our souls receive into them the seeds of an immortal nature. Now surely these graces are not of so little force, as that we can't perceive whether we have them or no; and if we dwell in Christ and Christ in us, which He will not do till we are regenerate, certainly we must be sensible of it. If his opinion be true, I must own I have always been in a great error; for I imagined that when I communicated worthily, i.e. with faith, humility, and thankfulness, my preceding sins were *ipso facto* forgiven me—I mean, so forgiven that unless I fell into them again I might be secure of their ever rising in judgement against me, at least in the other world. But if we can never have any certainty of our being in a state of salvation, good reason it is that every moment should be spent, not in joy but fear and trembling, and then undoubtedly in this life WE ARE of all men most miserable![80]

In addition to his fear of death, Wesley also discovered the misery of attempting to attain holiness through the works of the law. The cry of his heart was, "Lord save, or I perish! Save me . . . by such a faith as implies peace in life and in death," but every time his life was in danger, fear would grip his heart.[81] Battling doubt and fear, Wesley finally found the solution to his problem when he met Peter Böhler in 1738. Böhler was a Moravian missionary whom Wesley encountered upon his return to England after Wesley's disastrous Georgia experience. Böhler convinced Wesley that "the cause of that uneasiness was unbelief, and the gaining a true, living faith was the 'one thing needful.'"[82] Such faith, Böhler insisted, contained two fruits: power over sin and enduring peace from knowing one's sins were forgiven. Wesley was astonished and looked upon this simple solution as

79. Taylor, *Rules and Exercises of Holy Living*, 276.
80. Wesley, *Letters* June 18, 1725 (BE), 25:169–170.
81. Wesley, *Journal* January 8, 1738 (BE), 18:209.
82. Wesley, *Journal* May 24, 1738 (BE), 18:247.

"a new gospel."[83] However, it was not long after Wesley renounced all dependence upon his own works and prayed in earnest for "justifying, saving faith, a full reliance on the blood of Christ shed for *me*; a trust in him as *my* Christ, as *my* sole justification, sanctification, and redemption," that he had his heart-warming experience at Aldersgate.[84]

It quickly became evident that a living faith in Christ alone (absent from attempts to earn God's pardon) was truly the solution to Wesley's attainment of holiness and consequentially his triumph over the fear of death. "I have *now peace with God*, and *I sin not today*," Wesley recorded in his journal on May 25, 1738.[85] Even when the tempter suggested that fear remained in his heart, Wesley concluded, "Well may fears be within *me*; but I must go on, and tread them under my feet."[86] That he had genuinely conquered his "sin of fear" was demonstrated a year later in a letter to his brother Samuel Wesley. Although he did not indicate the reason why, John apparently thought he would die soon. He wrote, "I do not expect to see your face in the flesh. Not that I believe God will discharge you yet, but I believe I have nearly finished my course. O may I be found in him, not having my own righteousness."[87] Gone was the frantic fear and the terrified outcries. In its place was a calm, peaceful resolve. Earlier in the letter, Wesley reasoned with his skeptical brother about the reality of transforming faith. "I have seen . . . very many persons changed in a moment from the spirit of horror, fear, and despair, to the spirit of hope, joy, peace; and from sinful desires, till then reigning over them, to a pure desire of doing the will of God," Wesley argued.[88] It was the sort of change that Wesley had himself experienced. Despite the danger of riots, bouts of illness, and dangers that brought him to the brink of death, Wesley's anxiety over death was gone.[89] In its place was a heart filled with peace and love for God.

83. Wesley, *Journal* May 24, 1738 (BE), 18:248.
84. Wesley, *Journal* May 24, 1738 (BE), 18:248–49.
85. Wesley, *Journal* May 25, 1738 (BE), 18:251
86. Wesley, *Journal* May 25, 1738 (BE), 18:251.
87. Wesley, *Letters* April 4, 1739 (BE), 25:623.
88. Wesley, *Letters* April 4, 1739 (BE), 25:623.
89. Wesley's demeanor from Aldersgate forward was markedly different. On November 26, 1753, Wesley became so ill that he thought he would die. Rather than cry out to God in a panic, Wesley calmly sat down and penned his own epitaph to "prevent vile panegyric." Wesley, *Journal* November 26, 1753 (BE), 20:482. On a journey to Dublin, Wesley encountered stormy seas much like the earlier storm on the way to Georgia. Wesley slept peacefully despite the waves which crashed over the ship. Wesley, *Journal* April 1, 1762 (BE), 21:354.

Conclusion

It is evident from the preface Wesley included in every volume of sermons he published during his lifetime that even after he resolved his own fear of death the issue of mortality remained at the forefront of his life and theology. Wesley remarked,

> To candid, reasonable men I am not afraid to lay open what have been the inmost thoughts of my heart. I have thought, I am a creature of a day, passing through life as an arrow through the air. I am a spirit come from God and returning to God; just hovering over the great gulf, till a few moments hence I am no more seen–I drop into an unchangeable eternity! I want to know one thing, the way to heaven–how to land safe on that happy shore.[90]

Life was fleeting, and Wesley wanted to direct as many people as he could to heaven's shores. He knew that faith which resulted in holiness of heart and life was the only way to triumph over sin and the fear of death; therefore, he set out to craft a theology of holiness which triumphed over the doubts and anxieties which plagued the soul. As he developed his doctrine of holiness and his understanding of the Christian life, Wesley consistently returned to the theme of death. Freedom from the fear of death was not only a test of genuine holiness for Wesley, but death itself functioned as a motivating factor to obtain a pure heart. Holiness was undoubtedly the focus of Wesley's theology, but because his discovery of holiness as the *telos* of the Christian life was intertwined with his victory over the fear of death, the theme of death always remained closely linked to Wesley's doctrines of salvation, grace, and holiness.

---

90. Wesley, *Preface to Sermons* (BE), 1:104–5.

Chapter 2

DEATH

The Distortion of God's Design for Humankind

Introduction

TO APPRECIATE PROPERLY THE connection between holiness and the theme of death in Wesley's theology, Wesley's understanding of death itself must be examined. Most definitions of death characterize it as the cessation of life. While this description is undoubtedly true, it is ultimately problematic because one is immediately faced with the question: "What constitutes life?" In other words, death cannot be properly analyzed without addressing the essence of human existence. It is no accident, therefore, that Wesley grounded his conception of death in the first few chapters of Genesis. Based on his interpretation of the origins of life, Wesley did not accept that mortality was the Creator's original intent for creation; rather, death existed solely as a result of the Fall. It stood as the antithesis to the fullness of life which Wesley believed was a gracious gift sustained by God. In his sermons, Wesley utilized an almost formulaic pattern to chronicle the descent from humankind's pristine primal existence to the Fall and the advent of sin and death.[1] By subordinating death to the overarching theme of the

---

1. Wesley employed the creation-Fall-death pattern in many of his sermons to remind his hearers of the current state of the human race and their utter dependence upon the mercy of God. For some examples of this literary pattern see the following sermons: *Justification by Faith* (BE), 1:181–99; *Original, Nature, Properties, and Use of the Law* (BE), 2:4–19; *New Birth* (BE), 2:186–201; *General Deliverance* (BE), 2:436–50; *End of Christ's Coming* (BE), 2:471–84; *Trouble and Rest of Good Men* (BE), 3:531–41; *Heavenly Treasure in Earthen Vessels* (BE), 4:161–67; *mage of God* (BE), 4:290–303.

creation story, he revealed his primary focus was on the positive aspects of God's desires for humanity.[2] This perspective made death subject to the good will of God and hinted at Wesley's hope that God would restore all things to their creative purpose at the proper time. Like Jeremy Taylor, Wesley viewed death not only as a consequence of sin but also as a viable instrument to instruct humanity about the perniciousness of sin and the necessity of redemption. Furthermore, because death owed its very existence to sin, it did not have its own storyline in Wesley's theology and could not be understood outside of the grand narrative of salvation. Wesley's ultimate concern was to clarify that although all humans experience death, it is an outside intrusion into the essence of humanity.

Creation: The Context for Understanding Death

Wesley affirmed that "in the beginning" life was good and beautiful in its very essence because nothing separated the human soul from the divine. Humanity in the garden knew only love, peace, happiness and holiness.[3] As long as our first parents fulfilled the purpose of their existence (which, according to Wesley, was to "know, and love, and enjoy, and serve his great Creator to all eternity"), death remained nothing more than a theoretical construct for the created world.[4] To be sure, as Gen 2:17 made clear, death was recognized as a real possibility if faith was broken with the Creator.[5] However, Wesley highlighted the unspoken promise in this verse rather than the threat: "And as there is a *threatening* of *death* expressed in these words, so a *promise of life* is implied. The threatening death only in case of disobedience, implied, that otherwise he should not die. And even since the fall, the law of God promises life to obedience... since the tenor of it is, 'Do

---

2. Douglas Davies distinguished "the direction of thought" that creation follows: "Creation speaks the positive language of birth and development, of fullness, and the divine imagination set upon a widening relationship of God and the world in the broadest of cosmic senses: survival comes by expansion." Davies, *Theology of Death*, 5.

3. Wesley's first sermon at St. Mary's (*The Image of God*) addressed the topic of humankind's original righteousness. Outler noted that this was a commonplace idea which had been mediated to Wesley through the Cambridge Platonists and John Norris. Introduction to *Image of God* (BE), 4:290.

4. Wesley, *What Is Man?* (BE), 4:26. According to Wesley's notes on Genesis 3:21, the act of clothing Adam and Eve in animal skins was God's way of demonstrating what death was since dying was foreign to their understanding. Wesley, *ENOT*, 1:9.

5. "But God said, 'You shall not eat of the fruit of the tree that is in the middle of the garden, nor shall you touch it, or you shall die'" (NRSV).

this and live . . . ."⁶ It was the advent of sin which overturned the perfect life that God had intended for all humankind. Wesley asserted,

> All were perfect in beauty, and man, the lord of all, was perfect in holiness. And as his holiness was, so was his happiness; knowing no sin, he knew no pain. But when sin was conceived, it soon brought forth pain; the whole scene was changed in a moment. He now groaned under the weight of a mortal body and–what was far worse–a corrupted soul.⁷

Wesley maintained that God's design for humanity was never death or dissolution; rather, humankind was always meant to flourish in the graces of God and live in harmony with the rest of creation.

The *Imago Dei*: The Life of the Soul

Humanity shared a special connection with the divine since they alone were formed in the image of God. Wesley affirmed it was the *imago Dei* that set men and women apart from the rest of creation and made them uniquely capable of relating to their Creator.⁸ In its most general sense, Wesley considered the image of God as "the true life of the soul" whereby humanity reflected the same qualities as the Divine Being.⁹ This "life of the soul" consisted of three facets which Wesley described as the natural, political and moral image. Since the *imago Dei* encapsulated what Wesley meant by life and human flourishing in its fullest essence, it is against this backdrop that the true nature and substance of death is most clearly revealed.

---

6. Wesley, *Doctrine of Original Sin, Part V* (BE), 12:408. This section of Wesley's treatise was distilled from two sermons by Samuel Hebdon: *Man's Original Righteousness* and *God's Covenant with Adam* (1740).

7. Wesley, *Trouble and Rest of Good Men* (BE), 3:533.

8. This is not to say that by setting humanity apart Wesley devalued the rest of creation. In his sermon, *General Deliverance*, Wesley acknowledged that the animal kingdom had been subjected to the effects of sin and sympathized with their plight. *General Deliverance* (BE), 2:436–50.

9. Wesley was influenced by Henry Scougal's *The Life of God in the Soul of Man* (1677). In this work, Scougal described the image of God as participation with the very nature of God. He explained, "Religion being a resemblance of the divine perfections, the Image of the Almighty shining in the Soul of Man . . . it is a real participation of his Nature, it is a beam of the Eternal Light, a drop of that infinite Ocean of goodness, and they who are endued with it, may be said to have *God dwelling in their Souls, and Christ formed within them*." Scougal, *Life of God in the Soul of Man*, 9.

Undoubtedly, Wesley's reflections on the *imago Dei* were most directly influenced by two of his contemporaries—Matthew Henry and Isaac Watts.[10] In the opening volume of Matthew Henry's *Exposition of the Old and New Testament* (1707), the Presbyterian minister asserted that the image of God consisted of three things: nature and constitution, place and authority, and purity and rectitude.[11] In a nearly verbatim quote from Henry, Wesley described the divine image in his own *Notes on the Old Testament* in the following manner: 1) Humanity's nature: God is spirit; therefore, humans were made not in the physical image of God but were fashioned after the divine in their immortal, intelligent souls. 2) Place and authority: Humans are the governing authority over the rest of creation. 3) Purity and rectitude: Our primal parents naturally conformed to the will of God because they were formed in knowledge, righteousness, and true holiness.[12] Isaac Watts produced a similar model for the *imago Dei*. In his treatise *The Ruin and Recovery of Mankind* written in 1740, Watts categorized the image of God in the following format: 1) Natural image: This aspect "consisted partly in his spiritual, intelligent, and immortal nature, and the various faculties thereof . . . ."[13] 2) Political image: Humanity was made "lord and governor over all the lower creation."[14] 3) Moral image: "This principle of universal righteousness and holiness . . . in which Moses . . . represents man to be at first created."[15]

Wesley employed the same categories of the *imago Dei* that Isaac Watts used (natural, political, moral); although, Wesley stressed the role of love more than his counterpart did. David Rainey identified Wesley's particular emphasis on love as a link between Wesley's concept of salvation and

---

10. Wesley and his contemporaries inherited a well-developed Trinitarian model for the image of God from their Western Christian heritage. In his work, *On the Trinity*, Augustine pronounced that humanity bore the image of the Trinity which he described in terms of the mind, the knowledge of the mind, and love. He further developed his understanding of Mind to consist of memory, understanding and will. See *On the Trinity* Books IX and X for his full discussion. Augustine, "On the Trinity," 25–143. Wesley did not utilize Augustine's specific categorization of the divine image, but he did ascribe to the tri-part image.

11. Henry, *Matthew Henry's Commentary on the Whole Bible*, 1:10.

12. Wesley, *ENOT*, 1:7. Wesley borrowed most of his comments on the creation narrative directly from Matthew Henry's commentary. He abbreviated some of Henry's notes but changed very little of Henry's content regarding this passage.

13. Watts, "Ruin and Recovery of Mankind," 6:59.

14. Watts, "Ruin and Recovery of Mankind," 6:59.

15. Watts, "Ruin and Recovery of Mankind," 6:59.

his view of love as the reigning characteristic of God. Rainey noted, "For Wesley it was God's love that bound the Father, Son, and Holy Spirit together and it was this love that most adequately defined the three images of intelligence, governance, and morality that bound the human person into wholeness."[16] Because our original parents embodied the Creator's love, Wesley asserted that there was nothing which stood in the way of direct communion between the human and the divine. Indeed, Wesley declared:

> In this image of God was man made. 'God is love:' accordingly, man at his creation was full of love, which was the sole principle of all his tempers, thoughts, words, and actions. God is full of justice, mercy, and truth; so was man as he came from the hands of his Creator. God is spotless purity: and so man was in the beginning pure from every sinful blot. Otherwise God could not have pronounced *him* as well as all the other work of his hands, "very good." (Gen. i. 31.).[17]

Natural Image

Wesley believed that the natural image endowed humanity with understanding, will, and liberty. He termed the faculty of understanding, or the ability to "know," as the "most essential property of the spirit" since it is the natural image and all its capacities that mark humans as spiritual beings.[18] After all, it is the intellect which allows humankind to comprehend that which is "other" and gives them the ability respond as rational beings. Although humanity could never claim unlimited understanding, Wesley surmised that their knowledge was not clouded by error before the Fall.[19] The natural image also includes the "*will*, with various affections (which are only the will exerting itself various ways) that he might love, desire, and delight in that which is good."[20] Almost inseparable from the will is the endowment of liberty or, in other words, the ability to choose between good and evil. "Without this [liberty]," Wesley exclaimed, "both the will and the understanding would have been utterly useless. Indeed, without liberty man had been so far from being a *free agent* that he could have been

---

16. Rainey, "John Wesley's Doctrine of Salvation," 68.
17. Wesley, *New Birth* (BE), 2:188.
18. Wesley, *End of Christ's Coming* (BE), 2:474.
19. Wesley, *End of Christ's Coming* (BE), 2:474.
20. Wesley, *End of Christ's Coming* (BE), 2:474.

no *agent* at all."[21] Wesley went on to assert that understanding, the will, and at least a measure of liberty are necessary elements to create an intelligent being. Without a measure of freedom, Wesley explained, "there can be no moral good or evil, no virtue or vice"; for only where "an intelligent being knows, loves, and chooses what is good [or evil] can there be any vice or virtue."[22] Thus, the natural image imparts the God-given capacity for intellect, virtue, and morality in decision making which is absent in the animal realm.

Political Image

Wesley said less about the political image than the natural or moral aspects, yet it is a key component in determining humanity's placement within the rest of creation. Theodore Weber identified a twofold nature in Wesley's concept of the political image. First, it implied "an ordering of responsibility and stewardship in which humankind as a whole represents God in the governing of whatever else dwells on earth."[23] Secondly, it suggested a mediatory role in which humanity "also stands between God and the 'inferior creatures' as God's agent and representative."[24] Both aspects can be seen in Wesley's comments about the political image in his sermon *The General Deliverance*. He wrote, "So that man was God's viceregent upon earth, the prince and governor of this lower world; and all the blessings of God flowed through him to the inferior creatures. Man was the channel of conveyance between his Creator and the whole brute creation."[25] While the role as viceregent indicated a certain hierarchy of the created order, what is most notable is the relational aspect Wesley discerned in the political image. In other words, the political image allowed humankind to relate to the rest of the created order with the same love and grace that God had lavished upon them.

---

21. Wesley, *End of Christ's Coming* (BE), 2:475.
22. Wesley, *End of Christ's Coming* (BE), 2:475.
23. Weber, "Recovering the Political Image," 393.
24. Weber, "Recovering the Political Image," 393.
25. Wesley, *General Deliverance* (BE), 2:440.

Moral Image

By far, the most distinctive aspect of the *imago Dei* is the moral image. Humanity was formed, stated Wesley,

> Not barely in his *natural image,* a picture of his own immortality, a spiritual being endued with understanding, freedom of will, and various affections; nor merely in his *political image,* the governor of this lower world, having 'dominion over the fishes of the sea, and over the fowl of the air, and over the cattle, and over all the earth'; but chiefly in his *moral image,* which, according to the Apostle, is 'righteousness and true holiness'.[26]

It is the moral image which endows human beings with the character of God; indeed, the moral image is indicative of the Holy Spirit infusing humanity with the very nature of the divine.[27] It is because of this indwelling nature that Lindström defined the moral image in terms of permeating love, righteousness, and purity. "Just as God is love, so man at first was imbued with love. His whole being bore its imprint. It was the guiding principle of his disposition, thoughts, words, and deeds. Like the Creator, the creature was righteous, merciful, true, and pure."[28]

When Wesley concluded that the moral image was the cardinal facet of the *imago Dei*; he was not undermining the significance of the natural and political aspects in his elevation of the moral image. Rather, according to Collins, Wesley focused on the moral image for three reasons.[29] First, this aspect of the image distinguishes humanity from all other created beings. It is not reason (i.e. the natural image) that separates us from the beasts, Wesley claimed, "But it is this: man is capable of God; the inferior creatures are not."[30] Second, the moral image creates the possibility for sin because it signifies a relation to God which can be corrupted through evil influences. Third, the moral image is expressive of the moral law which Wesley defined

---

26. Wesley, *New Birth (BE),* 2:188.

27. Maddox noted that the natural image in humanity ". . .referred to those characteristics or faculties definitive of being human, while the moral Image of God referred to the 'character' of holiness and love that God intended for humanity." Maddox, *Responsible Grace,* 68.

28. Lindstrom, *Wesley and Sanctification,* 25.

29. For a more detailed discussion regarding Wesley's threefold foci on the moral image, see Collins's discussion on the topic. Collins, *Theology of John Wesley,* 55–57.

30. Wesley, *General Deliverance* (BE), 2:441.

as "a copy of the eternal mind, a transcript of the divine nature."[31] Collins proposed that the moral law provided Wesley with "an important window on the essence of the *imago Dei*, namely righteousness and holiness, [and] highlights the similarities between the nature of God as well as the nature of humanity as originally created."[32] Thus, the moral image not only provides the capacity for relationship with the Creator, it also defines the intended *nature* of that relationship.

The Fall: Sin as the Harbinger of Death in All its Forms

According to the Genesis account, only one thing could mar humanity's perfect existence and uninhibited communion with God—a violation of the Creator's injunction not to eat of the tree of the knowledge of good and evil. A simple statement heralded the calamity that would befall the entirety of creation if this commandment was not honored. "But of the tree of the knowledge of good and evil you shall not eat, for in the day that you eat of it you shall die" (Gen 2:17 NRSV). Adam and Eve's consumption of the forbidden fruit was more than an act of disobedience; rather, Wesley believed that humanity first doubted the validity and integrity of God's command.[33] Cox asserted, "Wesley summed up the nature of the fall of Adam by pointing out that his sin was unbelief—he chose to believe Satan rather than God."[34] This unbelief in the goodness and loving intent of the Creator struck a fatal blow to the loving relationship between the divine and humankind. The act of eating the fruit was the stroke that finalized

---

31. Wesley, *Original, Nature, Properties, and Use of the Law* (BE), 2:10.

32. Collins, *Theology of John Wesley*, 56.

33. Wesley espoused a two-covenant theology: a covenant of works which was based upon perfect obedience and was relevant to humanity prior to the Fall and a covenant of grace given to humankind after the Fall. He contrasted the two types of covenants in his sermon *Righteousness of Faith* (BE), 1:202–16. Wesley came by this theology through the *Westminster Confession* which defined the first covenant as "a covenant of works, wherein life was promised to Adam, and in him to his posterity, upon condition of perfect and personal obedience." *Westminster Confession*, "Chapter VII. 2.," 42. The *Confession* described the second covenant as "the covenant of grace; wherein He freely offereth unto sinners life and salvation by Jesus Christ, requiring of them faith in Him that they may be saved . . . ." *Westminster Confession*, "Chapter VII. 3.," 42.

34. Cox, "John Wesley's Concept of Sin," 18.

a rending of the loving connection between our primal parents and the Creator.

The moment this break in fellowship occurred death was introduced into the created world. Once a place of perfection for human flourishing, creation was now a fallen environment filled with corruption and death. Henceforth, Wesley declared that even while we are "'in the midst of life we are in death;' yea, 'the whole of creation groaneth together,' 'being in bondage to sin,' and therefore, to misery."[35]

In Wesley's theology, death was multifaceted because it was more than the demise of the physical body; it was the reversal of all that God had purposed for human life. Death represented the severing of a holy, loving relationship with God as well as the corruption of humanity's relationship with the rest of creation. In the moment Adam and Eve sinned, death manifested itself in three forms: spiritual death, physical (temporal) death and eternal death.[36]

> For the moment he tasted that fruit, he died. His soul died, was separated from God; separate from whom the soul has no more life than the body has when separate from the soul. His body likewise became corruptible and mortal; so that death then took hold on this also. And being already dead in spirit, dead to God, dead in sin, he hastened on to death everlasting, to the destruction both of body and soul, in the fire never to be quenched.[37]

Spiritual Death: The "Life of God" Lost

Since Wesley traced the origin of human death back to the first sin, it is little wonder that he viewed spiritual death as the source of both physical and eternal death. Wesley's definition of spiritual death was the defacement of the *imago Dei* or the "life of God" lost within the soul. In his sermon,

---

35. Wesley, *Trouble and Rest of Good Men* (BE), 3:533. The phrase, "in the midst of life we are in death," was part of the burial service found in the *Book of Common Prayer*. Wesley retained this language in his *Sunday Service* book for the Methodists of North America.

36. Johann Arndt also utilized the categories of spiritual, physical and eternal death. However, Arndt defined spiritual death not in terms of separation from God but as "Death to Avarice, Pride, Voluptuousness, Wrath, and all the other Sins and Passions of the corrupt Nature." Arndt, *Of True Christianity Four Books*, 1:97. Wesley published an abridgement of Arndt's *Of True Christianity* in the *Christian Library*.

37. Wesley, *Justification by Faith* (BE), 1:185.

The New Birth, Wesley explained that when Adam sinned, "he died to God, the most dreadful of all deaths. He lost the life of God: he was separated from him in union with whom his spiritual life consisted . . . the love of God was extinguished in his soul, which was now 'alienated from the life of God.'"[38] Separation from God caused a loss of purity, love, and inverted the characteristics of the *imago Dei* into their opposite traits. The natural image was corrupted because humanity's understanding, will, and liberty were turned away from God and used to serve selfish ends. No longer was human knowledge without error, nor did the will turn toward that which is good, pure, and true. Gone was the liberty to choose a life-giving relationship with the Creator; rather, humans were enslaved to the world's deceptive pleasures so that even that which brought forth superficial happiness caused destruction in the end. Runyon noted that after the Fall reason, the will, and freedom were "employed to rationalize our self-seeking goals, defend ourselves against our self-induced insecurities, and idealize our bondage."[39] The political image was also marred beyond recognition; no longer did humanity mediate grace to the rest of the creation. Rather, the created order was misused for humankind's perverse desires.

While all three facets of God's image were affected by the Fall none was as profoundly impacted as the moral image. The natural and political aspects were severely marred by sin, but the moral image was completely shattered. "The life of God was extinguished in his soul," Wesley lamented. "The glory departed from him. He lost the whole moral image of God, righteousness and true holiness . . . Thus was his soul utterly dead to God!"[40] This loss denied humanity the ability to participate in the transcendent nature of God. Wesley explained, "It is one thing to receive from God an ability to walk and speak, eat and digest, to be supported by his hand as a part of this earthly creation . . . and another, to receive from him a life which is his own likeness, to have within us something which is not of this creation . . . ."[41] The loss of the moral image, then, translated into a dimmed-down existence for humankind; without holiness and purity, humanity forfeited that which was necessary to realize the fullest aspects of the life God had intended for them.

---

38. Wesley, *New Birth* (BE), 2:189.
39. Runyon, *New Creation*, 20.
40. Wesley, *End of Christ's Coming* (BE), 2:477.
41. Wesley, *Holy Spirit* (Jackson), 7:511. This sermon was included in the Jackson edition but was authored by John Gambold not Wesley.

In Wesley's understanding, spiritual death was not only the destruction of humanity's communion with the divine but the distortion of all relationships. The image of God, particularly the moral aspect, served to facilitate ongoing harmony and fellowship among all creation. Runyon explained the nature of the moral image as, "neither a capacity within humanity nor a function that can be employed independently of the Creator, because it consists in a relationship in which the creature *receives* continuously from the Creator and mediates further what is received."[42] This description relates to Maddox's observation that Wesley distinguished four aspects of human relationship: relationship with God, other humans, animals, and with ourselves. With the defacement of the image of God, each of these aspects of relationship was adversely affected. Maddox explained,

> to enumerate, our understanding is darkened, our will is seized by wrong tempers, our liberty is lost, and our conscience is left without a standard. From this spiritual corruption spring our actual sins, which affect all four relationships definitive of human life. We no longer consistently love and serve either God or other humans; we neglect or actively terrorize the 'lower' animals; and, as a result, our own happiness and self-acceptance drain away.[43]

The relationships through which God meant to provide companionship and create a sense of belonging are instead the source of pain and isolation.

Original Sin: Spiritual Death Passed Down to the Human Race

Since the Fall, Wesley believed that the entire human race was wholly corrupted with inbred sin.[44] In other words, everyone entered the world with an inherited depravity which Cox defined as "that moral condition with which all men are born . . . spiritual death passed on to every child of Adam . . . ."[45] In his sermon, *Treasure in Earthen Vessels*, Wesley explained:

---

42. Runyon, *New Creation*, 18.

43. Maddox, *Responsible Grace*, 82.

44. Lindström noted that Wesley was at odds with the beliefs of the Enlightenment because he attributed our fallenness not to following a bad example but to a corrupt nature. Lindstrom, *Wesley and Sanctification*, 26.

45. Cox, "John Wesley's Concept of Sin," 19.

And 'in Adam all died.' For fallen Adam begat a son 'in his own likeness.' And hence we are taught to give a clear, intelligible account of the littleness and baseness of man. He is sunk even below the beasts that perish.... There is in every man born into the world (what is not in any part of the brute creation; no beast is fallen so low!) a 'carnal mind', which 'is enmity', direct enmity, 'against God.'[46]

Wesley derived his understanding of original sin partly from Henry Woolnor's case for traducianism. Wesley found Woolnor's argument for the universality of original sin compelling, and he abstracted Woolnor's work, *The True Originall of the Soule*, and published it in the *Arminian Magazine*. Woolnor made the claim that like produces like. God created humanity in the divine image, and after the Fall, Adam and Eve produced children after their own sinful image. Thus, every human being inherits both a corruptible body and a corrupted soul. Woolnor reasoned,

> because being wholy in *Adam*, according to the just law of nature, & so sinning potentially in him, he with us, and we with him being then actually one; the whole nature of mankinde is thereby so corrupted... and we are stained with originall sinne, and so are liable to Gods eternall wrath, so soone as we begin to be. It being a just and necessary law in nature, that as the roote is, such are the branches....[47]

Wesley believed so adamantly that spiritual death in the form of original sin tainted every soul that he made acceptance of this point a litmus test of true Christianity. "But here is the shibboleth: Is man by nature filled with all manner of evil? Is he void of all good? Is he wholly fallen? Is his soul totally corrupted?" Wesley asked. "Allow this, and you are so far a Christian. Deny it, and you are but an heathen still."[48]

Wesley's sentiments were not uniformly shared among his contemporaries. In 1740, John Taylor, a dissenting minister, published his treatise *The Scripture-Doctrine of Original Sin* which claimed that the only consequence of Adam's sin was physical death and not the universal corruption of human nature. Taylor argued that the cause of sin was the choice of one's own will and was not caused by corruption from Adam's sin.[49] He declared,

---

46. Wesley, *Heavenly Treasure in Earthen Vessels* (BE), 4:162.
47. Woolnor, *True Originall of the Soule*, 56.
48. Wesley, *Original Sin* (BE), 2:183–84.
49. For Taylor's full argument see: Taylor, *Scripture-Doctrine of Original Sin*, 128.

"Sin proceedeth from our own choice, as it necessarily must, and not from Adam's transgression."[50] Furthermore, in Taylor's view, physical death was not a punishment for original sin or a sign of universal inbred sin; rather, death was a method of divine discipline. He went so far as to claim that even the death of innocent children was a means of God's correction. He asserted, "Where the scriptures speak of death, or any calamity inflicted upon children, such calamities are represented as disciplinary to Parents."[51]

To Wesley, Taylor's view smacked of Pelagianism because it undermined the absolute necessity of God's grace. Deeply troubled by Taylor's assertions, Wesley wrote *The Doctrine of Original Sin According to Scripture, Reason and Experience* as a corrective to Taylor's claims. In this treatise, Wesley argued that physical death indicated the universal corruption of human nature. Children suffered and died, not as pawns in a cosmic game to discipline wayward parents, but because every human soul was born with a distorted image of God and is in a state of spiritual death. When Wesley declared, "[sufferings] have in them the nature of punishments, even on us and on our children. Therefore, children themselves are not innocent before God. They suffer; therefore, they deserve to suffer," he was not insinuating that any particular child deserved divine punishment.[52] His point was that God does not punish one person to cure the sin of another. *Everyone* faces suffering and physical death because *all* are under the unfortunate curse of sin. "Now, as these sufferings cannot be sent upon them [children] to correct their personal sins, so neither are they sent as a trial of their virtue . . . ," Wesley proclaimed.[53] Rather the death of innocents (such as children) indicted that all are "under some general curse, involved in some general punishment."[54] Without the understanding that original sin is the cause of death, God could be viewed as a capricious being that uses the death of innocents as an instrument of punishment. Against such a notion, Wesley declared, "It remains, that the death *expressed* in the original threatening,

---

50. Taylor, *Scripture-Doctrine of Original Sin*, 130.

51. Taylor, *Reply to the Reverend Mr. John Wesley's Remarks*, 25.

52. It helps clarify Wesley's arguments in this treatise to recognize that he was arguing against John Taylor's notion that death and suffering were means of improving virtue rather than a result of original sin. Wesley, *Doctrine of Original Sin, Part III* (BE), 12:310.

53. Wesley, *Doctrine of Original Sin, Part IV* (BE), 12:372.

54. Wesley, *Doctrine of Original Sin, Part IV* (BE), 12:372.

and *implied* in the sentence pronounced upon man, includes all evils which could befall his soul and body—death temporal, spiritual, and eternal."⁵⁵

Wesley's insistence upon the utterly noxious effects of sin was not a depreciation of the dignity of humankind; rather, to hold any other view was, for Wesley, a disregard of the pernicious nature of sin and an inaccurate reflection of humanity's unmitigated need for God's grace. Wesley reasoned, "If, therefore, we take away this foundation, that man is by nature foolish and sinful, 'fallen short of the glorious image of God,' the Christian system falls at once."⁵⁶ Bryant discerned a direct correlation between grace and original sin in Wesley's reasoning. "For Wesley, grace had no meaning without original sin, and furthermore salvation was rendered unnecessary .... The doctrine of original sin was as constitutive to Wesley's theology as the doctrine of grace.... If the doctrine of original sin falls, other doctrines fall with it."⁵⁷ Therefore, Wesley's theology of original sin should not be viewed in terms of a bleak anthropology but as an immense estimation of God's graciousness.

Three Dimensions of Death and Depravity

Recognizing that much was at stake in his doctrine of original sin, Wesley emphasized three dimensions of human depravity that are relevant to his understanding of spiritual death. First, sin strikes at the very root of what it means to be human. Humanity, created in the image of God, was designed to be intimately connected to both God and fellow human beings. Indeed, the very defining attribute of humanity is the capacity for relationship. Sin distorted this interrelatedness inherent to humanity so that when Adam sinned, the totality of the human race was affected. Tyson suggested Wesley's doctrine of sin cannot be understood outside the correlation between personal sin and the whole of humanity. He noted, "Imbedded in [Wesley's] model [is] the recognition that all sin has a personal quality; it is based in the will and conscience (or lack thereof) of individuals and their collectives.... Nor does Wesley see sin as a private matter between the individual and God—individual sin quickly has catastrophic ramifications."⁵⁸ Simply put, Wesley recognized that no one can opt out of human history or the

55. Wesley, *Doctrine of Original Sin, Part IV* (BE), 12:220.
56. Wesley, *Doctrine of Original Sin,* Introduction (BE), 12:158.
57. Bryant, "Original Sin," 524.
58. Tyson, "Sin, Self and Society," 86.

corporate fallen nature of the human race; thus, everyone is subject to death in all its forms.

Second, the absolute corrupting nature of original sin highlights the cruciality of God's freely bestowed grace. Because no one is exempt from inherited sin, the solution to the problem of sin and death lies completely outside the human realm.[59] Lindstrom declared, "Since the whole of mankind is involved in guilt and punishment and since human nature has been utterly perverted, man has no chance at all of saving himself by his own efforts. Instead, he is referred exclusively to God's grace in Christ."[60] More will be discussed about God's grace especially in terms of the divine response to the marred *imago Dei*; however, Wesley's embrace of total depravity indicated that he understood humanity was completely dependent upon God's grace for salvation due to their corrupted state.

Finally, Wesley was careful to draw a distinction between original sin and personal or actual sin. He was careful to clarify that no one will be damned solely for bearing the burden of original sin. Wesley illustrated this point by using the example of an infant who dies. The infant is obviously affected by original sin in that they are subject to death, but through God's grace, the guilt of that sin does not rest upon the child.[61] Wesley noted in his argument against Taylor,

> You add: '*Suffering* may happen where there is *no sin*, as in the case of brutes and infants . . .' Absolutely true. That is, where there is no *personal* sin, but only *sin imputed*. There was no *personal sin* in our blessed Lord there can be none either in brutes or infants. He suffered therefore for the sins of others, which were thus *imputed* to him. As is the sin of Adam to infants, who suffer death through him . . . .[62]

---

59. Tyson argued that an important aspect of Wesley's doctrine of original sin is its structural role in the grand narrative of salvation. "The fall of the first Adam provides the pattern for redemption through the second Adam (Christ)." Tyson, "Sin, Self and Society," 80.

60. Lindstrom, *Wesley and Sanctification*, 31.

61. For Wesley, the baptism of infants resulted in regeneration–a washing away of the guilt of original sin. He wrote, "it is certain, our Church supposes that all who are baptized in their infancy are at the same time born again." *New Birth* (BE), 2:197.

62. Wesley, *Doctrine of Original Sin, Part III* (BE), 12:319. Wesley's distinction here has considerable pastoral implications since suffering is not necessarily linked to personal guilt.

Although Wesley thought no one was culpable for inherited sin, this sin warped human nature in such a way that it inevitably led to actual, willful sin. In other words, original sin plunged humankind into the dark night of spiritual death, but it is their own sins that keep them there.

Physical Death

In Wesley's paradigm, there would be no physical death without the Fall. It was only after humanity sinned that death became an innate biological occurrence in the natural processes of life. In *The Theology of Death*, Davies proposed that "death can be framed as either natural, albeit still fraught with grief and potential anxiety, or as a supernatural evil to be countered by a supernatural good."[63] Wesley applied the latter description. His explanation for physical death was simple; it was a direct result of spiritual death. In *The Doctrine of Original Sin* Wesley declared, "He [Adam] would never have died if he had not sinned."[64] Just as Wesley defined spiritual death in terms of disconnection from the life of God, so he identified physical or temporal death in terms of separation. In spiritual death the rift is a relational one—disrupting communion between the human soul and the divine nature. In physical death, the rending entails the parting of the soul from the body.[65] To be sure, physical death also involves a relational disconnection from family, friends, and acquaintances. Wesley defined temporal death as, "leaving this world, these houses, lands, and all things under the sun . . . never to return . . . It is leaving these pleasures . . . leaving your acquaintance, companions, friends . . . ."[66] However, as Wesley went on to elaborate in this passage, death is also a devastating tearing of one's very "self." "It is leaving a part of yourself; leaving this body which has accompanied you so long. Your soul must now drop its old companion, to rot and moulder into dust. It must enter upon a new, strange, unbodied state. It must stand naked before God!"[67]

---

63. Davies, *Theology of Death*, 9.

64. Wesley, *Doctrine of Original Sin*, Part VII (BE), 12:452. This section of Wesley's treatise was an abridgement of Thomas Boston's *Four-fold State of Man* (1720).

65. Wesley, *What Is Man?* (BE), 4:25.

66. Wesley, *Word to a Condemned Malefactor* (Jackson), 11:179.

67. Wesley, *Word to a Condemned Malefactor* (Jackson), 11:179.

The Mystery of Death

In defining death as the soul dropping its "companion" (the body), Wesley identified himself as a dualist.[68] That is to say, he accepted the notion that the soul and body are distinct entities by distinguishing the spirit, "the highest principle in man, the immortal spirit made in the image of God . . . ," from the body, which he defined as "organized matter which every man received in the womb . . . ."[69] Wesley believed the soul or spirit was a direct gift from God, the "Father of Spirits;" therefore, it always retained a transcendent element which was beyond humanity's ability to fully comprehend.[70] In wrestling with the question, "What is our soul?" Wesley raised more questions for himself than answers. "It is a spirit, we know. But what is a spirit? . . . And where is the soul lodged? In the pineal gland? In the whole brain? In the heart? In the blood? In any single part of the body? Or . . . all in every part?"[71] He concluded that such speculations were beyond humankind's ability to comprehend, and any awareness that we possess an undying soul was ultimately a matter revealed through the spiritual sense of faith.[72] Ultimately, physical death retained a certain amount of mystery for Wesley because he recognized not only the complexity of the human body but also the inexplicable connection between body and soul. Wesley wondered at what point the soul left the body. Was it when respiration ceased, when the heart quit beating, or when the person grew stiff and cold? He noted that there were several cases in which these signs of death were

---

68. Wesley viewed the person to consist of dual substances: an eternal, immaterial soul and a temporal, physical body. Wesley reflected, "Yet the soul cannot dispense with [the body's] service . . . For an embodied spirit cannot form one thought but by the mediation of its bodily organs. For thinking is not (as many suppose) the act of a pure spirit, but the act of a spirit connected with a body . . . ." Wesley, *On the Fall of Man* (BE), 2: 405–406. This type of dualism can also be found in the writings of Augustine. For example, in *City of God*, Augustine noted the effect of the body upon the soul. Augustine, *City of God*, Book 19, Chapter 17.

69. Wesley, *Some Thoughts Upon 1 Thessalonians 5:23* (Jackson), 11:447.

70. Wesley, *ENOT*, 1:7.

71. Wesley, *Imperfection of Human Knowledge* (BE), 2:576. He went on to question how the soul and body are connected and concluded that even the wisest of people cannot answer such questions.

72. Wesley understood faith to be a spiritual sense which reveals the unseen realm to the otherwise blinded mind. "Faith is an evidence to me of the existence of that unseen thing, my own soul. Without this I should be in utter uncertainty concerning it. . . . But by faith I know it is an immortal spirit, made in the image of God . . . ." Wesley, *On the Discoveries of Faith* (BE), 4:30.

apparent, yet the person revived. Wesley finally concluded, "Therefore we can say no more than that death is the separation of the soul and body; but in many cases God only can tell the moment of that separation."[73]

Sin: The Ongoing Cause of Physical Death

Wesley believed that the soul and body are distinct entities, but he equally insisted that the body and soul are so intertwined it is impossible to define one's true "self" without taking both into account. Wesley reflected, "Indeed at present this body is so intimately connected with the soul that I seem to consist of both. In my present state of existence, I undoubtedly consist both of soul and body. And so I shall again after the resurrection to all eternity."[74] Consequently, this meant that in Wesley's theology sin did not just reside in the ethereal realm of spirit; rather, he contended the soul and body are so interwoven that sin (whether original or actual) had real, physical consequences. In terms of original sin, Wesley offered a psychosomatic theory in which original sin affected the body in such a way as to impede all of its processes.[75] Actual sin (whether inward or outward) also had the potential to affect the body in negative ways. For example, in his comments on Deut 5:17 ("Thou shalt not kill."), Wesley correlated the sin of gluttony with physical death. "Have you not tempted any one, to what might shorten his life? . . . Are you guilty of no degree of self-murder? Do you never eat or drink anything because you like it, although you have reason to believe, it is prejudicial to your health?"[76] Wesley also assumed that inward sins such as envy, inordinate grief, or uncontrolled passion could break down the body.[77] In 1778 he published a poem by a young woman in the Arminian

---

73. Wesley, *What Is Man?* (BE), 4:25.

74. Wesley, *What Is Man?* (BE), 4:23.

75. See the opening pages of Wesley's *Primitive Physick* or his sermon *The Image of God* (BE), 4:290–303 for a more detailed study of the body's process of deterioration. As was typical of his era, Wesley viewed the body in a mechanical sense. Thomas Oden explored Wesley's conjecture that eating the forbidden fruit caused the vessels of the body to lose flexibility. Wesley speculated that since the Fall the "juices" of the body adhere to the vessel walls until finally the channels fill up leading to death. Oden observed that Wesley effectively describes arterial build-up which leads to heart disease with a great deal of accuracy. Oden, *John Wesley's Scriptural Christianity*, 136.

76. Wesley, *ENOT*, 1:601.

77. This perspective has the potential to cast new light on Wesley's seventeen birthday journal entries in which he assessed his state of being. He testified to robust health

Magazine entitled, "To Health," which praised the vibrancy of innocence and youth. In the final stanza, the author of the poem suggested that her spiritual standing had a direct impact on her physical well-being:

> No Boist'rous Passion shook my troubled Frame,
> To fright thee [health] from my Breast, nor pining Care,
> Nor rankling Envy ever fester'ed there;
> Nor did Intemp'rance e'er my Blood inflame:
> And Grief, though long an Inmate of my Mind,
> To Hope and Cheerfulness her Place resign'd.[78]

Wesley recorded similar sentiments in *Primitive Physick* where he declared the love of God was the "Sovereign Remedy of all Miseries." This love "effectually prevents all the bodily disorders the passions introduce, by keeping the passions themselves within due bounds. And by the unspeakable joy and perfect calm . . . it gives the mind, it becomes the most powerful of all the means of health and long life."[79]

While Wesley observed a connection between sin and death, he did not make the error of equating sin with physical death. In other words, personal sin does not have to be present for illness or death to occur. All are affected by death and suffering because creation itself has been corrupted. Even the creaturely realm languishes because of the Fall. Wesley noted of the animal kingdom, "And not death alone came upon them, but all of its train of preparatory evils: pain, and ten thousand sufferings . . . likewise all those irregular passions, all those unlovely tempers (which in men are sins, and even in brutes are sources of misery) 'passed upon all' the inhabitants of the earth . . . ."[80] Indeed, the whole of creation will endure suffering until the moment of final redemption. Commenting on Rom 8:20–23, Wesley

---

despite his aging body. It is possible, perhaps even on a subconscious level, that the aging Wesley drew a correlation between his physical and spiritual condition. Such an association would explain the triumphant tone to these annual musings. On his seventy-second birthday he wrote, "How is this, that I find just the same strength as I did thirty years ago? That my sight is considerably better now and my nerves firmer than they were then? That I have none of the infirmities of old age and have lost several that I had in my youth?" Wesley, *Journal* June 28, 1774 (BE), 22:418.

78. Unknown, "To Health," October (1778), in Wesley, *AM,* 481.

79. Wesley, *Primitive Physick.* Wesley transcribed advice from Cheyne's work, *An Essay of Health and Long Life* for use within *Primitive Physick.* See Cheyne's Chapter VI, "On the Passions," in *Essay of Health and Long Life* for a more in-depth examination of the impact of the love of God on health and well-being.

80. Wesley, *General Deliverance* (BE), 2:444.

observed that all of creation is "literally in the pain of childbirth; to be delivered of the burden of the curse . . . to this very hour, and so on till the time of deliverance."[81]

For Wesley, sin was always the underlying cause of death even in the case of natural disasters or accidents. The biblical flood, for example, was the result of God's judgment upon sin. Relevant to his own day, Wesley openly wondered if the utter devastation suffered in the 1755 earthquake in Lisbon could be God's judgment upon the world for its flagrant sin. To those that scoffed at this idea, Wesley retorted,

> If by affirming, 'All this is purely natural,' you mean it is not providential, or that God has nothing to do with it, this is not true . . . unless you can prove that God never works in or by natural causes. But this you cannot prove; nay, none can doubt of his so working, who allows the Scripture to be of God. For this asserts, in the clearest and strongest terms, that 'all things' (in nature) 'serve him;' that (by or without a train of natural causes) He 'sendeth his rain on the earth;' that He 'bringeth the winds out of his treasure,' and 'maketh a way for the lightning and the thunder;' in general, that 'fire and hail, snow and vapour, wind and storm, fulfil his word.'[82]

However, Wesley did not believe God lashed out at the earth's inhabitants out of cruel wrath. The purpose of judgment on sin was to urge people to seek God's salvation. Wesley argued that God was not "an epicurean deity, who sits at ease upon the circle of the heavens, and neither knows nor cares what is done below," but as the Creator all things "cannot neglect the work of his own hands."[83] Wesley urged his readers to "make this gracious God our friend."[84] Then one need not fear death or destruction. In his sermon, *The Cause and Cure of Earthquakes*, Wesley advised, "He that believeth hath the witness in himself; hath the earnest of heaven in his heart; hath love stronger than death. Death to a believer has lost its sting; 'therefore will he not fear, though the earth be removed, and though the mountains be carried into the midst of the sea.'"[85]

---

81. Wesley, *ENNT*, 549.

82. Wesley, *Serious Thoughts Occasioned by the Earthquake at Lisbon* (Jackson), 11:6.

83. Wesley, *Serious Thoughts Occasioned by the Earthquake at Lisbon* (Jackson), 11:10.

84. Wesley, *Serious Thoughts Occasioned by the Earthquake at Lisbon* (Jackson), 11:10.

85. Wesley, *Cause and Cure of Earthquakes* (Jackson), 7:399.

To be clear, Wesley did not make the error of assuming all natural disasters which resulted in death were caused by God's wrath. Wesley adamantly denied that simply because God is sovereign over nature did not mean that "all death, or rage, or curse, wherever it is, must be said, in the language of Scripture, to be the wrath or vengeance of God."[86] Elsewhere, Wesley asserted that God did not make death and "neither hath he pleasure in the death of any living thing."[87] Death was the consequence of existing in a fallen world. However, Wesley was unwilling to accept that physical death acted randomly, nor did he place physical death within the realm of satanic control. He noted in his sermon, *The Important Question*, that, "the breath of man is not in his [Satan's] hands. He is not the disposer of life and death—that power belongs to the Highest."[88] Here Wesley's goal was to affirm that God reigned supreme over both life and death even though death was never the Creator's intent for humanity. This was an important distinction because, even though death was the result of evil, Wesley believed God remained firmly in control of the dying experience.

Death as Punishment

There were occasions when death could be the direct result of divine punishment. As the apostle John observed in 1 John 5:16, "There is a sin unto death." Wesley did not take the apostle's words to mean a specific sin which led to death (beyond what he cited as "total apostasy from both the power and form of godliness"); rather, he viewed a "sin unto death" to mean a sin which "God has determined to punish with death."[89] Wesley reported visiting a "poor backslider" whom he feared, "sinned a sin unto death–a sin which God has determined to punish by death."[90] There was no hint of condemnation in Wesley's journal entry about the dying man; indeed, the fact that he visited this man who had "given great occasion to the enemy to blaspheme" indicated Wesley's hope that God would heal his soul if not his body. Wesley noted that he had seen many people "(chiefly notorious backsliders from high degrees of holiness, and such as had given great occasion to the enemies of religion to blaspheme) whom God has cut short in

---

86. Wesley, *Extract of a letter to the Rev. Mr. Law* January 6, 1756 (Jackson), 9:483.
87. Wesley, *General Deliverance* (BE), 2:441.
88. Wesley, *Important Question* (BE), 3:195.
89. Wesley, *ENNT* (1 John 5:16), 919.
90. Wesley, *Journal* June 25, 1776 (BE), 23: 20–21.

the midst of their journey . . . ."[91] However, even in these instances, death was not meant to be a heartless punishment but rather a means whereby God captured the attention of the sinner so that reconciliation could occur. Wesley explained, "But in most of these cases it has been observed that 'mercy rejoiced over judgment'. And the person themselves were fully convinced of the goodness as well as the justice of God. They acknowledged that he destroyed the body in order to save the soul . . . So they died that they might live for ever."[92]

There were some cases, however, when death as divine punishment was received without a spirit of humility or reconciliation. Wesley recorded the story of a woman who had been a faithful believer but took "violent offense" at the actions of another person. Even after she became ill, she refused to set things right. Wesley wrote, "But as her illness increased, so did her anger. She often cried out, 'I cannot forgive, I will not forgive,' and intermixed with horrid shrieks, till she died."[93] Sometimes, for those who actively opposed the Methodist ministry or who were brazen sinners, death came swiftly and violently. Wesley documented the account of a clergyman from the Church of England who continually inveighed against the Methodists in his sermons and warned his listeners against any association with them. One Sunday, while about to embark on yet another rant against Wesley's followers he "was suddenly seized with a rattling in his throat, attended with an hideous groaning. He fell backward against the door of the pulpit, burst it open, and would have fallen down the stairs but that some people caught him . . . ."[94] He died the next Sunday. In yet another case, "an eminently profane man" swore to his friends that he would outlive all of them. Wesley wrote, "Instantly he began vomiting blood; and in ten minutes was stone-dead."[95] Wesley's point was not to scare people

---

91. Wesley, *Call to Backsliders* (BE), 3:218.

92. Wesley, *Call to Backsliders* (BE), 3:219.

93. Wesley, *Journal* February 5, 1767 (BE), 22:70. See also Wesley's account of Thomas B., a backslider who, "died stupid as an ox." *Journal* May 5, 1757 (BE), 21:101.

94. Wesley, *Journal* August 23, 1743 (BE), 19:331. See also Wesley's account of three farmers who violently opposed the spread of Methodism and kept many from hearing the preaching. All three of them were dead within a month. The third recognized his impending death as a punishment from God and begged to be spared, but Wesley noted, "The Lord would not be entreated." *Journal* May 30, 1759 (BE), 21:198-99. Benjamin Harris, whom Wesley labeled "the most impetuous" of all those involved in the George Bell perfectionism scandal, was "struck raving mad" and died two weeks later. *Journal* December 26, 1763 (BE), 21:401.

95. Wesley, *Journal* October 22, 1770 (BE), 22:257.

into submission; rather, he recognized that God's grace could not be flouted without running the risk of dire consequences.

The Soul's Existence After Physical Death

Although Wesley believed when the soul left the body it entered a "strange, unbodied state," he appeared to have some sense of the soul's "embodiment" before the final resurrection. Wesley theorized that Paul's division of humanity into three parts, "Your spirit and soul and body be kept sound and blameless . . ." provided some explanation to the mystery of the human soul.[96] In an essay dedicated to unravelling Paul's statement here, Wesley speculated that the "spirit" referred to "the highest principle" in a human– that part which was formed in the image of God and endued with "self-motion, understanding, will, and liberty."[97] The body was the "organized matter" formed in the womb while the soul denoted the "immediate clothing of the spirit."[98] By this Wesley reasoned that the soul sheaths the spirit both before and after death, so that the spirit remains unaffected by the death of the body but carries on in existence after the fact. Wesley surmised that from the beginning of the spirit's existence the soul was connected to the spirit and "consists of ethereal or electric fire, the purest of all matter. It does not seem to be affected by the death of the body, but envelopes the separate, as it does the embodied spirit; neither will it undergo any essential change, when it is clothed with the immortal body at the resurrection."[99]

After death, Wesley believed the spirit entered the realm of Hades which he defined as "the receptacle of separate spirits, from death to resurrection."[100] Wesley noted that the term Hades was frequently translated into English as "hell," but to think of Hades as simply a place for the damned was a misnomer. Rather, Hades was separated into two divisions: the abode of the unholy dead and the domain of holy, happy souls. Here the dead awaited the resurrection and the judgement in their respective

---

96. 1 Thess 5:23 NRSV.

97. Wesley, *Some Thoughts on an Expression of St. Paul* (Jackson), 11:447.

98. Wesley, *Some Thoughts on an Expression of St. Paul* (Jackson), 11:447.

99. Wesley, *Some Thoughts on an Expression of St. Paul* (Jackson), 11:448. Unfortunately, Wesley did not always abide by the careful distinction he made here between the "soul" and "spirit." Instead, he seemed to use "soul" and "spirit" interchangeably in most places.

100. Wesley, *On Faith*, 1791 (BE), 4:189.

places.[101] This did not mean that Wesley believed in the Roman Catholic notion of a particular judgement. Rather, he asserted, "The imagination therefore of one judgment at death, and another at the end of the world, can have no place with those who make the written Word of God the whole and sole standard of their faith."[102] However, this did not mean that the dead did not know their fate prior to the great judgment since Wesley reasoned when a soul stood naked before God outside the bounds of time it was "no longer possible to be deceived in the judgment which we pass upon ourselves."[103] In other words, the distractions of life, the world's allurements and the heart's own cunning could no longer shut out the eternal radiance of divine truth.

Souls awaiting the great judgment could not change their eternal fate. Wesley was well aware of those who attempted to offer an alternative to the Roman Catholic option of purgatory while still holding to the view that the repentant sinner could escape the antechamber of hell. Wesley referenced Archibald Campbell's work, *The Doctrines of a Middle State Between Death and the Resurrection* (1721), which suggested that departed souls such as the rich man in the story of the beggar Lazarus who retained a measure of "disinterested love" for their fellow humanity might have a chance of escaping their final doom.[104] However, Wesley heartily disagreed with Campbell's conclusion. Once a person entered the realm of eternity, the season of proving one's concern for God and others had passed. Wesley declared, "For *time* is no more: the time of our trial for everlasting happiness or misery is past. Our *day*, the day of man, is over; 'the day of salvation' is ended. Nothing now remains but the day of the Lord, ushering in wide, unchangeable eternity."[105]

Wesley was also well aware of several treatises published on the topic of "soul sleep" of which perhaps the most well known was Edmund Law's Appendix to the *Considerations on the Theory of Religion* (1755). Law refuted the idea of a conscious awareness after death. He argued that Scripture taught death was represented by "Sleep, by a negation of all Life, Thought, or

---

101. Wesley discussed the resurrection and judgment in great detail in his sermon *Great Assize* (BE), 1:354–375.
102. Wesley, *Good Steward* (BE), 2:293.
103. Wesley, *Good Steward* (BE), 2:292.
104. Wesley, *On Faith*, 1791 (BE), 4:190.
105. Wesley, *Good Steward* (BE), 2:289.

Action; by Rest or Home; Silence, Oblivion, Destruction, or Corruption."[106] The idea of a "compound *Being* or Person, [was] merely grounded on our *Ignorance*, and will prove equally against known Fact . . . as well as against the *Union* of two such heterogeneous principles, as those of our own Soul and Body are supposed to be."[107] Interestingly enough, Law garnered the support of John Taylor (the same Taylor who wrote *The Scripture-Doctrine of Original Sin*) who openly approved of Law's theory.[108] Wesley did not seem to consider this controversy much of a threat because his attitude was dismissive. He asked, "What then can we say to an ingenious man who has lately made a discovery that disembodied spirits have not only no senses . . . they are in a dead sleep from death to the resurrection! . . . What can we say but ingenious men have strange dreams . . . they sometimes mistake for realities."[109]

Quite to the contrary of soul sleep, Wesley spoke of the dead as though they retained consciousness, a recognizable form, and certain senses which allowed them to experience pain or pleasure. This is not to say that Wesley believed the soul retained its bodily senses; rather, the soul was "all eye, all ear, all feeling, all perception."[110] To illustrate his point Wesley used the example of a dream. "For does not the soul see, in the clearest manner, when the eye is of no use, namely in dreams? Does she not then enjoy the faculty of hearing without any help from the ear?"[111] Wesley also maintained that the dead would retain their knowledge, will, understanding, memory, and all the affections. He scoffed at those who believed the dead would neither recognize nor care about other souls in paradise. Citing the dying words of Thomas Halyburton who proclaimed that he was going to join his father, mother, and ten siblings who proceeded him in death, Wesley asked, "Would you have replied: 'What if you are going to them? They will be no more to *you* than any other persons; for you will not know them.' Not know them! Nay, does not all that is in you recoil at that thought?"[112]

---

106. Law, *Considerations on the Theory of Religion*, 367.

107. Law, *Theory of Religion*, 399.

108. There were other voices in the debate over soul sleep. See: Blackburne, *No Proof in the Scriptures*.

109. Wesley, *Good Steward* (BE), 2:290–291.

110. Wesley, *Human Life a Dream* (BE), 4:113.

111. Wesley, *Good Steward* (BE), 2:289.

112. Wesley, *On Faith*, 1791 (BE), 4:196–97.

Wesley was not simply being pastoral to allow the dying Halyburton to continue in his belief that he would join his beloved family in paradise to await the resurrection. Rather, Wesley cited the example of "the rich man" and Lazarus in Abraham's bosom; the rich man in this passage of Scripture clearly recognized Lazarus and Abraham even from afar. Furthermore, Wesley maintained that souls in paradise employed and grew in the holy tempers; thus, they must be able to relate to others in a meaningful way. A person cannot exercise gratitude for one's fellow beings if there is no awareness or recognition of them. Thus, Wesley reasoned, "For we know every holy temper which we carry with us into paradise will remain in us forever. But such is gratitude to our benefactors . . . And this implies that the knowledge of our benefactors will remain, without which it cannot exist."[113] In other words, even in the afterlife Wesley assumed there was no "solitary religion . . . no holiness but social holiness."[114]

Wesley believed the departed continued to develop and change so that souls continued to progress spiritually in whatever state they were in prior to death. That is to say, the evil soul continued in its wickedness while the righteous soul "will be continually ripening for heaven, will be perpetually holier and happier, till they are received into 'the kingdom prepared for them from the foundation of the world.'"[115] Wesley imagined the unholy souls joined the spirits of other sinful beings (both human and demonic) "howling and blaspheming, cursing God and looking upwards, till they are cast into 'the everlasting fire,'"[116] and were quite possibly employed by Satan to work havoc on those who do not know God-inflicting disease, temptations, natural disasters, and death. On the other hand, the righteous "will . . . advance in holiness, in the whole image of God wherein they were created! In the love of God and man, gratitude to their Creator, and benevolence to all their fellow-creatures," Wesley wrote.[117] Wesley found great

---

113. Wesley, *On Faith*, 1791 (BE), 4:197.

114. Wesley, Preface to a *List of Poetical Works* (Jackson), 14:321.

115. Wesley, *On Faith*, 1791 (BE), 4:191. Wesley mentions Archibald Campbell in this sermon. Campbell argued that it was possible for a repentant soul to escape the realm of the wicked; however, Wesley clearly disagreed with Campbell's conclusion. It is Campbell's citation of John Taylor that concerned Wesley's theology the most. Taylor essentially asserted that any final awareness of the person on the deathbed was simply a function of the brain and not a glimpse of the afterlife. See Law, *Considerations on the Theory of Religion*, 402.

116. Wesley, *On Faith*, 1791 (BE), 4:190.

117. Wesley, *On Faith*, 1791 (BE), 4:196.

comfort in the thought that holy souls may assist God's work by ministering alongside angels to the living. He reflected, "It is a pleasing thought that some of these human spirits attending us with, or in the room of, angels, are of the number of those that were dear to us while they were in the body."[118] Thus, in Wesley's theology, the righteous dead remained an integral part of the kingdom of God on earth and in the afterlife.

Eternal Death: Total Separation from God

In his essay, "Claiming a Death of Our Own," Lonnie Kliever summarized Wesley's theology of death in the following terms: "Because of original sin, physical and temporal death is the inevitable fate of all human beings. Because of actual sin, spiritual and eternal death is the deserved lot of all human beings."[119] Eternal death (which is pronounced at the great judgment) is the only type of death that encompasses both spiritual and physical death; therefore, it is the worst of the three forms and is rightly the most feared. Wesley defined eternal death as the irreversible and complete separation of a person from the Creator; it is the opposite of the communion entailed in a relationship of holy love. One of the defining marks of being created in the *imago Dei* entailed immortality of the soul; therefore, Wesley's understanding of eternal death did not encompass any form of annihilation.[120] It was a "vain thought" that death ended either the existence of the soul or the body. Rather, Wesley concluded, "It will put an end to neither the one nor the other; it will only alter the manner of their existence. But when the body 'returns to the dust as it was, the spirit will return to God that gave it.' Therefore, at the moment of death it must be unspeakably happy or unspeakably miserable."[121]

Although Wesley referenced eternal death throughout his writings, his most detailed description of eternal death is found in his sermon "On Hell" which was written in 1788. He used Mark 9:48 for his text which

---

118. Wesley, *On Faith*, 1791 (BE), 4:191.

119. Kliever, "Claiming a Death of Our Own," 280.

120. Wesley concluded, "The body is not the man; that man is not only a house of clay, but an immortal spirit; a spirit made in the image of God . . . We know all the things 'which are seen are temporal;'—of a changing, transient nature;—but 'the things which are not seen' (such as is the soul of man in particular) 'are eternal.'" Wesley, *What Is Man?* (BE), 3:460.

121. Wesley, *On Eternity* (BE), 2:367.

referenced the words of Jesus, "Where their worm dieth not, and the fire is not quenched." From this passage and many others like it, Wesley concluded that torment in the eternal fires of hell is precisely what Scripture means by eternal death.[122] Eternal torment stems from two sources which Wesley defined as "*poena damni*, what they lose, or *poena sensus*, what they feel."[123] Some of the "losses" are felt the instant the soul is severed from the body such as the privation of pleasure belonging to the bodily senses (touch, smell, taste). Also absent is that which Wesley termed "pleasures of the imagination"—nothing beautiful or honorable remains for those who are damned. Furthermore, they are separated from all the things which brought enjoyment and all the people they knew and loved. The most devastating loss of all is the recognition that joy is complete only in God's presence; therefore, forfeiting all hope of heaven and the opportunity to be in God's presence seals the person's utter misery. If, as Wesley proposed, the enjoyment of God is the *telos* of every person, to have the possibility of fulfilling one's true purpose completely removed makes one's very existence utterly wretched. Wesley concluded, "They will then know and feel that God alone is the center of all created spirits; and consequently that a spirit made for God can have no rest out of him ... Banishment from the presence of the Lord is the very essence of destruction to a spirit that was made for God. And if that banishment lasts for ever, it is 'everlasting destruction.'"[124]

Added to this utter devastation of being separated from God and every known good is what Wesley called *poena sensus* or the "punishment of sense." Here, Wesley made a distinction between Jesus's words "Where *their* worm dieth not," and "Where *the* fire is not quenched." Wesley understood "*the* fire" to be a generalized punishment; all in hell will suffer from the unquenchable flames while "*their* worm" he took to be personal in nature.[125] In other words, each soul will retain individual personhood and will

---

122. Wesley made the distinction between the "grave" and the place of a person's eternal existence. For instance, in his sermon *Dives and Lazarus* Wesley separated the current place of the rich man's torment from his place of eternal punishment. Those who die outside of a redemptive relationship with God await the final judgment in a place of pain and anguish from which there is no release.

123. Wesley, *Of Hell* (BE), 3:33.

124. Wesley, *Of Hell* (BE), 3:35.

125. Wesley acknowledged that even in this general punishment there could be varying degrees. He wrote, "'The fire' will be the same, essentially the same, to all that are tormented therein–only perhaps more intense to some than others, according to their degree of guilt." Wesley, *Of Hell* (BE), 3:37.

receive punishment for specific behavior. Wesley asserted that the measure of wickedness in a lifetime has a direct correlation to the amount of misery experienced in hell. In eternal death, a person suffers a guilty conscience, remorse, sorrow, and a sense of the wrath of God. Furthermore, all the unholy passions such as fear, anger, hatred, and jealousy consume the person since God's grace is no longer at work to check these affections of the heart. Ultimately, Wesley concluded, "the inhabitants of hell are perfectly wicked, having no spark of goodness remaining."[126] Although Wesley did not spell out exactly what he meant by having "no spark of goodness remaining," presumably he was referring to the withdrawal of God's grace.

Conclusion

Left unaided in the post-Fall condition, the *imago Dei* would remain in ruins, and spiritual, physical, and eternal death would be the fate of all since, as Wesley observed, "'through the offence of one' all are dead, dead to God, dead in sin, dwelling in a corruptible, mortal body, shortly to be dissolved, and under the sentence of death eternal."[127] However, because Wesley viewed all of creation as a gift of God's free grace, he was convinced that the Creator would not abandon humankind to a fate of hopeless death. Indeed, even in God's punishment of sin, Wesley found evidence of God's graciousness.

> He might justly have *chased him out of the world*, but he only chased him out of the garden. He might justly have 'cast him down to hell,' . . . but man was only sent to *till the ground out of which he was taken* . . . . His tilling the ground would be recompensed by his eating its fruits; and his converse with the earth, *whence he was taken*, was improvable to good purposes, to keep him humble, and to mind him of his latter end. Our first parents were excluded from the privileges of their state of innocency, yet they were not abandoned to despair; God's thoughts of love designing them for a second state of probation upon new terms.[128]

Wesley understood death in the context of God's creative intent for abundant life; therefore, his emphasis was on God's promises which described the potential for eternal life and happiness for all creation. Death

---

126. Wesley, *Of Hell* (BE), 3:40.
127. Wesley, *Justification by Faith* (BE), 1:185.
128. Wesley, *ENOT*, 19.

did not have the final word in Wesley's theology. Rather, as it will be examined in the following chapter, God graciously provided the means for everyone to overcome spiritual and eternal death.

Chapter 3

GRACE, REGENERATION, AND A GOOD DEATH

Introduction

WESLEY BELIEVED IT WAS possible by grace through faith in Christ for all of humanity to rise from the darkness of spiritual death and be re-united with their Creator in a relationship of holy love. Indeed, Wesley viewed salvation as the transition from spiritual death to the fullness of life. "By the righteousness of one, the free gift might come upon all unto justification of life, 'justification of life' as being connected with the new birth, the beginning of spiritual life, which leads us, through the life of holiness to life eternal, to glory," he proclaimed.[1] If followed to its proper end, the path of salvation led to glorification and eternal life. The new birth was the beginning of life in the Spirit; however, there were other points along Wesley's way of salvation (both prior to and after the new birth) which were marked by distinct interventions of God's grace. It was at these particular points that the correlation between Wesley's soteriology and his understanding of death was most clear. Therefore, an extensive analysis of his *ordo salutis* is necessary for an adequate interpretation of his theology of death.

---

1. Wesley, *On the Fall of Man* (BE), 2:411.

Sola Fide and Salvation

Upon his return to England from Georgia, Wesley met Peter Böhler and was heavily influenced by the Moravian's teaching about faith.[2] Wesley was captivated by Böhler's insistence that justification was a gift of grace which came through faith alone. While Wesley admitted that he had personally relied upon his own good works in the hope of salvation, the notion of *sola fide* was hardly foreign to the post-Reformation Church of England.[3] It is somewhat surprising, then, that it took some convincing for him to accept Böhler's definition of saving faith as a "sure trust and confidence which a man hath in God, that through the merits of Christ *his* sins are forgiven, and *he* reconciled to the favour of God."[4] What is more comprehensible was the point with which Wesley took the most issue—Böhler's claim that conversion was an instantaneous work. It had been ingrained into Wesley's understanding of salvation by the Caroline Divines (Jeremy Taylor in particular) that justifying grace was gradually bestowed only in conjunction with corresponding good works. That is, only those who were in some measure sanctified could be justified. Jeremy Taylor pointed out, "Our sins indeed are potentially pardoned, when they are marked out for death . . . when by resolving and fighting against sin we die to sin daily . . . when we are 'dead to sin, and are risen again unto righteousness,' . . . then we are truly, effectually, and indeed justified, till then we are not."[5] With

---

2. On the day he met Böhler, Wesley noted it was "a day much to be remembered." Wesley, *Journal* February 7, 1738 (BE), 18:223.

3. Wesley openly admitted that he had placed his hope of salvation partly on his own works and righteousness. See Wesley, *Journal* May 12, 1738 (BE), 18:248 and *Journal* April 22, 1738 (BE), 18:233–34.

4. Wesley, *Journal* April 22, 1738 (BE), 18:233–34. The *Homilies* record a similar definition of faith: "For the right and true Christian faith is, not only to believe that holy Scripture, and all the foresaid articles of our Faith are true; but also to have a sure trust and confidence in God's merciful promises, to be saved from everlasting damnation by Christ." "Of Salvation of Mankind" Part III, in *Certain Sermons or Homilies Appointed to Be Read in Churches in the Time of Queen Elizabeth*, 22.

5. Taylor, "Fides Formata," 3:292–93. To be sure, Taylor and the other Caroline Divines were not suggesting that anyone deserved or merited salvation. Bishop Bull clarified this in his remarks regarding St. James's claim that believers were justified by works and not faith alone. Bull observed, "'by works,' St. James does not mean that our works are the principle or meritorious cause of our justification." Rather, Bull concluded that good works were "the necessary condition for a man's justification, that is, that he may receive the forgiveness of sins, obtained through Christ, and become accepted of God to salvation." Bull, *Harmonia Apostolica*, 10–11. The true concern of the Caroline Divines revolved around the issue of antinomianism.

this interpretation of justifying faith in mind, Wesley recorded, "I could not understand how this faith should be given in a moment; how a man could *at once* be thus turned from darkness to light from sin and misery to righteousness and joy in the Holy Ghost."[6]

Determined to test the veracity of Böhler's assertions, Wesley searched the Scriptures for evidence and was amazed at what he found. "To my utter astonishment," Wesley declared, "[I] found scarce any instances there of other than *instantaneous* conversions."[7] Böhler also introduced Wesley to three people who gave witness "of their own personal experience that a true, living faith in Christ is inseparable from a sense of pardon for all past, and freedom from all present sins . . . . This faith was the gift, the free gift of God, and that he would surely bestow it upon every soul who earnestly and perseveringly sought it."[8] Wesley recorded in his journal that he "was now thoroughly convinced," and he invested the theological terminology handed down to him from his tradition with new meaning.[9] He exchanged a more gradual understanding of justification and regeneration (brought about by faith *and* works) with belief in immediate conversion which was separated from the necessity of works and accompanied by a sense of assurance.

Free Grace

It was not long before Wesley found for himself the justifying, sanctifying, assuring faith which was in accordance with his new model. On May 24, 1738, Wesley had his famous Aldersgate experience where he felt his "heart strangely warmed. I felt I did trust in Christ, Christ alone for salvation, and an assurance was given me that he had taken away *my* sins, even *mine*, and saved *me* from the law of sin and death."[10] It is noteworthy that Wesley marked Aldersgate as the moment when he personally appropriated "the free grace of God in Christ" since free grace, imbued with his newly acquired interpretation of immediacy, quickly became an underlying theme

---

6. Wesley, *Journal* April 22, 1738 (BE), 18:234. In this same entry, Wesley recorded his astonishment that he could scarcely find an example in Scripture of conversion that was not instantly wrought.

7. Wesley, *Journal* April 22, 1738 (BE), 18:234.

8. Wesley, *Journal* May 12, 1738 (BE), 18:248.

9. Wesley, *Journal* May 12, 1738 (BE), 18:248.

10. Wesley, *Journal* May 24, 1738 (BE), 18:250.

of his overall theology.[11] *Salvation by Faith* was the first sermon Wesley published after his heart-warming experience. He opened this sermon by proclaiming,

> All the blessings which God hath bestowed upon man are of his mere grace, bounty, or favour: his free, undeserved favour, favour altogether undeserved, man having no claim to the least of his mercies. It was free grace that 'formed man of the dust of the ground, and breathed into him a living soul', and stamped on that soul the image of God ... The same free grace continues to us, at this day, life and breath, and all things. For there is nothing we are, or have or do which can deserve the least thing at God's hand. 'All our works thou, O God, hast wrought in us. These therefore are so many more instances of free mercy: and whatever righteousness may be found in man, this also is the gift of God.[12]

The emphasis on "free grace" could not be more explicit; therefore, it is worthwhile to determine why the qualifier "free" was so important to Wesley and how it impacted his interpretation of the *ordo salutis* and his approach to death.

Several conceptions of grace can be found in Wesley's writings; however, his comments above outline his understanding of grace as freely bestowed divine favor. It was out of this favor that God created the world, and it is this same free grace that bestows every measure of goodness experienced by humankind. Wesley understood this favor to be nothing less than God's love for all humanity, and he often interchanged the terms "love" and "free grace" in his writings.[13] Further along in the sermon, he also described grace as divine power noting that through God's justifying grace, a believer is delivered from the guilt and power of sin. Wesley explained that through this power a believer is enabled to grow in Christ "'going on in the might of the Lord his God', 'from faith to faith', 'from grace to grace', until at length he comes unto a perfect man, unto the measure of the stature of the

---

11. Wesley, "To the Revd. Samuel Wesley, Jun." October 30, 1738 *Letters* (BE), 25:575.

12. Wesley, *Salvation by Faith* (BE), 1:117–18.

13. Wesley sometimes used the terms *grace* and *love* interchangeably. He noted, "By 'the grace of God' is sometimes to be understood that free love, that unmerited mercy, by which I a sinner, through the merits of Christ, am now reconciled to God." Wesley, *The Witness of Our Own Spirit* (BE), 1:309. See also: *Sermon on the Mount, III* (BE), 1:517; *Preface to a Treatise on Justification* (Jackson), 10:328; *Justification by Faith* (BE), 1:184–85; *Righteousness of Faith* (BE), 1:213; and *Circumcision of the Heart* (BE), 1:405.

fullness of Christ."[14] In other words, grace understood as divine power is nothing less than the Holy Spirit working in the lives of individuals.

Free Grace and Cooperant Grace

The qualification of saving grace as "free" marked a theological turning point for Wesley because it directly impacted the way he interpreted various species of grace received along the *ordo salutis*. It must be acknowledged that Wesley did not completely reject his former understanding of grace as divine and human cooperation.[15] To be sure, Wesley believed that God *always* initiated the work of redemption, but he also acknowledged that the gift of free grace empowered humanity to respond to God's work in their lives. "For first, God works; therefore you *can* work," Wesley declared. "Secondly, God works; therefore you *must* work."[16] Wesley even went as far as to say that "you must be 'workers together with him, (they are the very words of the Apostle); otherwise he [God] will cease working."[17]

Wesley also identified himself with Calvin's doctrine of free grace which was not based on any prior human working or response. At the Bristol Conference of August 1745, the question was posed, "Wherein may we come to the very edge of Calvinism?" To which the reply was made, "(1) In ascribing all good to the free grace of God; (2) in denying all natural free will and all power antecedent to grace; and (3) in excluding all merit from man, even for what he has or does by the grace of God."[18] Wesley staunchly affirmed that there were points along the path of salvation when God acted independently upon the human heart. For Wesley, these moments of utterly free grace included prevenient, justifying, initially regenerating, and entirely sanctifying grace. It was precisely at these points along the *ordo salutis* that Wesley's new interpretation of the immediacy of grace impacted his view of death and revolutionized his ministry to the dying. Unlike the

---

14. Wesley, *Salvation by Faith* (BE), 1:124–25.

15. Collins wrote extensively about Wesley's conception of grace as both free and cooperant. He pointed out that Wesley did not attempt to simultaneously hold a monergistic (work of God alone) and synergistic (divine–human cooperation) view of grace at all points along the *ordo salutis*. Collins alternatively categorized Wesley's view of grace along the lines of a Catholic emphasis (cooperant grace) and a Protestant emphasis (free grace). Collins, *Theology of John Wesley*, 155–64.

16. Wesley, *On Working Out Our Own Salvation* (BE), 3:206.

17. Wesley, *On Working Out Our Own Salvation* (BE), 3:208.

18. Wesley, *Minutes of Conference* August 2, 1745 (BE), 10:153.

Caroline divines who were reluctant to promise pardon to dying sinners because they thought the grace of justification required time and effort on the part of the believer, Wesley offered a real hope of salvation and assurance to even the most notorious of sinners because he by-passed an extended process of conversion due to his understanding of free grace.

Prevenient Grace as Free Grace

Even though Wesley was keen to emphasize human agency in working out one's own salvation, he realized that, due to the total depravity of human nature, the ability to respond to the offer of redemption must be initiated by God. Simply put, prevenient grace in Wesley's theology was God's initial action on behalf of humankind to raise them up from spiritual death.[19] In other words, no one had been left helpless in a state of "mere nature;" rather, as Cox noted, "in Wesley's view, man's present state is what he is by nature plus this prevenient grace. The very beginning of grace in man is in a sense a beginning of life."[20] Wesley explained this concept in the following matter:

> For allowing that all the souls of men are dead in sin by *nature*, this excuses none, seeing there is no man that is in a state of mere nature; there is no man, unless he has quenched the Spirit, that is wholly void of the grace of God. No man living is entirely destitute of what is vulgarly called 'natural conscience'. But this is not natural; it is more properly termed, 'preventing grace' . . . . Everyone has some measure of that light, some faint glimmering ray, which sooner or later, more or less, enlightens every man that cometh into the world.[21]

Outside the reception of preventing grace, humanity would be utterly helpless to respond to God. Therefore, prevenient grace is undoubtedly not only a species of free grace, but it is also an example of irresistible grace.

---

19. In his notes regarding *On Working Out Our Own Salvation*, Outler observed that *preventing* and *prevenient* were associated with the Spirit's work in drawing a person to God. Outler in Wesley, *On Working Out Our Own Salvation* (BE), 3:203. Thomas Noble also highlighted the role of the Holy Spirit's work in Wesley's doctrine of prevenient grace. "This grace was not some kind of created substance, some kind of medicine or causal force . . . it was God Himself, God the Holy Spirit present to the creature to re-create that freedom to believe and trust and follow and obey that was lost in the Fall." Noble, "John Wesley as a Theologian: An Introduction," 251.

20. Cox, *John Wesley's Concept of Sin*, 20.

21. Wesley, *On Working Out Our Own Salvation* (BE), 3:207.

Collins noted, "Since men and women in the natural state, according to Wesley, do not even have the freedom to accept or reject any offered grace, then this gift itself must be graciously and *irresistibly* restored."[22] Many are surprised to find the notion of irresistible grace in Wesley's theology; however, this is a clear example of Wesley's tightly crafted doctrine of free grace which must be held in careful balance with humanity's restored ability to respond to God's offer of salvation. Wesley viewed this tension as a part of the Arminian theological position since he noted, "The Arminians hold, that although there may be some moments wherein the grace of God acts irresistibly, yet, in general, any man may resist, and that to his eternal ruin, the grace whereby it was the will of God he should have been eternally saved."[23]

As foundational as this initial flush of God's grace is to the *ordo salutis*, Wesley did not view prevenient grace as salvific. Rather, as Herbert McGonigle observed, "While prevenient grace is not justifying grace, it is God's enablement to the sinner to respond to further grace. It is, therefore, a supernatural gift of God, and it gives to every human being that power of choice which is the prerequisite for all moral responsibility."[24] Wesley elaborated,

> Preventing grace, if we take everything that is entailed, is "all the 'drawings' of the 'Father', the desires after God, which, if we yield to them, increase more and more; all that 'light' wherewith the Son of God 'enlighteneth everyone that cometh into the world', *showing* every man 'to do justly, to love mercy, and to walk humbly with his God'; all the *convictions* which his Spirit from time to time works in every child of man.[25]

---

22. Collins, *Theology of John Wesley*, 80–81.

23. Wesley, *Question, 'What is an Arminian' Answered. By a Lover of Free Grace* (Jackson), 10:360.

24. McGonigle, "Arminius and Wesley on Original Sin," 106. McGonigle's assessment of preventing grace as "supernatural" is clearly in line with Wesley's teaching. Wesley equated the work of preventing grace with resurrection. He wrote, "Seeing all men are by nature not only sick, but 'dead in trespasses, and sins', it is not possible for them to do anything well till God raises them from the dead. It was impossible for Lazarus to 'come forth' till the Lord had given him life. And it is equally impossible for us to 'come' out of our sins, yea, or make the least motion toward it, till he who hath all power in heaven and earth calls our dead souls into life." Wesley, *On Working Out Our Own Salvation* (BE), 3:206–7.

25. Wesley, *Scripture Way of Salvation* (BE), 2:156–57.

Preventing grace enables humanity's ability to respond to God's gift of salvation, but it does not determine the nature of that response.

Prevenient Grace and Universal Redemption

Because preventing grace is irresistibly given to everyone, Wesley espoused the doctrine of universal redemption. By this Wesley did not mean that all *would* be saved; rather, he believed all *could* be saved since humanity's collective problem of spiritual death had been answered by God's universal extension of grace. Expounding upon John 3:16, Wesley declared, "God so loved the world . . . all men under heaven; even those that despise his love, and will *for that cause* finally perish. Otherwise not to believe would be no sin to them. For what should they believe? Ought they to believe that Christ was given for them? Then he was given for them."[26] In other words, if individuals remained separated from God it was not because God's loving favor was not extended to them but because they had rejected his overtures of free grace.[27]

It was noted earlier that Wesley embraced Calvin's doctrine of free grace since he agreed that salvation could not be merited through human efforts. However, Wesley's theology of prevenient grace was a significant departure from the Reformer's theology. Because prevenient grace opened the opportunity for all to respond (positively or negatively) to God's offer of salvation, this irresistibly bestowed grace was potentially salvific.[28] Colin Williams observed, "[Wesley] broke the chain of logical necessity by which the Calvinist doctrine of predestination seems to flow from the doctrine of original sin, by this doctrine of prevenient grace. This view of universal grace . . . 'free for all, and in all'–undoubtedly gave great impetus to the evangelistic appeal of his message."[29] Shortly after publishing his

---

26. Wesley, *ENNT*, 313.

27. Wesley found support for universal redemption in the Thirty-First Article which stated, "The offering of Christ once made, is that perfect redemption, propitiation, and satisfaction for all the sins of the whole world, both original and actual, and there is none other satisfaction for sin but that alone." Article XXI of the *Thirty-Nine Articles of Religion* in *Homilies*, Appendix not paginated.

28. Some have confused Wesley's doctrine of prevenient grace with Calvin's understanding of common grace. For the purposes of this discussion, the best distinction between the two is that preventing grace opened the opportunity for salvation while common grace does not fulfill a salvific role.

29. Williams, *John Wesley's Theology Today*, 44.

sermon *Salvation by Faith,* Wesley penned the controversial sermon *Free Grace.* Here Wesley publicly attacked the Calvinist doctrine of reprobation because he believed it denigrated the notion of free grace.[30] Specifically, Wesley took issue with the Calvinist notion that God's saving grace was not extended to *all* of humanity but only to a select few.

Wesley believed the Calvinist position cast aspersions on the character of God because it maintained that Christ did not die for the sins of the whole world and that God's salvific love did not truly pertain to all humankind. Such a view irrevocably damned an entire swath of humanity to death in all its forms. Wesley countered, "The grace or love of God, whence cometh our salvation is free in all, and free for all."[31] Restating the Calvinist position on this point, Wesley wrote, "To this some have answered: 'No: it is free only for those whom God hath ordained to life, and they are but a little flock. The greater part of mankind God hath ordained to death; and it is not free for them. Them God hateth; and therefore before they were born decreed they should die eternally."[32] Wesley's source for the Calvinist position on this matter likely included *A Practical Discourse of God's Sovereignty* written by Elisha Coles in 1673. In his discourse, Coles argued that portions of Scripture which spoke of the universal love of God and of God willing all to be saved could not possibly be taken literally. He declared, "For, there is nothing more plain . . . that the general Import of Election, is, to *chuse One* or *more out of Many:* Which necessarily implys the *leaving,* or not *chusing* of some; and consequently, the *Not-willing* of Salvation to all, *Universally.*"[33]

George Whitefield was heavily influenced by Coles's writing, and he argued against Wesley along similar lines. "But, blessed be GOD!—Our LORD knew for whom he died . . . For these, and these only, he is now interceding; and with their Salvation, he will be fully satisfied."[34] Whitefield went on to charge Wesley with "making Man's Salvation depend on his own

---

30. Wesley, *Free Grace* (BE), 3:545. The publication of this sermon was the source of a bitter disagreement between Wesley and George Whitefield and resulted in a division between the men and their followers. Wesley summarized the consequences with the following words: "So there were now two sorts of Methodists, so called, those for *particular* and those for *general* redemption." Wesley, *Short History of Methodism* (BE), 9:370. Despite the conflict, Wesley was convinced he was "indispensably obliged to declare this truth to all the world." Wesley, *Free Grace* (BE), 3:544.

31. Wesley, *Free Grace* (BE), 3:544.

32. Wesley, *Free Grace* (BE), 3:545.

33. Coles, *Practical Discourse of God's Soveraignty,* 73.

34. Whitefield, *Letter from the Reverend Mr. George Whitefield,* 28.

Free-Will" since Wesley asserted that, enabled by prevenient grace, everyone had the opportunity to respond positively to justifying and regenerating grace. Whitefield took issue with Wesley's assertion that Christ's death procured the freedom to choose or reject salvation because he believed that this position made salvation entirely dependent upon a person's self-will. He urged Wesley to rewrite his sermon and "entitle it, *Free Grace Indeed. Free, not because free to all; but free, because GOD may with-hold or give it to whom and when he pleases*."[35] Wesley refused to back away from his assertions because he could not accept that a God of love would damn anyone to eternal death without first giving that person the opportunity to choose life. Thus, Wesley's conception of prevenient grace stood in contrast to his Calvinist contemporaries because it provided everyone a foundation of hope in a context of spiritual, physical, and eternal death.

Prevenient Grace, Universal Redemption, and Infant Mortality

Wesley's conception of preventing grace and universal redemption also shaped his theology regarding the fate of children who died in infancy. With such dire infant mortality rates, the eternal fate of young children was an issue of real concern for eighteenth-century parents.[36] The strict Calvinist position taught that no one could have complete certainty about who was elected to salvation and who was set apart for damnation. This was especially true of infants since they had neither time nor opportunity to demonstrate any leanings toward God's grace. Wesley's position was that there could be no personal sin in infants, and they were considered innocent before God.[37] However, strict Puritans such as Samuel Willard, argued that a child's innocence of personal sin was no guarantee of salvation.

In his work, *The Mourners Cordial against Excessive Sorrow*, Willard reminded his readers that children, "were only *innocent vipers*, that were as full of the poyson and malignity of sin as ever they could hold, and would have vented this venome of theirs as soon as they had gotten a little strength and understanding . . . ."[38] Willard encouraged Christian parents not to

---

35. Whitefield, *Letter from the Reverend Mr. George Whitefield*, 29.

36. Entire works were dedicated to this tender topic such as the Rev. J. Malham's text which was written to comfort grieving parents. Malham, *Infant Salvation*.

37. Wesley, *Doctrine of Original Sin, Part III* (BE), 12:319.

38. Willard, *Mourners Cordial*, 77.

mourn for their dead children as those who have no hope since "there is a connexion between the promise and the precept, the more fruitful we are in our obedience to God, the clearer is our evidence that the promise belongs unto us."[39] Therefore, parents who were faithful in their Christian duties to the child (through the acts of baptism, prayer, and godly instruction) could have a greater hope than an unbeliever that their son or daughter would be saved from the fires of hell. However, Willard almost negated this hope with the declaration, "That Saving Grace is not absolutely tied to the visible covenant . . . His Grace is free. So that being in the Covenant and under the terms of it, doth it not make an infallible truth that such an one must & shall be Saved."[40] Furthermore, he acknowledged that even if the conditions were met to receive God's promises, "God is not under any positive engagement to this or that person to do it for him."[41] A parent's personal faith could not bring any certainty of the infant's eternal well-being since, as Willard reiterated, "God is not obliged or brought in debt unto us . . . . We ourselves when we have done all we can, and served God with the greatest integrity, are still *saved by grace* . . . And so much our Children too: God hath the liberty to do with his own what he will, we cannot beforehand with him."[42] Stannard soberly noted that "there was probably not much consolation in the fact that some Puritans, though not all, believed that [the child], if marked for damnation, would at least receive the 'easiest room' in that pit of eternal fire or torment."[43]

Wesley refused to espouse this teaching. He agreed with the Calvinist position that all infants were stained by original sin, "but it is equally true," he stated, "that, by the righteousness of one, the free gift came upon all men' (all born into the world, infant or adult) 'unto justification.' Therefore no infant ever was, or ever will be, 'sent to hell for the guilt of Adam's sin;' seeing it is cancelled by the righteousness of Christ, as soon as they are sent into the world."[44] Wesley also embraced the Anglican ritual of infant baptism which taught that through the "mystical washing away of sin" God would "look upon *this Child*; wash *him* and sanctify *him* with the Holy Ghost; that *he* being delivered from thy wrath, may be received into the ark

39. Willard, *Mourners Cordial*, 80.
40. Willard, *Mourners Cordial*, 76.
41. Willard, *Mourners Cordial*, 76.
42. Willard, *Mourners Cordial*, 78.
43. Stannard, *Puritan Way of Death*, 52.
44. Wesley, *Letters* "Letter to John Mason" November 21, 1776 (Telford), 6:239.

of Christ's Church."⁴⁵ Thus, not only was the infant covered by preventing grace but was also regenerated and "born anew of water and the Holy Ghost."⁴⁶ Only those who were guilty of actual sin (which Wesley defined as a willful violation of a known law of God) could be in danger of eternal punishment. Since infants were incapable of committing willful sin against God's law, there was no fear of eternal damnation for them. Elsewhere Wesley asserted, "No kind of assurance (that I know), or of faith, or repentance, [is] essential to their salvation who die infants."⁴⁷

Wesley's notions of preventing grace and the offer of universal redemption deeply impacted the way Arminian Methodists interpreted the death of their children. There is no better testimony to the appropriation of prevenient grace than Sally Wesley's letter to Charles informing him of the death of their infant son. In this heartbreaking letter, Sally noted the contrast between her hope and that of a Calvinist parent.

> It was a hard struggle before he could depart, he was dying all yesterday . . . he screamed three times about half an hour before he died that he could be heard from Nurse's Parlour to the other side of the street not Thro' guilt, (That is my comfort) but thro' extreme pain; perhaps were I of Calvin's opinion, I might have attributed it to a different cause, but glory be to a Redeemer's Love in declaring (for the consolation of distressed Parents) that of such is the kingdom of Heaven.⁴⁸

Free Grace and the New Birth

As important as the universal bestowal of preventing grace was to humanity, Wesley argued that a person in this state cannot truly enjoy life as God intended because "though he is a living man, he is a dead Christian."⁴⁹ To be sure, Wesley celebrated any positive transformation that took place in the soul as evidence of God's grace at work; however, it was to the peril of

---

45. Wesley, *Sunday Service of the Methodists in North America*, 139–40. Wesley's service of infant baptism was nearly identical to that contained in the *Book of Common Prayer*.

46. Wesley, *Sunday Service of the Methodists in North America*, 139.

47. Wesley, *Letters* "Letter to the Revd. Samuel Wesley, Jun." April 4, 1739 (BE), 25:622.

48. Wesley, "Sally Wesley to Charles Wesley."

49. Wesley, *New Birth* (BE), 2:192.

the soul to remain in a state of preventing grace without moving forward toward the new birth. Wesley warned that care must be taken "not, on the one hand, to despise the day of small things, nor on the other, to mistake any of these partial changes for that entire, general change, the new birth; that total change from the image of the earthly Adam into the image of the heavenly, from an earthly, sensual, devilish mind into the mind that was in Christ."[50] The new birth was God's gracious solution to the first type of death since it entailed renewal of the image of God that was lost when humanity sinned in the garden. Like creation and prevenient grace, the new birth was a work of God's free grace alone and was just as miraculous as raising a person from physical death.[51] Wesley insisted, "No man is able to work it in himself. It is a work of omnipotence. It requires no less power thus to quicken a dead soul than to raise a body that lies in the grave. It is a new creation; and none can create a soul anew but he who first created the heavens and the earth."[52] Reflecting upon Wesley's use of creation language in relation to the new birth, Lee noted, "It seems that Wesley is assuming an ontological change—re-birth—that transforms our inmost being. With this *new* exchange, we are empowered to conquer the image and likeness of our destroyer in us and 'to return from the gates of death to perfect soundness. . . .'"[53]

Wesley understood the new birth to consist of two elements: justification and regeneration. If either of these elements were missing, then the new birth had not yet occurred. In his sermon *The New Birth*, Wesley emphasized that justification (in the Christian sense) and regeneration occur simultaneously, "the former relating to that great work which God does *for us*, in forgiving our sins; the latter to the great work which God does *in us*, renewing our fallen nature."[54] Thus, to divide one from the other is a misrepresentation of Wesley's view of salvation.[55] Hoo-Jung Lee observed,

---

50. Wesley, *On Living without God* (BE), 4:174.

51. Anderson observed, "The work of making a person holy, of bringing a person to birth, belongs to the Triune God. By analogy to physical birth, we do not give birth to ourselves nor, by analogy to the raising of Lazarus, do we raise ourselves from the dead." Anderson, "Day of New Beginnings," 232.

52. Wesley, *Earnest Appeal* (BE), 11:48.

53. Lee, "Doctrine of the New Creation," 24–25.

54. Wesley, *New Birth* (BE), 2:187.

55. Even though Wesley understood justification and regeneration to be two distinct works of grace, he sometimes used the term justification to refer not simply to pardon but to the whole of salvation. For example, he stated, 'Justification' taken in its largest

"For Wesley salvation is not only a pardoning, justifying act of God as evidenced in faith ... but the transforming, renewing act of God as Spirit that aims at the *wholeness* of humanity in the restored image of God."[56] Since justification and regeneration constitute the new birth, Wesley applied the qualification of free grace to both doctrines. It was the qualification of free grace which distinguished him from the holy dying tradition of the Caroline Divines. Therefore, it is helpful to consider each element of the new birth separately.

Justifying Grace as Free Grace

Prior to meeting Böhler, Wesley's error had been the belief that he must attain a holy life before he could receive God's justifying grace—an idea that had been communicated to him by Jeremy Taylor (among others). In his journal Wesley recorded, "After we had wandered many years in the *new path* of *salvation by faith and works*; about two years ago it pleased God to show us the *old way* of *salvation by faith only*."[57] From that point forward, Wesley stressed the "free gift" of justification. "Justification is the act of God, pardoning our sins, and receiving us again to his favour," he declared. "This was free in him, because undeserved by us, undeserved, because we had transgressed his law, and could not, nor even can now perfectly fulfil it."[58] With his newfound understanding, Wesley concluded that such efforts

---

sense, implies a deliverance from guilt and punishment, by the atonement of Christ actually applied to the soul of the sinner now believing on him, and a deliverance from the power of sin, through Christ 'formed in his heart.' So that he who is thus justified or saved by faith is indeed 'born again.'" Wesley, *Salvation by Faith* (BE), 1:124.

56. Lee, "Doctrine of the New Creation," 35.

57. Wesley, *Journal* June 22, 1740 (BE), 19:153. Wesley blamed his misunderstanding in part on his mentor William Law. He wrote a scathing letter to his former mentor in which he complained, "Under this heavy yoke I might have groaned till death, had not a holy man, to whom God lately directed me ... answered ... 'Believe and thou shalt be saved.' ... This faith, indeed, as well as the salvation it brings, is the free gift of God.... Now, Sir, suffer me to ask, How will you answer it to our common Lord, that you never gave me this advice?" Wesley, *Letters* "To the Revd. William Law" May 14, 1738 (BE), 25:541.

58. Wesley, *Principles of a Methodist Farther Explained* (BE), 9:179. From 1738 forward, Wesley's writing was laced with the notion of justification as "free," a sheer gift of God's grace. See: *Treatise on Baptism* (Jackson), 10:190; *On the Fall of Man* (BE), 2:411; *Death of George Whitefield* (BE), 2:342; "To the Author of *The Craftsman*" July 8(?), 1745 (BE), 26:148–49; and "Preface to Journal Four" (BE), 19:117.

were not only in vain but contributed to the condition of spiritual death. He admonished, "For they being ignorant of . . . the justification that flows from his mere grace and mercy, freely forgiving our sins through the Son of his love . . . and seeking to establish their own righteousness' . . . as the ground of their pardon and acceptance,) . . . consequently seek death in the error of their life."[59]

One of Wesley's hallmark works on justification was his sermon *Justification by Faith*. In this sermon, Wesley stated that God's gracious gift of justification was the first act of grace which brought about actual restoration of new spiritual life. He wrote, "So that for the sake of his well-beloved Son . . . God now vouchsafes on one only condition (which himself also enables us to perform) both to remit the punishment due to our sins, to reinstate us in his favour, and to restore our dead souls to spiritual life, as the earnest of life eternal."[60] The "condition" of which Wesley spoke was, of course, faith; however, faith as a condition of pardon did not mean that justification was not a gift of grace alone. Rather, he noted that the faith leading unto justification was itself given as a gift of free grace so that justification was wholly an act of divine favor. "Of yourselves cometh neither your faith nor your salvation," argued Wesley. "'It is the gift of God,' the free, undeserved gift–the faith through which ye are saved, as well as the salvation which he of his own good pleasure, his mere favour, annexes thereto. That ye believe is one instance of his grace; that believing, ye are saved, another."[61] This view made Wesley confident his understanding of justification was as firmly planted in the doctrine of free grace as the Calvinist tradition.[62] He reasoned, "It is true, repentance and faith are privileges and free gifts. But this does not hinder their being conditions too. And neither Mr. Calvin himself, nor any of our Reformers, made any scruple of calling them so."[63]

---

59. Wesley, *Righteousness of Faith* (BE), 1:203. In this sermon, Wesley argued that obedience to the law was not the means of salvation under the new covenant. He noted that the Adamic covenant before the Fall was "Do this and live," but the covenant under Christ was "Believe and live." Wesley, *Righteousness of Faith* (BE), 1:204.

60. Wesley, *Justification by Faith* (BE), 1:186.

61. Wesley, *Salvation by Faith* (BE), 1:126.

62. Because of his view of free grace Wesley could legitimately maintain his claim that he was only a hair's breadth from Calvinism. Wesley, *Letters* "To John Newton" May 14, 1765 (Telford), 4:298.

63. Wesley, *Letters* "To a Gentleman at Bristol" January 6, 1758 (Telford), 3:246.

Regenerating Grace as Free Grace

Regeneration was no less a miraculous gift of free grace than justification was. Even as faith (the condition of pardon) was provided as a free gift of God's grace so was the "inward righteousness" or "holiness of heart" (the fruit of regeneration) given as "[God's] own free gift through Christ, and his own work by his almighty Spirit."[64] Therefore, Wesley proclaimed, "As soon as ever, through the free grace of God in Christ, we 'receive forgiveness of sins,' we receive likewise 'a lot among those which are sanctified, by faith which is in him.' Sin has lost its power: It has no dominion over those who are under grace, that is, in favour with God."[65] In other words, at the same time that God freely bestowed pardon for sin, the newly-born Christian actually became holy and exercised power over sin through the indwelling of the Spirit. This inseparable connection between regeneration and the new birth explains why Wesley did not draw a distinction between the two. In fact, Wesley often used the terms "new birth" and "regeneration" interchangeably.

In Wesley's understanding, regeneration encompassed two related but separate forms of transformation. Naglee helpfully explained, "First he saw it as a single act of God in which a 'new birth' takes place as the first radical change of human nature worked by the Holy Spirit. Secondly, he saw it as a continuing work of the Spirit within the believer, bringing him to the reality of the moral image of God fully restored."[66] The initial sanctification of the new birth functioned to reverse the curse of spiritual death. According to Wesley, the new birth was "that great change which God works in the soul when he brings it into life; when he raises it from the death of sin to the life of righteousness. It is the change wrought in the whole soul by the almighty Spirit of God when it is 'created anew in Christ Jesus.'"[67] Wesley explained that before a person is born of God, "he has, in a spiritual sense, eyes and sees not . . . ears, but hears not . . . . His other spiritual senses are all locked up; he is in the same condition as if he had them not."[68] But after the new birth all this was changed so that the person was alive unto God. Wesley exclaimed, "And now he may properly be said *to live* God having

---

64. Wesley, *Sermon on the Mount, IX* (BE), 1:643.
65. Wesley, *Sermon on the Mount, VI* (BE), 1:586.
66. Naglee, *From Font to Faith*, 43.
67. Wesley, *New Birth* (BE), 2:193–94.
68. Wesley, *New Birth* (BE), 2:192.

quickened him by his Spirit, he is alive to God through Jesus Christ... God is continually breathing, as it were, upon his soul, and his soul is breathing unto God. Grace is descending into his heart, and prayer and praise ascending to heaven."[69]

Regeneration in Wesley's second sense was "the first point of sanctification, which may increase more and more unto the perfect day."[70] Wesley recognized that while regeneration entailed vivification of the soul toward God it also paradoxically included the mortification of any trait which was contrary to the renewed moral image. Much like Wesley's understanding of regeneration, the mortification associated with the new birth had both instantaneous and on-going aspects. On the one hand, at the moment of the new birth the believer decisively died to willful sin and the allures of the world; yet on the other hand, the new birth was the point at which a believer began to mortify the sinful nature. "From the time of our being 'born again' the gradual work of sanctification takes place," Wesley explained. "We are enabled 'by the Spirit' to 'mortify the deeds of the body', of our evil nature. And as we are more and more dead to sin, we are more and more alive to God."[71]

Instantaneous Conversion: A Fruit of Free Grace

A result of Wesley's emphasis on free grace was his insistence that the new birth was an instantaneous event. Certainly, Wesley did not dismiss the reality of growth in grace as a vital part of the spiritual journey, but he determined that neither justification nor regeneration in terms of the new birth was gradual work. The new birth, Wesley reflected, was not a "progressive work carried on in the soul by slow degrees from the time of our first turning to God. This is undeniably true of sanctification; but of regeneration, the new birth, it is not true."[72] Furthermore, regeneration in Wesley's view, was "not 'gaining habits of holiness;' . . . It is not a natural,

---

69. Wesley, *New Birth* (BE), 2:193.
70. Wesley, *On God's Vineyard* (BE), 3:507.
71. Wesley, *Scripture Way of Salvation* (BE), 2:160.
72. Wesley noted, "This [the new birth] is a part of sanctification, not the whole; it is the gate of it, the entrance into it. When we are born again, then our sanctification, our inward and outward holiness begins.... A child is born of a woman in a moment, or at least in a very short time. Afterward he gradually and slowly grows up to the measure of the full stature of Christ." Wesley, *New Birth* (BE), 2:198.

but a supernatural change; and is just as different from the gradual 'gaining habits,' as a child's being *born* into the word is from his *growing* up into a man. The *new birth* is not, as you suppose the *progress*, or the *whole*, of sanctification, but the *beginning* of it . . . ."[73] This meant salvation was not a distant goal that one hoped to achieve; rather, as Wesley asserted, "It is a present thing; a blessing which, through the free mercy of God, ye are now in possession of."[74]

For Wesley, there were only two prerequisites necessary for salvation: 1) to be a sinner in need of redemption and 2) to believe that one's sins were forgiven through the merits of Christ. The first requirement was naturally met by all humanity due to the universality of the sinful nature. The second requirement was fulfilled through God's willingness to freely give the faith required for salvation. Thus, Wesley surmised it was sheer ignorance of God's desire to freely redeem all humankind that caused people to reject immediate pardon and instead attempt to earn God's forgiveness. He asserted that God had purchased a better covenant than the covenant of works, and Wesley called every person to "'Believe and live;' believe, and thou shalt be saved; now saved, both from the guilt and power of sin, and, of consequence, from the wages of it."[75]

Free Grace and the Holy Dying Tradition

The perspective of free grace and its fruit of instantaneous conversion opened an entirely new avenue of ministry for Wesley. If God's grace was instantaneously available to everyone, then the doors of salvation must be flung open wide to those who had no time to spare for a drawn-out conversion. The first person to whom Wesley proclaimed immediate salvation by faith alone was a prisoner awaiting execution. Wesley recorded in his journal,

> Accordingly, Monday 6, I began preaching this new doctrine, though my soul started back from the work. The first person to whom I offered *salvation by faith alone* was a prisoner under sentence of death. His name was Clifford. Peter Böhler had many times desired me to speak to him before. But I could not prevail

---

73. Wesley, *Doctrine of Original Sin, Part II* (BE), 12:300.
74. Wesley, *Scripture Way of Salvation* (BE), 2:156.
75. Wesley, *Righteousness of Faith* (BE), 1:204.

on myself so to do, being still (as I had been many years) a zealous asserter of *the impossibility of a death-bed repentance.*[76]

It was little wonder that Wesley "started back" from the idea of offering salvation to this man on the brink of death. The entirety of the English holy living and holy dying tradition which had so heavily influenced his spiritual development as a young man spoke against the possibility of a deathbed repentance. Furthermore, as McKenzie noted, "By the early eighteenth century, Anglican clergymen had more and more difficulty with the traditional notion that one's final moments were of critical spiritual significance, and that a 'good death' could outweigh a less than exemplary life."[77] The general assumption in the eighteenth century mind was that even for relatively benign people, the possibility of a deathbed repentance was slim. For those who had lived a notorious life of sin, the possibility of repentance was nearly non-existent.

Jeremy Taylor shaped much of Wesley's early thinking on the subject of deathbed repentance, and Taylor asserted that repentance was more than regret or sorrow over sin; rather, it was a "renewing of a holy life, a living the life of grace."[78] In other words, repentance was intertwined directly with holy living; therefore, repentance and consequentially pardon could not be actualized in a short period of time. For sinners to demonstrate true repentance, Taylor declared they must have made "a purchase of the contrary graces, by the labours of great prudence, watchfulness, self-denial and severity. *Nothing that is excellent can be wrought suddenly.*"[79] Thus, the timing of repentance was crucial since as Taylor purported, "A Repentance on our Death-bed, is like washing the Corps, it is cleanly and civil, but makes no change deeper than the skin."[80]

One can hardly find fault for the rationale behind Taylor's theology. God's desire for humanity was for them to live holy lives in Jesus Christ; therefore, deliberately rejecting the holiness offered to humankind through Christ with the intention of a quick deathbed repentance was the worst possible dismissal of God's mercy and a willful repudiation of the gospel promises made by Christ. Thus, Taylor insisted repentance was to be completed—not begun—upon the deathbed; "it must by that time be arrived to

---

76. Wesley, *Journal* March 6, 1738 (BE), 18:228.
77. McKenzie, *Tyburn's Martyrs*, 183.
78. Taylor, *Rule and Exercises of Holy Living*, 277.
79. Taylor, *Rule and Exercises of Holy Living*, 277.
80. Taylor, *Rule and Exercises of Holy Dying*, 145.

Contrition, that is, it must have grown from Fear to Love, from the passions of a Servant to the affections of a Son . . . For to hate sin, out of the love of God, is not the Felicity of a new Convert or an infant-Grace . . . ."[81]

Justification in the Holy Dying Tradition

Taylor's theology of repentance naturally shaped his conception of pardon for sin. Gregory Mesimore explained Taylor's view of God's forgiveness in the following terms: "Taylor's view of pardon is like the incoming tide. If pardon is initially well received, (demonstrated by a putting away of sins and a putting on of holiness) then it will slowly continue to advance."[82] This advancement of holiness and the cultivation of holy habits took time and effort that a dying person did not have. Thus, in Taylor's mind, the probability of a dying person receiving God's pardon was highly unlikely. Taylor made it clear that, like repentance, God's pardon was not immediately accessible. "No man is to reckon his pardon immediately upon his returns from sin to the beginnings of a good life . . . For a holy life being the condition of the Covenant on our part, as we return to God, so God returns to us, and our state returns to the probabilities of pardon."[83]

One must be careful not to jump to the conclusion that Taylor proposed works—righteousness; however, his understanding of justification was such that a person must first live a life of holiness before claiming God's acceptance and forgiveness. In other words, a person must be in some measure sanctified before he or she could be justified. Mesimore noted, "It is here that the synergy of Taylor comes through most forcefully; Christ's death alone will not justify the sinner but neither will a holy life be adequate."[84] Thus, Taylor's words in the introduction to *Holy Dying* were chilling for the one who has waited too long to repent and seek God's pardon.[85] Taylor intoned,

81. Taylor, *Rule and Exercises of Holy Dying*, 152.
82. Mesimore, "Way of Salvation," 51. Mesimore noted that Wesley made subtle, but highly significant, changes to Taylor's theology in his publication of Taylor in the Christian Library. One example of this is a portion where Taylor's original version reads "and if he does repent, timely and entirely, that is, live a holy life he shall be forgiven and saved." Wesley writes, "and if he does repent and believe, he shall be forgiven and saved." Mesimore, "Way of Salvation," 205.
83. Taylor, *Rule and Exercises of Holy Living*, 275.
84. Mesimore, "Way of Salvation," 56.
85. C. Fitzsimons Allison charges Taylor with pastoral cruelty for, among other

> But concerning sinners really under the arrest of death, God hath made no death-bed covenant, the Scripture hath recorded no promises, given no Instructions, and therefore I had none to give, but only the same which are to be given to all men that are alive, because they are so, and because it is uncertain when they shall be otherwise.[86]

For known sinners, such as the prisoners to whom Wesley ministered, the prospects of pardon were grim. Condemned prisoners at Newgate were warned in a sermon,

> That though Repentance be never too late before God when it is true, yet it seldom happens to be true when it is so very slow and late; and that God who has promised Pardon to the Penitent, has no where promised the Grace of Repentance to those that continually turn their backs upon it, and wilfully neglect the Opportunities of it.[87]

In this context, sinners caught by an unexpected death were offered little hope that God's grace would be extended to them. However, if grace was truly free for all and free in all, then Wesley reasoned it must apply even to the worst of sinners at the hour of their death.

Wesley in Contrast with His Contemporaries

Wesley's contention that God's grace could be genuinely offered to condemned malefactors was received with a great deal of skepticism.[88] William

---

reasons, denying that God loves sinners. Allison, "Pastoral Cruelty of Jeremy Taylor's Theology," 123–31. While some of Allison's accusations are the result of misunderstanding Taylor's full-orbed theology and failing to comprehend the true intent behind some of Taylor's comments, Allison does have a valid point. Some of Taylor's theology was extreme and could lead a person to despair. The Caroline divine dismissed biblical examples such as the pardon of the thief on the cross as irrelevant to the common person since the forgiveness of the thief was not applicable to those baptized in the new covenant.

86. Taylor, introduction to *Rule and Exercises of Holy Dying*, para. 7. Taylor affirmed God's mercy in a general sense, but did not offer the assurance of forgiveness to specific individuals.

87. Crooke, *Two Sermons Preach'd before the Condemn'd Criminals at Newgate, 1695*, 8.

88. Outler observed that Wesley's departure from the established Anglican view was indeed significant. The remedy for original sin within traditional Anglican soteriology was through participation in the life of the church and the sacrament of baptism. The evangelical conversions which resulted from the Methodist revival caused Wesley to

Hogarth, a popular eighteenth-century satirist, demonstrated the pejorative attitude many of Wesley's contemporaries held toward the Methodist offer of deathbed grace. In his series "Idleness and Industry," Hogarth portrayed the lives of two young apprentices: Frances Goodchild, a man of virtue, hard work, and diligence and Tom Idle, a lazy, self-indulgent youth. Goodchild appeared in the series leading a life of piety and faithfulness to both personal and social duties. He was rewarded for such conscientiousness by becoming the Lord Mayor of London. In contrast, Idle neglected his duties toward God and society. He was pictured gambling in the churchyard, stealing, and frequenting prostitutes. The eleventh print in Hogarth's series entitled "The Idle Prentice Executed at Tyburn" revealed Idle's reward for a life squandered on evil pursuits. In this print, Idle was shown riding in the executioner's cart toward the nearby gallows. Standing in the cart next to him, a Methodist pointed heavenward while Idle, leaning upon his own coffin desperately clutching a book, gazed upward with mouth agape (presumably) in prayer.

Two details of the print clearly indicate Hogarth's placement of the Methodist in the cart with Idle was meant to be derogatory. First, the contrast between the Methodist minister and the Anglican Ordinary was notable. The Ordinary (identifiable by his cassock) led the way to the gallows in an enclosed carriage. Protected from the crush of the chaotic rabble, the Ordinary carried out his official duty to both society and the condemned man in a respectable manner. On the other hand the Methodist minister stood exposed with the criminal sharing both his shame and the jeers of the crowd.[89] It is possible with this placement of the minister that Hogarth was suggesting the Methodists belonged among those who rebelled against the very fabric of a stable, established society.[90] The second detail revealing Hogarth's distain was the caption under the print which read, "Proverbs Chap: I. Vers: 27:28. When fear cometh as desolation, and their destruction cometh as a Whirlwind: when distress cometh upon them. Then they shall call upon God, but he will not answer." To Hogarth and many others,

---

rethink the new birth and the antidote for sin. Outler, Introduction to Wesley, *New Birth* (BE), 2:186.

89. Silas Told, a Methodist who dedicated himself to ministering to the prisoners at Newgate, admitted that the first time he rode in the executer's cart "it was not without much shame, because I perceived the greater part of the populace considered me as one of the sufferers." Told, *Life of Silas Told*, 73.

90. For insight into Hogarth's portrayals of Methodists see Krymanski, "We See a Ghost," 235–51.

Methodists wasted their time, energy, and reputations distilling false hope to convicts for whom little actual hope was left.

Wesley's doctrine of free grace, specifically his view that both pardon (justification) and regeneration were freely and immediately offered to the worst of sinners, was a departure from the holy living and dying tradition of his day and set him at odds with others in the established church. His doctrine of immediate pardon riled fellow Anglican clergymen because they believed it smacked of antinomianism and encouraged people to postpone repentance until their deathbed. Furthermore, the charge of being a papist was leveled against Wesley from all sides. Whitefield accused Wesley of being a papist because he thought Wesley's belief that people had the ability to either choose or reject God's justifying and regenerating grace was a reiteration of the Catholic doctrine of "salvation by works."[91] Conversely, most Anglicans realized Wesley was not preaching "works righteousness," but as William VanReyk noted, "The idea of a last-minute death-bed repentance had long been associated with Catholicism."[92] Taylor expressed this notion in the introduction to his *The Rule and Exercises of Holy Dying*. He noted, "In the Church of Rome they reckon otherwise concerning Sick and Dying Christians than I have done. For they make profession, that from Death to Life, from Sin to Grace, a man may very certainly be Changed, though the Operation begin not before his last hour."[93]

While Wesley claimed there was no difference between his theology and the official doctrine of the Church of England, he did acknowledge that there was a difference between his teaching and the ideas of other clergy. He recognized that many of his fellow clergymen claimed "holiness or good works were the *cause* of justification and "good works as the *condition* of justification."[94] Furthermore, he asserted that there were many who "so vehemently contend that a man must be sanctified, that is holy, before he

---

91. Some Anglican detractors may have simply been repeating Whitefield's charges against Wesley. In his rebuttal against Mr. Church's accusations of "popery" Wesley contended, "I am afraid you advance here a wilful untruth, purely *ad movendam indiviam*. For you cannot but know, (1.) That there is not one word of preaching Popery, either in page 71 or 77. And (2.) That when Mr. C. and two other Predestinarians (as is relation page 73) affirmed they had heard both my brother and me many times preach Popery, they meant neither more nor less thereby than the doctrine of universal redemption." Wesley, "Answer to the Rev Mr. Church's Remarks" (Jackson), 8:400.

92. Van Reyk, "Christian Ideals of Manliness," 145–46.

93. Taylor, introduction to *Rule and Exercises of Holy Living*, para. 8.

94. Wesley, *Journal* September 13, 1739 (BE), 19:96.

can be justified; especially by such of them as affirm that universal holiness or obedience must precede justification."[95] Wesley insisted it was ministers such as these who preached a type of justification by "faith *and* works" that were the true papists. "Now, do I preach *this*?" Wesley questioned. "I did for ten years: I was (fundamentally) a Papist and knew it not."[96] Such a statement, combined with Wesley's active ministry among condemned malefactors, created a sense of animosity between Wesley and his fellow clergymen. Furthermore, his observation that people who were not religious in any way were "the more ready to cry to God as mere sinners, for the free redemption which is in Jesus" than those within the church, only heightened the tension since it seemed to elevate the common criminal above those who had spent a lifetime laboring for justification in the holy living tradition.[97] Indeed, Wesley observed that in nearly every pulpit that he proclaimed the message of "free salvation by faith in the blood of Christ. I was quickly apprised that . . . I am to preach no more."[98]

Free Grace and the Gallows

While Wesley's peers were irritated by his message to the dying, those on the outskirts of society eagerly received his teaching. Houlbrooke proposed that it was precisely because of Wesley's emphasis on free grace that his ministry was so successful among those who had been left untouched by the church. Houlbrooke made the case that, "It was among the poor, the sick, and condemned criminals, who misfortune had rendered especially receptive to the message of free grace, that Wesley found some of his best opportunities of saving souls."[99] This conclusion was supported by Wesley's own reports. For example, Wesley recorded that he went to Sandgate in Newcastle, "the poorest and most contemptible part of town."[100] At first those who gathered to hear him hardly knew what to make of Wesley and

---

95. Wesley, *Justification by Faith* (BE), 1:191.
96. Wesley, *Journal* August 27, 1739 (BE), 19:89.
97. Wesley, *Journal* April 1, 1743 (BE), 19:322.
98. Wesley, *Journal* May 14, 1738 (BE), 18:239–40. In a short period of time, Wesley was banned from St. Ann's, St. Lawrence's, St. Katherine Cree Church, Great St. Helen's, St. John's Wapping, St. Benet's, Paul's Wharf, and St. Antholin's for preaching "free salvation." See *Journal* entries for May 7–19, 1738 (BE), 18:237–41.
99. Houlbrooke, *Death, Religion and the Family in England*, 179.
100. Wesley, *Journal* May 30, 1742 (BE), 19:268–69.

his street preaching, but after he expounded upon the text "I will heal their backsliding, I will love them freely," the people nearly trampled him "out of pure love and kindness."[101] One of the results of Wesley's ministry was, according to Houlbrooke, "a reinvigoration of the notion of joyful dying" among those in the social strata who had been overlooked by the Anglican Church and had never before heard the message of free grace proclaimed.[102]

Notwithstanding the criticism, Wesley was eager to visit prisoners as often as he could to offer them the message of free salvation.[103] For these poor souls, the established tradition told them there was no time to follow the long path of repentance and holy living; therefore, they had little hope of finding peace with God. Wesley's message of free grace turned the established view upside down and gave the condemned prisoners reason to believe God would yet accept them. Wesley proclaimed, "When they know there is yet forgiveness with him, they will cry aloud that he would blot out their sins also, through faith which is in Jesus. And if they . . . seek him . . . [and] refuse to be comforted till he come; 'he will come, and will not tarry.' And he can do much work in a short time."[104]

Newgate prison was the proving ground for Wesley's message of free grace and instantaneous conversion. In his journal, Wesley recorded the response to the text, "God willeth all men to be *thus* saved." Prisoners "dropped on every side as thunderstruck."[105] Wesley marveled at one wom-

---

101. Wesley, *Journal* May 30, 1742 (BE), 19:268–69. Wesley drew crowds which numbered in the thousands who were eager for the message of "free salvation," "free grace" and "free forgiveness." See *Journal* entries for "free grace" April 10, 1739 (BE), 19:48; "free forgiveness" April 14, 1739 (BE), 19:48; "free grace" April 29, 1739 (BE), 19:52; "free forgiveness" October 5, 1739 (BE), 19:101; "free forgiveness" August 30, 1743 (BE), 19:335; "free salvation" March 10, 1761 (BE), 21:310.

102. Houlbrooke, Death, *Religion and the Family in England*, 179.

103. See Wesley, *Journal* September 17, 1738 (BE), 19:12. He wrote here, "I went to the condemned felons, in Newgate, and offered them free salvation."

104. Wesley, *Salvation by Faith* (BE), 1:127. Not every prisoner readily accepted the Methodist message of free pardon. For example, Matthew Henderson, a young man executed on April 25, 1746 was reported to complain about "the officiousness of a certain methodist, who sent him a letter signed, R. F.—the contents of which . . . gave him so much dislike, that he had not the patience to go through with it, and declared in chapel, that they must be very deluded persons to think their sins to have been washed away seventeen hundred years ago, and that they have nothing more to do than to believe in the blood of Christ." *Ordinary of Newgate's Account*, April 1746.

105. Wesley, *Journal* April 26, 1739 (BE), 19:51. Charles Yrigoyen counted more than sixty-five visits recorded in Wesley's journal to the Newgate prison in London and the Newgate prison in Bristol between the years 1738 to 1775. Charles Yrigoyen, "I Was in Prison and You Visited Me," 14.

an who was under such heavy conviction from the Spirit that it seemed she would die; however, "immediately [God's] abundant kindness was showed, and she loudly sang of his righteousness."[106] Wesley went back to Newgate the next day and found that it still "rang with the cries of those whom the Word of God cut to the heart, two of whom were in a moment filled with joy, to the astonishment of those that beheld them."[107]

One of the most extreme examples of this emphasis was recorded by Thomas Butts in a letter to Charles Wesley. Butts related his experience of witnessing the execution of ten prisoners. He managed to accompany three of the prisoners in the executioner's cart as it was being drawn to Tyburn, and during the short journey, he examined two of the prisoners who had previously heard Charles preach. Butts recorded, "I examined these two whether they would chuse to die or live; they declar'd they chose to Die, strongly believing [the] Lord would have Mercy upon their Souls; and that, tho they were sensible there must be a great change wrought in them, yet they also knew [the] Lord was able to effect it in a short Time."[108] Perhaps slightly less dramatic than a conversion experienced literally at the foot of the gallows, was Wesley's recollection of Richard Varley's execution. Varley was condemned for highway robbery, and one week after his sentencing, "the Lord touched his heart." Scarcely a day later, "God, who is rich in mercy, applied the blood of his Son, and convinced him, he had forgiven him all his sins."[109] There is no doubt that the prisoners themselves credited the doctrine of free grace with their new-found salvation. At the place of execution, Varley "took cheerful leave of his friends" and publicly proclaimed, "Glory be to God for free grace!" His last words were, 'Lord Jesus, receive my soul.'"[110]

It should not be assumed that Anglican Ordinaries did not take their ministry to condemned malefactors seriously. Many Ordinaries possessed a deep sense of responsibility for the spiritual well-being of the prisoners under their care. However, there was a general sense that one could not be certain of the effectiveness of ministry to people who had committed

---

106. Wesley, *Journal* April 26, 1739 (BE), 19:52.
107. Wesley, *Journal* April 27, 1739 (BE), 19:52.
108. Butts, "Letter to Charles Wesley" April 14, 1743.
109. Wesley, *Journal* December 1, 1756 (BE), 21:82.
110. Wesley, *Journal* December 1, 1756 (BE), 21:82.

such heinous crimes against God and society. Stephen Roe, an Ordinary of Newgate, reflected,

> We are, indeed, in general obliged to perform the best offices of piety and charity we can . . . for the worst of dying sinners and criminals; but the success is wholly unknown and uncertain to us . . . . 'Tis impossible for us, for any but the Searcher of Hearts, to know . . . [if] they have outsinned their day of Grace and Salvation . . . For however presumptuous and ignorant men may flatter themselves, and each other, that it is never too late to repent (and tho' perhaps this may be true of a sincere repentance) yet we are assured, by the highest authority, that . . . there is a time when these good things are hid from mens eyes, and the door of mercy is shut."[111]

It was also true that prison chaplains were stereotypically characters who left much to be desired. McKenzie noted that this tainted reputation was not entirely ungrounded. She cited the example of John Allen who served as the Ordinary at Newgate from 1698 to 1699. After only six months on the job, he was dismissed for receiving bribes, stealing money sent to the prisoners from their families, and printing inflammatory fabrications of the prisoners' confessions in the Ordinary's *Account*.[112] Both John and Charles Wesley observed several instances when they observed seeming indifference on the part of the Ordinary toward the prisoners under his care. Robert Southey recorded Charles's ministry to some condemned criminals in Newgate during John's absence in Germany. Southey noted, "The ordinary on these occasions, made a sorry figure. 'He *would* read prayers,' Charles says, 'and he preached most miserably.'"[113] Wesley published *Some Account of the Life and Death of Matthew Lee* wherein Lee himself had little good to say about the ministers attending to the prisoners. Their apparent lack of concern was cause for despair.

> Being informed there was a minister belonging to the Goal, who would help him in his addresses to the Almighty God: he answered, 'Why don't he then? Why don't he come and instruct me? Why don't he wrestle with God for me?' I see no regard paid to the immortal Souls of any that are confined here. They are running head-long to hell, and no one seeks to stop them. None prays with;

---

111. *Ordinary of Newgate's Account*, March 7, 1764.
112. McKenzie, *Tyburn's Martyr's*, 130.
113. Southey, *Life of Wesley*, 1:154. See footnote.

none admonishes, reproves, exhorts them; but he that is filthy, is left to be filthy still. What! Have the prisoners in Newgate immortal souls! And yet no one regardeth them?[114]

Faith in the Face of Execution

It was the Ordinary's task to provide spiritual direction to the prisoners and to keep those condemned to die safely between the dangers of despair and presumption. Samuel Rossell printed a handbook for prisoners called *The Prisoner's Director* which provided the appropriate response of faith for every type of prisoner.[115] Rossell believed that offering the possibility of forgiveness was necessary to keep the condemned from despair; on the other hand, he cited Peter's words to Simon Magus, "Repent therefore of this thy Wickedness, and pray God, if perhaps the Thought of thy Heart may be forgiven thee."[116] Rossell continued, "He saith not, and *so certainly it shall be,* this possibly might be too confident a Presumption to depend upon: but *if perhaps, that,* an humble hope may be allowed to seek after."[117] Thus, Rossell held out "a humble hope" that condemned criminals who repented of their sins could be forgiven, but only if this repentance took on a certain form. True repentance for the malefactor included confession not just to God but Rossell declared,

> Where the Sin against God is complicated with Injustice towards Men, (as in condemned Malefactors it always is) there it is requisite that the Sinner confess to Man, and shew his Zeal against Unrighteousness, by discovering the Combinations of Wickedness that he hath been accepted with; for it is hardly conceivable, that they thoroughly repent of their Unrighteousness, who at their Death desire it should go unobserved, and unreformed, and unpunished in others.[118]

In other words, part of the requirement for pardon was not simply confession to God but confession to the Ordinary. This confession was

---

114. Wesley, *Some Account of the Life and Death of Matthew Lee,* 12–13.

115. This book was filled with prayers and instructions for prisoners while they waited for either execution or release. It also contained a sort of *ars moriendi* for those who were awaiting execution.

116. Rossell, *Prisoner's Director,* 69–70.

117. Rossell, *Prisoner's Director,* 70.

118. Rossell, *Prisoner's Director,* 65–66.

then translated to the entire community through the Ordinary's *Account*—a publication which contained the confessions of those awaiting execution. The problem with this requirement was the well-known fact that Ordinaries supplemented their income with the *Account*. Of course, the most profitable issues of the *Account* contained the most explicit and intriguing confessions; the public found it especially fascinating when the accused informed on any others who were party to the crime. While Rossell undoubtedly had the best intentions in mind when he called for a full confession to both God and man, it was difficult for some prisoners to believe an Ordinary could remain objective. One of the charges leveled against the Methodists was that their optimistic theology (which promised immediate pardon and the assurance of heaven to the worst of sinners) closed the lips of the prisoners. Instead of delivering colorful confessions to the Ordinaries, the prisoners spent their last days rejoicing in the goodness and mercy of God.

The validity of the prisoner's repentance was also judged by the demeanor of a malefactor. The condemned were expected to sustain a sense of self-abasement and accept death as a rightful punishment for his or her crimes. Crooke, in his sermon to the prisoners at Newgate, minced no words in describing how the rest of society viewed their deplorable condition:

> And indeed sad is the State, deplorable the Condition you have brought your selves to, adjudged by the Laws of your Countrey, and by them account unworthy any longer to live, unworthy to tread this Earth, or breathe this Air; and that no further good, no other benefit to Mankind can be expected from you, but only by the Example of your Death ... to warn others from the same Ruin for the future.[119]

Therefore, the acceptable attitude for condemned malefactors (at least for those who desired any chance of divine pardon) entailed shame over sinful actions and humility before God and others. Repentance which was not accompanied by this posture was considered dubious. Rossell noted, "These Confessions where they are accepted with God, are always accompanied with a deep Sorrow and Contrition of Spirit, for those Sins that we acknowledge, otherwise they are hypocritical; but together with this they are often a Sacrifice acceptable to God."[120]

---

119. Crooke, *Two Sermons Preach'd before the Condemn'd Criminals at Newgate*, 2.
120. Rossell, *Prisoner's Director*, 66.

Assurance in the Face of Death

For Wesley, the element of instantaneousness extended beyond salvation itself and encompassed the privileges of redemption. To be sure, Wesley understood that new believers would grow in the graces they had been given; however, there was nothing required on the part of the newly born child of God to receive these gifts of grace.[121] It took neither time nor effort on the part of the new believer to appropriate the initial benefits of the new birth and experience the effects of spiritual life. This was an important theological distinctive for individuals facing imminent death. Even though the condemned and dying had little time or opportunity to improve upon the grace they had been given, they could still enjoy the privileges that accompanied the new birth such as assurance of salvation and the love of God. While Wesley agreed that all people should demonstrate appropriate humility before God, he also was adamant that the marks of the new birth (faith, hope, and love) were readily bestowed upon all who believed. Thus, even the worst of sinners could be confident that through the love of God they were saved from sin and eternal death.

Wesley's claim that assurance was the common privilege of all believers was unusual among eighteenth-century Anglicans. Susanna Wesley claimed she had no idea that the witness of the Spirit was offered to all who believed before John brought up this notion. Rather, she thought it was the privilege of a select few.[122] However, Wesley considered assurance to be a key sign of spiritual life. It implied confidence in one's right-standing with God and bestowed "the testimony of our own spirit or conscience that we walk 'in simplicity and godly sincerity;' but, secondly and chiefly, the testimony of the Spirit of God, 'bearing witness with', or to, 'our spirit, that we are the children of God; and if children, then heirs; heirs of God, and joint-heirs with Christ.'"[123] This knowledge had a profound impact upon the way in which believers faced death since those who were born of God did not need to fear judgment or condemnation. Wesley insisted that true believers,

> ... cannot fear any longer the wrath of God; for he knows it is now turned away from him and looks upon him no more as an angry

---

121. Wesley often called the marks of the new birth "privileges," and he essentially equated these marks with the new birth itself. Wesley, *Marks of the New Birth* (BE), 1:417.

122. Wesley *Journal* September 3, 1739 (BE), 19:93–94.

123. Wesley, *Marks of the New Birth* (BE), 1:423.

judge, but as a loving Father. He cannot fear the devil, knowing he has 'no power, except it be given him from above'. He fears not hell, being an heir of the kingdom of heaven. Consequently, he has no fear of death, by reason whereof he was in time past for so many years 'subject to bondage'.[124]

It is no surprise that Ordinaries, who attempted to guide prisoners along a path of humility, found Wesley's doctrine of assurance spiritually dangerous. The confidence with which common criminals proclaimed the assurance of salvation flew in the face of the prescribed formula of genuine repentance. It is likely that if the condemned had simply laid claim to *some* hope that they might be saved, opposition to Wesley's ministry may not have been so severe.[125] However, Methodists outraged Ordinaries such as Stephen Roe. Roe reported the case of a prisoner who was asked on the eve of his execution whether he was assured of salvation. The prisoner answered that he "dare not say more than that he earnestly hoped he should be saved." When the Methodist replied that he could be utterly certain of forgiveness, it was nearly too much for Roe to bear. Roe lamented, "Such crude assertions as these . . . shew a forward presumption at least, and that they know not what spirit they are of; so far from being safe and sure guides to others, that they know not how to conduct themselves; and if the blind lead the blind, you know the dreadful consequence!"[126] The doctrine of assurance contradicted the best wisdom of the day. Malefactors were instructed to not fear despair, "but fear Presumption, and groundless Hopes of Future Happiness; willingly retain Sorrow and Anguish with you, they are the most decent Company for you to appear in; will do most good on others and sooner lead you to Heaven, than the bold mistaken Pretenses of Peace and Assurance."[127]

Nevertheless, Methodist converts did not refrain from confidently proclaiming their faith in God's pardon and the assurance of their salvation. Their impending execution was meant to incite a proper amount of trepidation and encourage continued confession and sorrow over sin. However, Wesley's message of free grace and immediate acceptance with

124. Wesley, *Spirit of Bondage and Adoption* (BE), 1:261–62.

125. The condemned were encouraged to pray for "the Grace, thus to employ *myself*, that I may have some Taste of thy Mercy, and that the Fear of Death may be abated by some Hope, that, when *my Soul* shall be parted from *my Body, it* may be received into everlasting Mansions . . . ." Rossell, *Prisoner's Director,* 74.

126. *Ordinary of Newgate's Account,* May 1758.

127. Crooke, *Two Sermons Preach'd before the Condemn'd Criminals at Newgate,* 30.

God resulted in declarations of faith and hope in the face of death itself. One condemned malefactor declared: "I am perfectly at Ease & have not the least Doubt, the least Fear of Death; for to Day I shall be with him in Paradise."[128] When questioned under the gallows at Tyburn whether he was sure that his sins were forgiven, this same prisoner replied, "I speak it with Humility, I am sure of it. To the Goaler he said as surely as you knock off these Fetter so surely has [He] knockt off the Fetters of Sin from my Soul. Many like words he spoke full of Joy & Confidence & love to us, the Spectators & Officers."[129]

Conclusion

It is not difficult to understand why Wesley and his Methodist cohorts galled the patience of Anglican Ordinaries with their declarations of free grace, instantaneous pardon, and assurance. It did not help that some Methodists intentionally interfered with the Ordinary's ministry to the prisoners fearing that the chaplains would attempt to dissuade the converts from their faith. One Methodist admitted, "To prevent the Ordinary's troubling them I immediately began singing, 'Behold, the Saviour of mankind, Nailed to the shameful tree.'"[130] McKenzie observed,

> Individual Methodists not only challenged the Ordinary's pastoral authority over convicts, but Methodism generally threatened to cast the *Account* into disrepute, throwing into sharp relief the increasingly problematic issue of free grace in regard to those of known ill life–for, after 1740, John Wesley openly preached a radical and peculiarly optimistic brand of free grace, divorced from its older Calvinist predestination moorings; that is, free not only for the elect, but for any that truly repented, the greatest of sinners not excepted.... Thus Methodists' visitors offered–and converts trumpeted–assurances of the forgiveness of sins and the promise of salvation in terms that no orthodox mid-eighteenth-century Anglican clergyman could easily countenance.[131]

For Wesley, it was worth sharing in a malefactor's shame, defying long-standing traditions, and confronting the establishment for the license

---

128. Anonymous, Letter (possibly to Charles Wesley) November 11, 1738.
129. Anonymous, Letter (possibly to Charles Wesley) November 11, 1738.
130. Letter (possibly to Charles Wesley) November 11, 1738.
131. McKenzie, *Tyburn's Martyrs*, 182.

to proclaim that God's grace was free *for all* and *in all*. He had seen firsthand the devastation wrought by the prevailing theology. Wesley recorded the unfortunate ordeal of seeing four brothers executed for their crimes. Despite receiving absolution from their priest, Wesley observed that they were still terrified of dying. One of the men was so frightened his shrieks of horror could be heard almost a mile away. After watching the scene unfold, Wesley penned the following words: "O what but love can cast out the fear of death! And how inexpressibly miserable is that bondage!"[132]

In contrast to this tragic story, is the testimony of a condemned man whom Wesley counseled shortly before the poor man's execution.[133] After spending much time in prayer, the man received assurance of God's love. "'I am now ready to die,' he proclaimed. 'I know Christ has taken away my sins; and there is no more condemnation for me.' He demonstrated the same composed cheerfulness when he was carried to execution. In his last moments he was the same, enjoying a perfect peace, in confidence that he was 'accepted in the Beloved.'"[134] Such a message would not and could not be readily received by those who embraced the traditional understanding of repentance and faith in the holy living and holy dying motif. It was Wesley's message of hope which allowed the worst of sinners and the outcasts of society to face death with the dignity of a bold faith in the forgiveness, mercy, and love of God.

---

132. Wesley, *Journal* July 7, 1762 (BE), 21:372.

133. This was probably Clifford, the first person to whom Wesley offered salvation by faith alone.

134. Wesley, *Journal* March 27, 1738 (BE), 18:232–33.

Chapter 4

PROGRESSIVE SANCTIFICATION
The Mortification of the Sinful Nature

Introduction

WHILE WESLEY FIRMLY ASSERTED that God's pardon was freely available to sinners who faced an imminent death, he agreed with the holy living tradition that a deathbed repentance was not the ideal nor should it be the norm. God could save sinners on the brink of eternity, but the best preparation for death was to have the testimony of a holy life. In his notes on Gal 5:26, Wesley explained, "If we are indeed raised from the dead, and are alive to God, by the operation of His Spirit [then] *let us walk by the Spirit.* Let us follow His guidance, in all our tempers, thoughts, words, and actions."[1] The new birth (much like natural birth) was meant to be the entrance to the Christian life not the portal to death. A last-minute conversion was a backward approach to redemption since physical death was meant to be the seal of a transformed life. Regeneration began the process of sanctification which brought the believer into conformity with the Spirit; however, as life in the Spirit blossomed, the issue of death once again rose to the forefront in Wesley's theology. In this instance, the "death" which emerged was not in reference to spiritual death (it was already conquered in justification and initial regeneration); rather, it was the gradual death of the sinful nature which still remained in the child of God. There were deeper levels of grace and holiness to be obtained and still much work to be done in the believer's

1. Wesley, *ENNT*, 698.

heart if the problem of sin were to be fully addressed. The only way forward was to lead a dying life; that is, a life spent mortifying all the remaining traces of sin in a believer's heart.

The Remaining Sinful Nature

Although the new birth provided the solution to spiritual death, the issue of sin was still an area of deep concern for Wesley. He did not accept the supposition that believers were completely purified from all sin the moment they were born of God. In 1741, Wesley met with Count Zinzendorf to discuss the issue of justification and sanctification. During this meeting, Zinzendorf claimed that believers were utterly purified at the moment of justification and could not increase in their love for God. He declared, "A babe in Christ is as pure in heart as a father in Christ. There is no difference."[2] Indeed, Zinzendorf professed to be so pure after the initial flush of grace was bestowed in the new birth that he and his followers did not need to practice the spiritual disciplines which led to the mortification of the sinful nature. "We reject all self-denial," he asserted. "We trample upon it. We do, as believers, whatsoever we will, and nothing more. We laugh at all mortification. No purification precedes perfect love."[3]

Wesley was appalled by such a view, and he warned new believers that they would "feel two principles in themselves, plainly contrary to each other: 'the flesh lusting against the spirit,' nature opposing the grace of God."[4] Citing the ninth Article of Religion to support his position, Wesley declared, "Original sin . . . is the corruption of the nature of every man . . . And this infection of nature doth remain, yea, in them that are regenerated . . . ."[5] He admitted it was common to imagine that all sin was removed due to the transformation of the new birth. However, Wesley explained that the sinful nature was "stunned . . . not dead" and would eventually make its

2. Wesley, *Journal* September 3, 1741 (BE), 19:214.

3. Wesley, *Journal* September 3, 1741 (BE), 19:215. Wesley found Zinzendorf's position so disturbing that he denounced the doctrine as "wholly *new*; never heard of in the church of Christ from the time of his coming into the world till the time of Count Zinzendorf." Wesley, *On Sin in Believers* (BE), 1:333.

4. Wesley, *Scripture Way of Salvation* (BE), 2:159.

5. Wesley, *On Sin in Believers* (BE), 1:318. The second homily, "On the Misery of Man," outlined the nature and depth of original sin and pointed out that actual sins flowed out of that fatal flaw. "On the Misery of Man" in *Certain Sermons or Homilies Appointed to Be Read in Churches*, 12–17.

presence known.[6] Wesley defined the sin which remained as an "infection of nature" or as a "heart 'bent to backsliding,' still ever ready to 'depart from the living God;' a propensity to pride, self-will, anger, revenge, love of the world, yea, and all evil: a root of bitterness which if the restraint were taken off for a moment, would instantly spring up."[7] Elsewhere, he described the sinful nature as "any disposition contrary to the mind of Christ."[8] Wesley concluded there were two forces at work in the believer: the carnal nature and the Spirit of God—each rivaling the other for control.

Wesley held to a twofold understanding of sin: sin as an act (a willful transgression against a known law of God), and sin as a condition (the taint of original sin).[9] According to Wesley's definition, nothing was sin "properly speaking" unless it was an intentional violation of God's law; therefore, as long as a new born believer did not submit to the desires of the sinful nature and commit an act of willful sin, the person was holy. A person "may be in God's favour though he *feel* sin;" Wesley wrote, "but not if he *yields* to it. *Having sin* does not forfeit the favour of God; *giving way to sin* does. Though the flesh in *you* 'lust against the Spirit' you may still be a child of God."[10] Wesley was optimistic that those born of God would be able to resist the temptation to commit willful acts of sin since a true believer was "enabled 'by the Spirit' to 'mortify the deeds of the body,' or our evil nature. And as we are more and more dead to sin, we are more and more alive to God."[11] To be clear, Wesley did not believe the presence of the sinful nature discounted the work of justification and regeneration, nor did he believe that the carnal nature made a believer utterly unholy. Rather, beginning with the initial gift of holiness bestowed at the new birth, there were degrees of holiness along the path of salvation. "Every babe in Christ is holy,

---

6. Wesley, *Scripture Way of Salvation* (BE), 2:159. Wesley made a similar point in his sermon, *Deceitfulness of the Human Heart*: "Sin is then overcome, but it is not rooted out; it is conquered, but not destroyed." (BE), 4:157.

7. Wesley, *Repentance of Believers* (BE), 1:341.

8. Wesley, *On Sin in Believers* (BE), 1:320.

9. This is distinct from Calvin's view of the sinful nature. Calvin explained that Augustine only viewed the sinful nature as "sin" after a person followed the desires of the carnal nature and acted upon it. "We, on the other hand, deem it sin when man is tickled by any desire at all against the law of God. Indeed, we label 'sin' that very depravity which begets in us desires of this sort." In other words, Calvin did not differentiate between willful sin and the sinful nature. Calvin, *Institutes*, Book III, Chapter III, Sect. 10, 1:602–3.

10. Wesley, *On Sin in Believers* (BE), 1:332.

11. Wesley, *Scripture Way of Salvation* (BE), 2:160.

and yet not altogether so. He is saved from sin; yet not entirely . . . ." Wesley declared.[12] According to Wesley, the carnal nature "*remains*, though it does not *reign*."[13] In other words, a true believer was released from the guilt and power of actual sins through the new birth but grappled with the being of sin until the work of sanctification was complete.

To be wholly purified in this lifetime was an attainable goal. Wesley distinguished himself from his Reformed counterparts, the holy living tradition, and the Catholic Church by teaching that entire sanctification (the death of the sinful nature) was not only possible, but it was absolutely necessary to receive in this lifetime. He declared, "The Papists say, 'This can't be attained till we have been a sufficient time in purgatory.' The Dissenters say, 'Nay it will be attained as soon as the soul and body part.' The old Methodists said, 'It may be attained *before* we die: a moment after is too late.'"[14] To be cleansed from *all* sin (both sin as act and sin as a condition of the heart) was the *telos* toward which every believer must aim. Wesley explained, "We expect to be 'made perfect in love . . . .' We expect to be 'cleansed' from all our idols, 'from all filthiness,' whether 'of flesh or spirit;' to be 'saved from all our uncleannesses,' inward or outward; to be 'purified as he is pure.'"[15]

Wesley embraced a carefully nuanced position regarding the remaining sinful nature. On the one hand, he acknowledged that believers still deserved punishment and death because of their sinful condition. On the other hand, the penalty of spiritual death had been turned away through the advocacy of Christ. Wesley reasoned,

> . . . this is to be cautiously understood, and in a peculiar sense. For it is certain, 'there is no condemnation for them that are in Christ Jesus,' that believe in him, and in the power of that faith 'walk not after the flesh, but after the Spirit.' . . . what they deserve does not come upon them because . . . [Christ's] life and death and intercession still interpose between them and condemnation.[16]

---

12. Wesley, *On Sin in Believers* (BE), 1:327.

13. Wesley, *On Sin in Believers* (BE), 1:327.

14. Wesley, *Minutes of Conference, Annual Minutes, 1768* (BE), 10:363. Wesley repeated this same argument in the *Large Minutes, 1770–1772* (BE), 10:906 and the *Large Minutes, 1780–1789* (BE), 10:927–28. However, in the *Large Minutes, 1780–1789*, Wesley changed the term "Dissenters" to "Calvinists."

15. Wesley, *Satan's Devices* (BE), 2:140.

16. Wesley, *Repentance of Believers* (BE), 1:344–45.

As long as a believer "walked after the Spirit," all was well. However, if a believer was inattentive to the presence of the carnal nature, it could have in Wesley's words "fatal consequences." Believers could be lulled into thinking the carnal nature was already removed which, in turn, could leave new believers "exposed to all the assaults of the world, the flesh and the devil."[17] The believer would then be left vulnerable to the wiles of sin and decline into a state of death once again. Therefore, constant vigilance against the influence of sin along with forward progress toward the goal of inward and outward purity was the duty of every believer. "You cannot stand still," Wesley wrote to a struggling Methodist. "You know this is impossible. You must go forward or backward. Either you must recover that power and be a Christian altogether, or in a while you will have neither power or form, inside nor outside."[18]

An unhealthy fixation with the sin which remained was also dangerous since it could lead to discouragement and a sense of despair over one's unworthiness.[19] Wesley advised believers who felt hopeless about the discrepancy between their condition and the degree of holiness which was yet to be attained to "see that prize of thy high calling, not as Satan represents it, in a horrid dreadful shape, but in its genuine native beauty; not as something that *must* be, or thou wilt go to hell, but as what *may* be, to lead thee to heaven."[20]

Progressive Sanctification

Just as he had a twofold understanding of sin, Wesley also held to a dual concept of sanctification. He viewed sanctification as both an instantaneous event (as in the new birth when the person was raised from spiritual death and in entire sanctification which will be examined in the next chapter) and an ongoing process. The process of sanctification was initiated at the new birth and entailed growth in grace which continued throughout the

---

17. Wesley, *On Sin in Believers* (BE), 1:333.

18. Wesley, *Letters* "To John Trembath" August 17, 1760 (Telford), 4:103. Wesley made the same argument in a letter to Elizabeth Ritchie. He wrote, "But some of them, watching unto prayer, went on from faith to faith; while the others, being less watchful, seemed to stand still, but were indeed imperceptibly backsliding." Wesley, *Letters* "To Elizabeth Ritchie" January 19, 1782 (Telford), 7:103.

19. See Wesley's full argument in *Satan's Devices* (BE), 2:138–51.

20. Wesley, *Satan's Devices* (BE), 2:149.

believer's life. Wesley explained, "From the moment we are justified there may be a *gradual sanctification*, or a growing in grace, a daily advance in the knowledge and love of God."[21] In regeneration, all the holy virtues had been planted in the heart through a divine act of free grace, but the holy tempers needed to be cultivated in order to produce the fruit of righteousness. At the Bristol Conference in August 1745, Wesley noted that in justification "the seed of every virtue is then instantaneously sown in the soul. From that time the believer gradually dies to sin and grows in grace."[22] Therefore, the one that is born of the Spirit continues "'from faith to faith', 'from grace to grace', 'until at length he comes unto a perfect man, unto the measure of the stature of the fullness of Christ.'"[23]

The process of sanctification highlighted the conjunctive nature of Wesley's theology in which he recognized that the transformation of the human soul required both an act of free grace on the part of God along with humanity's full cooperation with the divine work. Wesley reasoned that because God had first acted on behalf of the person, the believer was enabled to respond to the grace previously given. In terms of the ongoing process of sanctification or growth in grace, he declared, "God worketh in you; therefore you can work . . . . God worketh in you; therefore you must work."[24] Wesley's synergism of grace was a careful balance between the scriptural statements, "Without me ye can do nothing" and "I can do all things through Christ that strengtheneth me."[25] On the one hand, believers were utterly reliant on the benevolence of God for any progress in the Christian faith. On the other hand, believers were responsible to "work out their own salvation" fully expecting their efforts would result in an increase in holiness. Maddox noted, "Put in slightly different terms, Wesley was convinced that, while we *cannot* attain holiness (and wholeness) apart from God's grace, God *will* not affect holiness apart from our responsive participation."[26] Wesley illustrated this synergism of cooperant grace in his encouragement of one follower to: "Grow in grace every hour, the more the

---

21. Wesley, *Minutes of Conference, Annual Minutes, 1768* (BE), 10:363.

22. Wesley, *Bristol Conference*, August 1–3, 1745 (BE), 10:154. Wesley recorded this declaration again in the *Doctrine Minutes*, 1749 (BE), 10:790.

23. Wesley, *Salvation by Faith* (BE), 1:124–25.

24. Wesley, *On Working Out Our Own Salvation* (BE), 3:206, 208.

25. Wesley, *On Working Out Our Own Salvation* (BE), 3:208. Here Wesley cited Matt 19:6 and Phil 4:13.

26. Maddox, *Responsible Grace*, 148.

better. Use now all the grace you have ... but also now expect all the grace you want! This is the secret of heart religion–at the present moment to work and believe.... Give yourself up to [Christ] without delay; and, as you can, without reserve."[27]

Progressive Sanctification and the Metaphor of Death

The process of sanctification not only entailed the positive qualities of vivification of the holy tempers but also the mortification of the being of sin. Therefore, Wesley utilized the imagery of death to express the manner in which believers should treat any thoughts or desires that were not in conformity to the renewed *imago Dei*.[28] "Put to death, slay with a continued stroke ... uncleanness–in act, word, or thought ... every passion which does not flow from and lead to the love of God," Wesley declared.[29] In essence, the process of sanctification was the gradual destruction of the carnal nature. Wesley warned his followers that Christ "cannot *reign* where sin *reigns;* neither will he *dwell* where any sin is *allowed*;" yet, he also conceded that Christ "*is* and *dwells* in the heart of every believer who is fighting against all sin; although it be 'not' yet 'purified....'"[30] Of course the believer was not left alone in the struggle against sin. Even though the carnal nature and Spirit were in conflict with one another and the Spirit "opposed your evil nature," Wesley guaranteed believers that "being thus strengthened by the Spirit, ye may not fulfill the desire of the flesh, as otherwise ye would do."[31] The believer was empowered to successfully overcome the sinful nature by producing works suitable for repentance. These works, which Wesley defined as works of piety and works of mercy, included mortification of the

---

27. Wesley, *Letters* "To Ann Foard" October 14, 1767 (Telford), 5:56.

28. The language of mortification and vivification was also key to Calvin's theology. For Calvin, the very act of repentance entailed "mortification of the flesh and vivification of the spirit." Calvin, *Institutes,* (Book III, Chapter 3, Sect. 8), 1: 600. See also Calvin's references to mortification regarding participation in Christ's death (Book II, Chapter 16, Sect. 7),1:512 and mortification in the act of baptism (Book IV, Chapter 15, Sect.11), 2:1311–12. Unlike Wesley, Calvin did not believe that the sinful nature could be remedied in this lifetime. He wrote, "For lust never actually dies and is extinguished in men until, freed by death from the body of death, they are completely divested of themselves." (Book IV, Chapter 15, Sect.11), 2:1311–12.

29. Wesley, *ENNT* (Col 3:5), 748.

30. Wesley, *On Sin in Believers* (BE), 1:323.

31. Wesley, *ENNT* (Gal 5:16), 696.

sinful will. Works suitable for repentance were not necessary to full salvation "in the *same sense* with faith or in the *same degree*."[32] However, Wesley noted that such works were "so necessary that if a man willingly neglect them he cannot reasonably expect that he shall ever be sanctified in the full sense . . ."[33] In other words, believers must die to the sinful nature to grow into the fullness of Christ.

Living the Dying Life

It was in his understanding of sanctification as an ongoing work that Wesley was most closely aligned with the holy living/holy dying tradition. A glance at the works that he edited and republished for his followers indicate Wesley was in agreement with his theological mentors that the Christian life was an extended preparation for death.[34] Along with Jeremy Taylor's *The Rule and Exercises of Holy Living and Holy Dying*, Wesley published selections from Thomas Goodwin's *Tryal of a Christian's Growth*, Richard Lucas's *An Enquiry after Happiness*, William Law's *A Serious Call to a Devout and Holy Life*, and extracts from the works of John Owen, Richard Baxter and Henry Scougal to name but a few. All these works emphasized the necessity of holy living in preparation for death. Wesley also recommended Nathaniel Spinckes's *The Sick Man Visited and Furnished with Instructions, Meditations and Prayers* which expressed, "there is none, how young, how healthful, how active, how lively, how strong soever, but ought to make it his continual Care thus to prepare himself for a better State."[35] Spinckes was explicit in his teaching that none who had delayed a holy life would see God, yet Wesley readily advised his followers to use this material when ministering to the ill.[36] Wesley took seriously William Law's assertion that,

> We are obliged to live unto God in the same manner that we are to die unto God . . . . For as the Reasons of Wisdom and Holiness are not founded in Death, so do they receive no Alternation by the

---

32. Wesley, *Scripture Way of Salvation* (BE), 2:167.
33. Wesley, *Scripture Way of Salvation* (BE), 2:164.
34. Although Wesley borrowed heavily from holy living literature (often from the Puritan tradition), Karl Ganske observed that Wesley removed any phrases which suggested that the sinful nature could not be completely mortified in this lifetime. Karl Ganske, "Religion of the Heart and Growth in Grace," 206–7.
35. Spinckes, *Sick Man Visited*, 134.
36. Wesley, *On Visiting the Sick* (BE), 3:392.

Approach of Death; there is no Wisdom and Holiness but what is equally necessary, whether I am twenty *Years* or twenty *days* from Death.[37]

The best use of life, therefore, was to prepare for the sober reality of death. Indeed, Richard Baxter went so far as to suggest that life itself was pointless if preparation for eternity was not seriously undertaken. In *The Saints' Everlasting Rest*, Baxter lamented, "Have we not had all our life-time to prepare to die; so many years to make ready for one hour; and are we so unready and unwilling yet? What have we done? Why have we lived?"[38] On a very practical note, Richard Lucas observed that great evils (such as physical death) were rarely handled well by people who could not cope with hardships of a slighter nature; therefore, living well in the little affairs of life trained a person to face greater trials with composure.[39] Wesley himself witnessed the correlation between those who lived holy lives and those who died well. One of the highest compliments he paid to his own followers was that they "died as they lived."[40] Wesley was so intrigued by the notion of a good death that he asked his preachers to send him accounts of Methodist deaths. Special note was made of believers such as Thomas Wardrobe who prepared for death by living the dying life. "Were I to repeat half what he spoke I should write you three hours," reported the witness who related Wardrobe's final hours to Wesley. "It shall suffice at this time to say, that as he lived the life, so he died the death of a Christian."[41] Even Methodists with "weak talents," like Joseph Guilford, could be distinguished in their death by their commitment to holy living. Wesley wrote of Guilford, "Surely never before did a man of so weak talents do so much good! He died as he lived, in full triumph of faith, vehemently rejoicing and praising God!"[42]

---

37. Law, *Practical Treatise upon Christian Perfection*, 161.

38. Baxter, *Saints' Everlasting Rest*, 305.

39. Lucas, *Enquiry after Happiness*, 143. In Lucas's warning, there are echoes of à Kempis's earlier admonishment, "Oh how wise and happy is he that now laboreth to be such a one in his life, as he wisheth to be found at the hour of his death!" Wesley took seriously à Kempis's claim, "For he that loveth God with all his heart, is neither afraid of death nor punishment, nor of judgment, nor of hell; for perfect love gives secure access to God. But he that takes delight in sin, what wonder is it if he is afraid, both of death and judgment?" à Kempis, *Imitation of Christ*, 74.

40. Wesley, *Journal* June 16, 1777 (BE), 23:55.

41. Wesley, *Journal* May 30, 1756 (BE), 21:56. This entry contained a letter from Mr. Gillies to John Wesley regarding Thomas Wardrobe's death.

42. Wesley, *Journal* May 18, 1777 (BE), 23:50.

Wesley elevated the stories of Methodists such as Wardrobe and Guilford because they demonstrated the type of preparation necessary for a good death. Such rigorous effort was work for the living not the dead or dying. Those who were close to death attested to the difficulty of waiting until the end of life to repent of sinfulness. For example, as one Methodist lay dying of a fever, she expressed her relief that she had used her life to prepare for death. She exclaimed, "O what would become of me, if I had all the work of religion to begin now, when I cannot keep my mind a moment fixt on one object!"[43] Therefore, as Lester Ruth noted, "The goal for a Methodist was to live in such a way—faithful to Christ, denying the world and self—that she or he would answer in the face of death, 'I am ready.'"[44]

Mortification of Self-Will

Living the dying life began with the mortification of self-will. Wesley believed it was "an essential part of human nature, indeed of the nature of every intelligent being" to have a will, but in fallen humanity the will often exalted itself against the will of God.[45] Thus, the sinful will along with "all its evil passions, appetites, and inclinations" must be put to death.[46] Wesley explained that "true believers in Him have thus *crucified the flesh*—Nailed it as it were, to a cross, whence it has no power to break loose, but is continually weaker and weaker."[47] Wesley admitted that a believer's crucified nature "often struggles to break from the cross."[48] Therefore, the way forward was to practice self-denial since, Wesley reasoned, "the nature of self-denial . . . is the denying or refusing to follow our own will, from a conviction that the will of God is the only rule of action to us."[49]

In a sermon dedicated to the topic of self-denial, Wesley explained that there was a difference between bearing a cross and taking up one. "Bearing a cross" was not properly self-denial since it meant enduring hardship that had been placed upon the believer without the person's consent. "Taking up a cross" was true self-denial because "we willingly embrace the will of God,

---

43. Wesley, "Account of the Death of Mrs. Dorothy Wright" *AM* (February 1790), 77.
44. Ruth, *Early Methodist Life and Spirituality*, 289.
45. Wesley, *Repentance of Believers* (BE), 1:337.
46. Wesley, *ENNT* (Gal 5:24), 697–98.
47. Wesley, *ENNT* (Gal 5:24), 697–98.
48. Wesley, *On Sin in Believers* (BE), 1:329.
49. Wesley, *Self-Denial* (BE), 2:242.

though contrary to our own."⁵⁰ Wesley was quick to point out that self-denial was not punishing one's self; rather, it was a cutting away of those pleasures that interfered with a person's ability to wholly love and serve God. The proper path of self-denial entailed engaging in works of piety (such as prayer, meditation, fasting, and reading Scripture) as well as works of charity (feeding the hungry, visiting the sick, and clothing the naked).⁵¹ These works were to be undertaken not simply when the believer found it convenient but especially when it was tiresome or inopportune.

Mortification of Worldly Desires

Another species of self-denial or mortification of self-will was the crucifixion of worldly desires. Wesley described love of the world as a "strong propensity to 'love the creature more than the Creator,'" the desire to gratify the "imagination with something great, or beautiful, or uncommon," to long for honor and recognition or "a desire and love of praise . . . and . . . a proportionable *fear of dispraise*."⁵² In his commentary on Gal 6:14, Wesley noted that those who had crucified the world and its fleshly desires were "dead to all worldly pursuits, cares, desires, and enjoyments."⁵³ The world offered many real pleasures; however, these same pleasures viewed through the lens of faith, were shown to be temporary gratifications. Death to the world and its pursuits allowed believers to align themselves with the enduring will of God rather than the fleeting whims of the transitory realm. Wesley admitted that taking up the cross and rejecting the world could prove to be a difficult task since the diversions of the world were tangibly present. However, Wesley reminded his followers that the lasting reality of true life was found in the spiritual realm with Christ and not in the temporary goods the world could offer. He wrote, "*For ye are dead*—To the things on earth. *And your* real, spiritual *life is hid* from the world, and laid up *in God, with Christ*—Who hath merited, promised, prepared it for us, and given us the earnest and foretaste of it in our hearts."⁵⁴

Believers were called to surrender everything in which they had invested themselves—even that which was good—to the greater glory of

---

50. Wesley, *Self-Denial* (BE), 2:244.
51. Wesley, *Self-Denial* (BE), 2:247–48.
52. Wesley, *Repentance of Believers* (BE), 1:338–39.
53. Wesley, *ENNT*, 700.
54. Wesley, *ENNT* (Col 3:3), 748

God. Such humble submission was actually an investment in the eternal realm, since as Bishop Hall reflected, "I will carry that treasure with me by giving it, which the worlding loseth by keeping it; so while his corpse shall carry nothing but a winding-cloth to his grave, I shall be richer under the earth, than I was above it."[55] Wesley understood that a capitulation of this magnitude often carried with it the painful sting of death. He noted, "True humility is a kind of self-annihilation."[56] Laying down the self and all its accomplishments required the deepest levels of trust and humility. It meant that the best of one's efforts (even those that were performed for the good of others) had to be laid at the foot of the cross. In his treatise, *Farther Thoughts upon Christian Perfection*, Wesley observed,

> Good works do not receive their last perfection, till they, as it were, lose themselves in God. This is a kind of death to them, resembling that of our bodies, which will not attain their highest life, their immortality, till they lose themselves in the glory of our souls, or rather of God, wherewith they shall be filled. And it is only what they had of earthly and mortal, which good works lose by this spiritual death . . . And by this means it prevents their being corrupted by pride, vanity, or any evil mixture. But this cannot be done otherwise than by making these good works in a spiritual manner die in God, by a deep gratitude, which plunges the soul in him as in an abyss, with all that it is, and all the grace and works for which it is indebted to him . . . .[57]

Even though the perception was false, Wesley recognized that those who were on the path leading to Christian perfection felt as if they were stepping off a cliff into the abyss.

Always an optimist, Wesley suggested that believers view death to self-will and temporal desires not as a painful sacrifice but as an occasion to be formed more closely to the *imago Dei*. It was also an investment toward the attainment of perfection. Wesley wrote, "Let him in all things deny his own will, however pleasing, and do the will of God, however, painful. Should we not consider all crosses . . . as what they really are, as opportunities of embracing God's will at the expense of our own? And consequently as so many steps by which we may advance toward perfection?"[58] Thus, the

---

55. Hall, *Meditations and Vows*, 447.
56. Wesley, *Farther Thoughts Upon Christian Perfection* (BE), 13:126.
57. Wesley, *Farther Thoughts Upon Christian Perfection* (BE), 13:130.
58. Wesley, *ENNT* (Matt 16:24), 83.

dying life called for believers to embrace the mortification of the fallen self and the corrupted world—not in a morbid fashion whereby one embraced sacrifice and suffering for the sake of suffering alone. Rather, knowing that mortification of the sinful nature simply stripped away only that which hindered humanity from a life-giving relationship with the divine, believers could more easily sever ties to anything that did not align itself with God's intent for their well-being.

The Process of Sanctification as Preparation for Physical Death

Wesley likened the death of the sinful nature to the death of the body. Both mortification of the sinful nature and physical death were typically preceded by a process of gradual decline and entailed the preparation for a translation from one state of being to another type of reality. In physical death, the change was from the physical world to the supernatural realm; in the death of the carnal nature, the transformation was qualitative—a change from being partially holy to entirely holy. Wesley linked the two types of death in his following explanation:

> A man may be dying for some time; yet he does not properly speaking, die, till the instant the soul is separated from the body; and in that instant he lived the life of eternity. In like manner, he may be dying to sin for some time; yet he is not dead to sin, till sin is separated from his soul; and in that instant he lives the full life of love. And as the change undergone, when the body dies, is of a different kind, and infinitely greater than any we had known before, yea, such as till then it is impossible to conceive; so the change wrought, when the soul dies to sin, is of a different kind, and infinitely greater than any before, and than any can conceive till he experiences it.[59]

Those who did the work of sanctification in mortifying the sinful nature had already anticipated the existential and spiritual struggles of the death bed. In undertaking the change entailed in the death of the carnal nature, believers faced the challenges of death in a forthright way and, in essence, did the work of the deathbed in advance. In other words, sanctification was a "practice run" for physical death. Gregory Schneider noted, "We might characterize evangelical religion fairly as an effort to steal a

---

59. Wesley, *Christian Perfection*, 11:402.

march on death, a strategy for conquering death by living a dying life."[60] Wesley expressed this same sentiment in a poem published in the *Arminian Magazine*:

> For this [death] habitually prepared,
> Death could not find him off his guard,
> A man who daily died:
> A stranger in the vale of tears,
> Whose life for more than forty years,
> Confessed The Crucified.[61]

Physical Death as a Motivation for Mortification

Wesley viewed physical death in terms of both punishment and promise. Death was the result of sin and was a sign that all had fallen short of God's holy intent. For believers, however, death could also be seen as an escape from the sinful world and the opportunity to be with Christ. Lester Ruth noted that this dual understanding of death acted as a tremendous incentive for early Methodists to pursue deeper levels of holiness.

> As a punishment, the approach of death could be lifted up as a warning to the complacent and the ungodly. As promise . . . death could be offered as opportunity . . . . Methodists connected death's exhortatory value to the paradox of death's known and unknown qualities. Death was coming (the known quality) but one never knew exactly when (the unknown aspect). The result was a vivid concern for readiness for death.[62]

In terms of the process of sanctification, death could serve as a helpful motivator to prevent actual sin and encourage believers in their efforts to mortify the sinful nature. Since death was contained within the larger context of God's providence, it could also be used as a beneficial tool in the capable hands of the Creator. After all, as Lucas noted, "That as God orders all the particular Events of Life to the Good of those that love Him, so much more must He dispose this biggest Event, to their Interest and Benefit."[63]

---

60. Schneider, "Ritual of Happy Dying among Early American Methodists," 353.
61. Wesley, "On the Death of Mr. Thomas Lewis," *AM* (January 1783), 49.
62. Ruth, *Early Methodist Life and Spirituality*, 289.
63. Lucas, *Extract from an Enquiry After Happiness*, 156.

Wesley was not naïve when it came to human nature. He understood that the reality of death brought certain truths into sharp focus and served as a powerful motivator for most people to make certain their spiritual standing. Furthermore, imminent death often made the eternal realm seem an almost tangible reality. The undeniable fact that one was leaving behind one's closest friends, life's work, and best accomplishments made the mortification of self-will and worldly desires easier to accept. Contemplating the end of one's earthly existence allowed time and opportunity to examine one's standing with God in a focused and honest way. Wesley believed that to leave such matters until the very end of life unnecessarily burdened the dying process with uncertainty and anxiety and left no room for a person to engage in works suitable for repentance if they were found lacking. Therefore, he encouraged people to think about the end of their lives as a means to improve their spiritual progress. "Do you never think about [death]?" he asked in his address titled, "A Word to an Unhappy Woman." "Why do you not? Are you never to die? Nay, it is appointed for all men to die. And what comes after? Only heaven or hell. Will the not thinking of death, put it farther off? No; not a day; not one hour."[64]

The refusal to contemplate the end of one's earthly existence was a glaring indication that something was wrong with the person's spiritual well-being and suggested that the process of sanctification had been derailed. The desire to avoid the subject of death altogether demonstrated that the individual either lacked spiritual awareness or was engaged in self-deception. If a believer put off facing the difficult questions in the here and now, it had the potential to place the person's soul in eternal peril. Wesley reminded those who wished to disregard death, "You can neither conquer nor escape [death] ... Death levels all; it mingles in one dust the gentleman, soldier, clown, and beggar; it makes all these distinctions void. When life ends, so do they. Holy or unholy, is the one question then."[65] Believers who were actively engaged in mortifying the sinful nature were not intimidated by questions about death or contemplation of the subject because they were already preparing themselves for their inevitable demise.

Of course, the best weapon against the being of sin was not the external pressure of death but genuine repentance over the carnal nature. When Wesley spoke of repentance over the being of sin, he defined it as an honest acknowledgment regarding the state of the heart and a loathing for one's

---

64. Wesley, "Word to an Unhappy Woman" (Jackson), 11:171.
65. Wesley, *Advice to a Soldier* (Jackson), 11:200–201.

sinful condition. This type of repentance was "one kind of self-knowledge," Wesley wrote. "The knowing ourselves sinners, yea, guilty, helpless sinners, even though we know we are children of God."[66] Until this type of repentance was in place, "until God unveils the inbred monster's face, and shows them the real state of their souls. Then only, when they feel the burden will they groan for deliverance from it," Wesley concluded.[67]

Wesley was skeptical of people who were only motivated to repent when death stared them in the face. Despite his firmly held optimism that God both could and would save sinners who faced imminent death, Wesley admitted that at times he was uncertain of whether such people were genuinely interested in a relationship with God. He wrote, "I visited two persons in Newgate, who were under sentence of death. They seemed to be in an excellent temper, calmly resigned to the will of God. But how much stress can be reasonably laid on such impressions, it is hard to say: So often I have known them vanish away as soon as ever the expectation of death was removed."[68] Nevertheless, Wesley did not discount the idea that the threat of death could be a helpful tool in perfecting repentance over the being of sin.

Freedom from the Fear of Death

Not only did physical death serve as an incentive for the mortification of the sinful nature, the threat of death also tested the genuineness of a person's subsequent repentance and pursuit of holiness. Wesley found death to be a sobering corrective in his own life. Martin Schmidt noted that it was precisely "the fear of death which aroused in him ultimate questions."[69] During

---

66. Wesley, *Repentance of Believers* (BE), 1:336.

67. Wesley, *Repentance of Believers* (BE), 1:351. Ideal repentance was not coerced. Rather, as Isaac Ambrose explained, "When a man lays violent hands on his sins; when he cuts them off, being yet in their flower, and strength, and power, and vigour; when he pulls up those weeds before they wither in themselves, this is true mortification." Ambrose, *Looking unto Jesus, a View of the Everlasting Gospel*, 236. Wesley republished Ambrose's work in the *Christian Library*.

68. Wesley, *Journal* November 18, 1784 (BE), 23:335. Wesley was skeptical of a response simply based on fear or guilt. He noted, "I visited a poor dying backslider, full of good resolutions. But who can tell when these imply a real change of heart? And when they do not, when they spring from fear only, what will they avail before God?" Wesley, *Journal* January 3, 1757 (BE), 21:84.

69. Schmidt, *John Wesley*, 1:217.

his early years the question, "Are you afraid to die?" revealed the true state of Wesley's own spiritual condition. Collins noted, "To be sure, just as with the illuminating and accusatory power of the moral law, such an uncomfortable question, through the grace of the Holy Spirit, could cut to the quick and break through the layers of self-deception and self-justification in which the sinful soul had placed its trust."[70] Therefore, Wesley's intense questioning about one's attitude toward death was not a tactic to frighten those who were anxious about dying. Instead, it was an opportunity to examine how deeply the grace of God had penetrated the soul.[71]

Because Wesley believed physical death only posed a danger if a person's spiritual standing was in jeopardy, the specter of death was not a threat to the child of God. Instead, death was an opportunity to prove the efficaciousness of God's grace. Facing the reality of one's own demise subjected all the holy virtues to extreme scrutiny. If believers demonstrated a sense of peace, joy, happiness, assurance, faith, and love under the trial of death, it was a good indication that they had genuinely experienced the transformation of the new birth and were progressing in the faith. If the prospect of death brought fear, uncertainty, unhappiness or the loss of peace, individuals should re-examine their standing with God. Fear of death could be an indication that there were still areas in which the believer was unwilling to detach themselves from the world and the pleasures it had to offer. Furthermore, Wesley knew it was easy to trust in the comforts of life or in one's own merits when all seemed well; however, the threat of death stripped away all false pretenses. A true believer, Wesley declared, is "delivered from the wrath and the curse of God, from all sense of guilt and condemnation, and from all that horror and fear of death and hell whereby he was 'all his life' before 'subject to bondage.'"[72]

Fears Inconsistent with Sanctifying Grace

Wesley was sensitive enough to understand that the fear of death was not a simple matter since it could have a variety of causes. He turned to the Anglican Homily "An Exhortation Against the Fear of Death" to help

70. Collins, "John Wesley and the Fear of Death as a Standard of Conversion," 56.

71. Wesley understood that there were some believers who lacked assurance because of bodily or mental infirmities; however, such persons were the exception and not the rule.

72. Wesley, *Law Established Through Faith* (BE), 2:29.

categorize the types of uncertainty a person might experience. According to the sermon, most people commonly feared death for the following reasons: (1) Fear of leaving their pleasures, possessions, family, or friends. (2) Fear of pain or illness leading up to death, and (3) Fear of condemnation by God and everlasting damnation.[73] Believers undergoing sanctification should not be afraid of leaving behind pleasures, possessions, family, or friends since they were in the process of mortifying anything that would displace God as their highest love. Wesley went so far as to state that "whatever takes our heart from [God], or shares it with him, is an idol; or, in other words, whatever we seek happiness in, independent of God."[74] If individuals were afraid to depart and be with Christ because their hearts were entangled with earthly concerns, Wesley inferred that the person was dealing with a problem of disordered loves (at best) or idolatry (at worst).[75] Wesley offered a series of questions to help individuals examine themselves for disordered love: "Have you no choice as to life or death? And have you no choice as to the manner of your death? Are you not afraid of the pain of dissolution? Can you freely part with all your friends here?"[76]

Fear of condemnation was a sign that one not only lacked the ongoing grace of sanctification but the very gifts and graces of the new birth. Wesley insisted that those born of God were free from "all servile fear, from that 'fear which hath torment', from fear of punishment, from fear of the wrath of God, whom they now no longer regard as a severe master, but as an indulgent Father."[77] He made no attempt to hide his alarm over the spiritual condition of Mrs. Cummins, a follower who apparently demonstrated signs of trepidation at the thought of dying. He urged her, "O make haste! Be a Christian, a real Bible Christian now! You may say, 'Nay, I am a Christian already.' I fear not. (See how freely I speak.) A Christian is not afraid to die. Are you not? Do you desire to depart and be with Christ?"[78]

---

73. "An Exhortation Against the Fear of Death" in Wesley, *Homilies*, 57–58.

74. Wesley, *Spiritual Idolatry* (BE), 3:104–5.

75. Wesley seemed to have difficulty making allowances for strong relational bonds which sometimes caused him to appear unsympathetic when dealing with issues of grief.

76. Wesley, *Letters* "To Elizabeth Ritchie" June 16, 1777 (Telford), 6:266.

77. Wesley, *Salvation by Faith* (BE), 1:122.

78. Wesley, *Letters* "To Miss Cummins" June 8, 1773 (Telford), 6:30–31.

Fear That May Coincide with Sanctifying Grace

Wesley conceded that some real Christians feared death not because of condemnation or misplaced love but out of anxiety over the physical pain of death.[79] Wesley developed this line of thought in a letter to his father by reasoning, "The material part of us being thus liable to corruption, pain is necessary to make us watchful against it, and to warn us of what tends toward it; as is the fear of death likewise, which is of use in many cases that pain does not reach.... But if pain and the fear of death were extinguished, no animal could long subsist."[80] Wesley concluded that in this case the fear of death is necessary since without it humans would lack the wherewithal to preserve their lives. Furthermore, the threat of physical suffering could be beneficial to believers since it was a reminder that true rest cannot be found within this earthly realm.[81]

Misguided philosophies or confused reasoning could also cause anxiety over death. For example, the eighteenth century brought with it a growing sentiment, especially among the well-educated, that death brought with it personal extinction. In the essay *Fame and the Afterlife*, Keith Thomas noted, "A persistent theme in Elizabethan and Jacobean drama was the dread of personal annihilation after death, the fear that life might indeed be a tale told by an idiot, signifying nothing."[82] Wesley, himself, seemingly grappled with the notion of extinction. In 1766, he wrote a letter to Charles in which John expressed that he did not feel endangered by the wrath of God, but neither did he have any more certainty "of the eternal or invisible world than [I have] now; and that is [none at all], unless such as fairly shines from reason's glimmering ray."[83] Wesley went on to remark in this letter, "I have no more fear than love. Or if I have [any fear, it is not that of falling] into hell but of falling into nothing."[84] Wesley's comments here are

79. Wesley understood the prospect of pain could cause alarm. He observed that 'whoever is uneasy on any account (bodily pain alone excepted) carries in himself his own conviction that he is so far an unbeliever.' Wesley, *Journals* December 28, 1737 (BE), 18:207.

80. Wesley, "To the Revd. Samuel Wesley" January 15, 1731 *Letters* (BE), 25:265.

81. à Kempis declared, "Adversity is profitable because trouble and sorrow cause us to desire to die and be with Christ." à Kempis, *Imitation of Christ*, 43.

82. Thomas went on to suggest that many of the upper class did not believe in an afterlife, but they found it politically savvy to perpetuate the idea of eternal punishment and reward to control the masses. Thomas, "Fame and the Afterlife," 233-34.

83. Wesley, *Letters* "To Charles" June 27, 1766 (Telford), 5:16.

84. Wesley, *Letters* "To Charles" June 27, 1766 (Telford), 5:16.

somewhat baffling since they did not accurately reflect his spiritual journey. However, if one places Wesley's remarks in the context of annihilation, his woeful annotations make more sense. In his sermon, *The Case of Reason Impartially Considered* (1781), Wesley reflected upon a point in his life "many years ago" that he learned "by sad experience" he could not prove either the existence of God or an afterlife through reason alone.[85] He had asked himself the question, "What, if that saying of a great man be really true . . . 'Death is nothing, and nothing is after death?' How am I sure that this is not the case; that I have not followed cunningly devised fables?"[86]

Degrees of Assurance

Wesley also acknowledged that there are varying degrees of assurance bestowed throughout the Christian life. In a letter written to Dr. Rutherford in 1768, Wesley described three degrees of assurance: (1) A consciousness of being in God's favor which may be weakened by returns of doubt or fear. (2) Full assurance of faith which Wesley described as being assured of being "now in the favour of God" which excludes all doubt or fear (typically associated with entire sanctification). (3) Full assurance of hope by which Wesley meant assurance of everlasting salvation.[87] Wesley conceded that some genuine believers may lack assurance altogether, but this condition would be very unusual and generally be caused by some sort of bodily disorder or sheer ignorance of the promise of assurance. Wesley believed it was the general privilege of all believers to have some measure of certainty which would drive away the fears associated with both spiritual and physical death. As believers grew in grace and holiness through the process of sanctification, they possessed more assurance, and the fears associated with death diminished. Not all believers had the same extent of confidence in the face of death because they varied in degrees of holiness. In his comments on Rom 8:38-39, Wesley remarked, "And hereby they are 'persuaded' (though perhaps not all at all times, or with the same fullness of persuasion) 'that neither death, nor life, nor things present, nor things to come, nor height, nor depth, nor any other creature, shall be able to separate them from the

---

85. Wesley, *Case of Reason Impartially Considered* (BE), 2:593-94.

86. Wesley, *Case of Reason Impartially Considered* (BE), 2:594. Outler noted that Wesley quoted here from Seneca. See footnote 30. In this sermon, Wesley also brought up the anecdotal last words of Thomas Hobbes who reportedly said, "I am taking a leap into the dark." *Case of Reason Impartially Considered* (BE), 2:595.

87. Wesley, *Letters* "To Dr Rutherford" March 28, 1768 (Telford), 5:358.

love of God, which is in Christ Jesus our Lord.'"[88] However, Wesley was entirely convinced of God's faithfulness to genuine believers so that at the time of death grace would be given as it was needed. In a letter to Miss Bishop, Wesley gave the following reassurance, "Faith is given according to our present need. You have now such faith as is necessary for your living unto God. As yet you are not called to die. When you are, you shall have faith for this also. To-day improve the faith you have, and trust God with tomorrow."[89] In other words, those living the dying life had nothing to fear in terms of temporal death.

Conclusion

Wesley adamantly disagreed with those who thought the problem of sin was totally resolved in the new birth. Such a view left a believer vulnerable to the being of sin which remained even in those who were justified and regenerated. The proper approach to the Christian life, therefore, was progressive mortification of the carnal nature whereby a believer grew in holiness and the grace of God. The death of the sinful nature was accomplished through cooperating with the grace of God, but Wesley found contemplating physical death could encourage the process of sanctification. Keeping one's mortality in view was a reminder that life was a precious gift from God and should not be squandered on penultimate pursuits. Wesley admonished his followers, "You have no time to lose; see that you redeem every moment that remains. Remove everything out of the way, be it ever so small . . . that might anyways obstruct your lowliness and meekness, your seriousness of spirit, your single intention to glorify God, in all your thoughts and words and actions."[90] Those who fully invested their lives in the pursuit of glorifying God had nothing to fear from death; rather death became yet another opportunity for the grace of God to be made manifest.

---

88. Wesley, *Salvation by Faith* (BE), 1:123.

89. Wesley, *Letters* "To Mary Bishop" April 17, 1776 (Telford), 6:213. Wesley gave similar counsel in one of his sermons: "Most true: you have not *now* the power which you do not *now* stand in need of. You are not able at *this time* to conquer that enemy; and at *this time* he does not assault you. With the grace you have now you could not withstand the temptations which you have not. But when the temptation comes the grace will come. In greater trials you will have greater strength. When sufferings abound, the consolations of God will in the same proportion abound also. So that in every situation the grace of God will be sufficient for you." Wesley, *Sermon on the Mount, IX* (BE), 1:647.

90. Wesley, "Advice to Methodists with Regard to Dress" (Jackson), 11:475–76.

Chapter 5

ENTIRE SANCTIFICATION AND DEATH

Introduction

THE MORTIFICATION OF THE sinful nature was not an indefinite process in Wesley's theology; rather, the process of sanctification led to the moment when the grace of entire sanctification was actualized. Unlike most of his contemporaries, Wesley believed that the death of the carnal nature was not only a possibility but was a necessary work of grace for all believers to experience before they died. The doctrine of Christian perfection was at the heart of Wesley's theology from the beginning of his ministry, and it was in the context of this central doctrine that Wesley drew upon the motif of death most frequently. He found the metaphor of death helpful in explaining not just the gradual mortification of the sinful nature but in describing its actual expurgation. Wesley's connection between death and entire sanctification went much deeper than mere metaphor because it was at the deathbed of saintly Christians that he was convinced perfection was actually possible. This chapter will examine not only how Wesley utilized death metaphorically for inward heart holiness but also how perfection related to physical death.

Christian Perfection as the Highest Degree of Love

Wesley offered the following definition of entire sanctification to his brother Charles: "By perfection, I mean the humble, gentle, patient love of God and man ruling all the tempers, words, and actions, the whole heart and the whole life."[1] He specifically applied this definition of Christian perfection to the re-creation of the moral image whereby the lingering divisive effects of sin were wiped clean.[2] He explained in his sermon, *On Perfection*, "Now the moral image of God consists . . . 'in righteousness and true holiness.' By sin this is totally destroyed. And we can never recover it till we are 'created anew in Christ Jesus.' And this is perfection."[3] Later in the same sermon, Wesley declared that believers are left with "no room to doubt but God will thus 'renew' us 'in the spirit of our mind,' and 'create us anew' in the 'image of God, wherein we were at first created.'"[4] The new birth removed the threat of spiritual death by restoring a right relationship with God, and Christian perfection furthered the fortification against spiritual demise through a complete restoration of the moral image. Thus, Christian perfection meant nothing less than the divinely bestowed ability to once again relate to God from a heart motivated solely by love, true righteousness and holiness.

At first glance, the work of perfection appears no different from the benefits imbued in the new birth. In his sermon, *On Patience*, Wesley addressed this very issue. Christian perfection was not "a new *kind* of holiness"[5] he observed; rather, it was love which was qualified by complete purity.[6] Wesley went on to explain, "Love is the sum of Christian

---

1. Wesley, *Letters* "To Charles" September n.d., 1762 (Telford), 4:187. Wesley's explanation of perfection is especially significant here since the purpose of this particular letter was to clarify the exact nature of Christian perfection.

2. Wesley wrote, "Ye know that the great end of religion is to renew our hearts in the image of God, to repair that total loss of righteousness and true holiness which we sustained by the sin of our first parent. Ye know that all religion which . . . stops short of this. . . is no other than a poor farce and a mere mockery of God, to the destruction of our own soul." Wesley, *Original Sin* (BE), 2:185.

3. Wesley, *On Perfection* (BE), 3:75.

4. Wesley, *On Perfection* (BE), 3:77. Wesley used similar language in his preface to the 1740 edition of *Hymns and Sacred Poems*. Here Wesley likened entire sanctification to nothing less than a new creation whereby God "giveth them a single Eye and a clean Heart. He stamps upon them his own Image and Superscription; He createth them anew in Christ Jesus . . . [and] bringeth them into the Rest which remaineth for the People of God." Wesley, *Hymns and Sacred Poems*, xi.

5. Wesley, *On Patience* (BE), 3:174.

6. Collins suggested that holiness and love cannot simply be equated; rather, he noted

sanctification; it is the one *kind* of holiness which is found, only in various *degrees*, in the believers who are distinguished by St. John into 'little children, young men, and fathers.' The difference between one and the other properly lies in the degree of love."[7] In other words, the love and faith of some believers may be "mingled with doubts or fears"[8] or be mixed with pride, anger or residual self-will, but the one who was entirely sanctified had "no mixture of any contrary affections."[9] Wesley clarified that a perfected believer "now loves God with all his heart, and with all his soul, and with all his mind, and with all his strength, so Jesus now reigns alone in his heart, the Lord of every motion there."[10]

The purity of entire sanctification was not simply a void of inordinate or distracting affections but also the embodiment of the holy tempers—the chief of which was love. Wesley declared, "It is not only a negative blessing, a deliverance from all evil dispositions implied in that expression, 'I will circumcise the heart,' but a positive one, likewise, even the planting all good dispositions in their place."[11] Perfection, then, was the compilation of the fruit of the Spirit within the heart. "Love, joy, peace; long-suffering, gentleness, goodness, fidelity ... meekness, temperance .... What a glorious constellation of graces is here! Now suppose all these to be knit together in one, to be united together in the soul of a believer–this is Christian perfection,"[12] rejoiced Wesley. In a positive sense, perfection was the closest humanity could come to reaching their *telos* this side of heaven. Entire sanctification purified "the *relation* between God and humanity such that the *imago Dei*, especially the moral image, has been renewed in its glory and splendor. The creature, once steeped in sin, now reflects the goodness of the Creator in a remarkable way."[13]

---

that they "represent two distinct classes of words: the one indirectly relational, expressing the quality of a relationship; the other directly so. Thus, Wesley's view of holiness as purity represents a *qualitative* designation that reveals the integrity and the beauty of the relations of love." Collins, *Theology of John Wesley*, 7.

7. Wesley, *On Patience* (BE), 3:175.
8. Wesley, *On Patience* (BE), 3:175.
9. Wesley, *On Patience* (BE), 3:176.
10. Wesley, *On Patience* (BE), 3:176.
11. Wesley, *On Discoveries of Faith* (BE), 4:37. Elsewhere, Wesley described perfection as, "love excluding sin; love filling the heart, taking up the whole capacity of the soul." Wesley, *Scripture Way of Salvation* (BE), 2:160.
12. Wesley, *On Perfection* (BE), 3:75.
13. Collins, *Theology of John Wesley*, 302.

Indeed, many of those who testified to the grace of entire sanctification felt their hearts so remarkably renewed in the divine image that God's presence seemed to consume their entire being. Thomas Hitchens, for example, declared, "I am sanctified, Soul, Body and Spirit. I am whiter than Snow. I am washed in the Blood of my Redeemer. *Why, I am all God.* My heart is full of God: O let them who hear me now praise thee for ever and ever."[14] Much of Methodist hymnody regarding Christian perfection also reflected the feeling of being utterly consumed by the divine nature.[15] For example, one hymn intoned:

> Break off the yoke of inbred sin,
> And fully set my spirit free.
> I cannot rest till pure within,
> *Till I am wholly lost in thee.*[16]

In yet another poem by Charles Wesley, it was recorded:

> Now let me gain perfection's height
> Now *let me into nothing fall,*
> Be *less than nothing in my sight,*
> And feel that *Christ is all in all.*[17]

Put in its simplest terms, Christian perfection was an all-consuming love; it was God's Spirit reigning in the heart without rival.

Christian Perfection as Death to the Sinful Nature

It is clear from Wesley's description of perfection that sanctifying love was a radically purifying element.[18] Such purity went beyond sincerity or proper intentions; it was the reality of a heart purged from inbred sin. "A person may be sincere who has all his natural tempers, pride, anger, lust, self-will, but he is not perfect till his heart is cleansed from these, and all its other

---

14. Hitchens, *Short Account of the Death of Thomas Hitchens*, 10. Italics are mine. Wesley originally published this account in 1745.

15. Charles Wesley penned most of these hymns, but John exercised a large enough editorial role over the hymns that they must be taken into account on this matter.

16. Wesley, "Hymn 377" (BE), 7:550. Emphasis mine.

17. Wesley, "Promise of Sanctification" (BE), 2:124. Emphasis mine.

18. Stanley Johnson described the love entailed in Wesley's doctrine of Christian perfection, as "the principal dynamic which as a fire burns up the dross of sin." Johnson, "Christian Perfection as Love for God," 55.

corruptions," declared Wesley.[19] Wesley pronounced that after a person was "thoroughly convinced of inbred sin, of the total corruption of his nature," God would "take it all away... purify his heart and cleanse him from all unrighteousness."[20] In the third discourse of his *Sermon on the Mount*, Wesley further elaborated on this point:

> The pure in heart are they whose hearts God hath 'purified even as he is pure'; who are purified through faith in the blood of Jesus from every unholy affection; who, being cleansed from all filthiness of flesh and spirit, perfect holiness in the loving 'fear of God'. They are... purified... from every desire but to please and enjoy God, to know and love him more and more... so that now they love the Lord their God with all their heart, and with all their soul, and mind, and strength.[21]

The totality of purification entailed in entire sanctification made the image of death a convenient illustration for Wesley because he believed the sinful nature was not simply subdued but destroyed.[22] This point was made extremely clear in his sermon *On Repentance in Believers*. He noted that in the work of Christian perfection "the evil root, the carnal mind, is destroyed; and inbred sin subsists no more."[23] Accordingly, whenever Wesley spoke of perfection, he heavily utilized the language of death. For example, the terms "mortify," "die" and "kill" appeared in just four lines of a hymn on the topic. The hymn intoned,

---

19. Wesley, *Further Thoughts upon Christian Perfection* (BE), 13:100. Henry Knight expressed the matter in these terms: "Salvation is not a divine plan to act as if we have no sin, but to replace the sin we actually have with love." Knight, "Love and Freedom 'By Grace Alone' in Wesley's Soteriology," 65.

20. Wesley, *On Patience* (BE), 3:175.

21. Wesley, *Upon Our Lord's Sermon on the Mount*, Discourse Three (BE), 1:510–11.

22. Wesley's views on entire sanctification often put him at odds with his contemporaries. George Whitefield declared, "I do not expect to see indwelling sin finished and destroyed till I bow down my head and give up the ghost! There must be Amalekites left in the Israelite's land to keep his soul in action, to make him humble, and drive him constantly to Jesus for pardon and forgiveness." Wesley, "Letter from the Revd. George Whitefield" *Letters* September 25, 1740 (BE), 26:32. Most Anglicans agreed with Whitefield's assumption that the being of sin could not be removed before death. However, Wesley's view was not without precedence. Both Thomas Drayton and Robert Gell proposed that the sinful nature must be removed in this lifetime. See Drayton, *Proviso or Condition of the Promises*, and Gell, "Some Saints Not without Sin for a Season, Sermon 20."

23. Wesley, *Repentance of Believers* (BE), 1:346.

> My old affections mortify,
> Nail to the cross my will,
> Daily and hourly bid me die,
> Or altogether kill.[24]

Elsewhere, when asked to describe what entire sanctification was like, Wesley explained, "A man may be dying for some time; yet he does not, properly speaking, die, till the instant the soul is separated from the body . . . . In like manner, he may be dying to sin for some time; yet he is not dead to sin, till sin is separated from his soul; and in that instant he lives the full life of love."[25] Just as physical death meant the end of one's bodily existence, Christian perfection was the death knell for the sinful nature.

It is easy to understand why Wesley's doctrine of entire sanctification was often misunderstood. Not only did the term "perfection" make people believe Wesley was preaching some sort of unattainable spiritual state, but some of Wesley's Methodist counterparts began preaching a variation of Christian perfection which suggested that those who enjoyed this blessing would never sin or die. Much of the confusion was spawned from the perfectionist sect led by George Bell and Thomas Maxfield.[26] Bell's ministry was the epitome of the charge of "enthusiasm" which was often leveled against the Methodists. After attending one of Bell's gatherings, William Briggs (a loyal Methodist) wrote to Charles Wesley expressing dismay at what he observed. Briggs related that the doctrine of entire sanctification was explained using "such expressions of their perfection & union with God as I never before heard of;" furthermore, the entire event was punctuated by Bell's vehement prayers in which he was "screaming for some token of almighty power to work the mighty change in those present."[27] The tenor of the meeting was such that Briggs initially thought a brawl had broken out between Bell's followers and a handful of people who expressed disagreement with the doctrine which was presented.[28] According to Luke Tyer-

24. Wesley, "Hymn 352" (BE), 7:519. See Section VII: "Groaning for Full Redemption" in *A Collection of Hymns* for forty-seven more hymns on the topic.

25. Wesley, *Plain Account of Christian Perfection* (BE), 13:175.

26. It is unclear exactly what role Thomas Maxfield played in the whole affair. That he was involved is without doubt; however, the extent to which he involved in the whole debacle has been disputed.

27. Newport and Lloyd, "George Bell and Early Methodist Enthusiasm," 95. The letter was written by William Briggs to Charles Wesley on October 28, 1762.

28. Newport and Lloyd, "George Bell and Early Methodist Enthusiasm," 96. It turned out this impression was not the case, but his disgust with the whole scene was evident in his plea a few lines later never to be asked again to attend one of Bell's meetings.

man's account, Bell openly declared that God could only be found within the assembly of his followers, and he and his followers were "more holy than our first parents and incapable of falling."[29] David Stark noted that Bell also encouraged a "believe and receive" or a "name it and claim it" theology whereby some testified that they had been perfected when Bell laid hands on them.[30] Most germane to the subject at hand was Bell's claim that he would not die. It is unclear if Bell made this claim because he thought he was too holy to die, or if it was based on his prophecy that the world would end on February 28, 1763. Whatever the case, Wesley was forced to defend himself against such claims.[31]

In 1762, Wesley penned a short treatise called *Cautions and Directions Given to the Greatest Professors in the Methodist Societies* where he listed the recent misinterpretations of entire sanctification. Here, he called the notion that one was not "liable to bodily Death, or Pain. Or Grief. Or Temptation" the very height of enthusiasm.[32] The same year, Wesley wrote to Thomas Maxfield using a similar list of misconceptions about Christian perfection; Wesley added that he disliked the supposition a person could "be absolutely perfect; that he can be infallible, or above being tempted; or that the moment he is pure in heart he cannot fall from it."[33] Furthermore, Wesley took the step of warning his societies "of the *enthusiasm* which was breaking in by means of two or three weak though good men, who from a misconstrued text in the Revelation inferred that they should not die."[34] Wesley concluded that the development of such bizarre ideas was born of the desire to constantly seek some new gift of grace without the recognition that love was the point of it all. He summarized this point in the following statement: "Love is the highest Gift of GOD, humble, gentle, patient Love:

---

29. Tyerman, *Life and Times of the Rev. John Wesley*, 2:434. For further discussion on the controversy see Goodwin, "Setting Perfection Too High," 86–96 and Newport, "George Bell, Prophet and Enthusiast," 95–105.

30. Stark, "Peculiar Doctrine Committed to Our Trust," 180.

31. After much investigation into the matter, Wesley thought it necessary to publicly distance himself from Bell's extreme views. In two separate letters to the *London Chronicle*, Wesley denounced Bell's teaching and his prophecy that the world would end on February 28, 1763. Wesley, *Letters* "Letter to the Editor of the *London Chronicle*" January 7, 1763 (Telford) 4:200–201 and February 9, 1763 (Telford), 4:202–3.

32. Wesley, *Cautions and Directions Given to the Greatest Professors in the Methodist Societies* (London 1762), 5.

33. Wesley, *Letters* "To Thomas Maxfield" November 2, 1762 (Telford), 4:192–94.

34. Wesley, *Journal* February 5, 1762 (BE), 21:350.

That all Visions, Revelations, Manifestations whatever, are little things compared to Love."[35]

Christian Perfection Properly Explained

After the Bell and Maxfield scandal, Wesley exerted much time and effort into clearly articulating his views of entire sanctification. Wesley did not claim Christian perfection erased the effects of the fall; even the entirely sanctified were subject to the ongoing consequences of sin which included (among other things) the death of the body. Rather, as noted earlier, perfection served to reinstate the original purity of the human heart. This renewal of purity, however, was not a claim for Adamic or angelic perfection.[36] Humanity's condition after the Fall made it impossible to unerringly fulfill every point of the moral law; furthermore, it was not Wesley's desire to revert back to a pre-Fall condition. He was instead teleologically focused on attaining the promises of the gospel. That is, instead of perfection of performance or a "covenant of works," believers after the Fall were under a new "covenant of grace."[37] The requirements of the law were fulfilled by the believer's love for God and neighbor rather than by perfect obedience. Wesley insisted, "Faith working or animated by love is all that God now requires of man. He has substituted (not sincerity, but) love, in the room of angelic perfection."[38]

Because entire sanctification was neither Adamic nor angelic perfection, no one was exempt from the consequences of sin. In other words, *all* believers were fallible, fragile beings and were subject to temptation, error, unwitting sin, and physical death. In *A Plain Account of Christian Perfection*

---

35. Wesley, *Cautions and Directions Given to the Greatest Professors in the Methodist Societies*, 6.

36. Skevington Wood asserted that after the Fall humanity cannot go back to an Adamic perfection since, "Adamic perfection signifies perfect obedience to every point in this law. Holiness must be perfect in degree and continue without intermission throughout the whole life." Perfection of performance was impossible after the Fall. Wood, "Love Excluding Sin," 13.

37. Wesley discussed the difference between the Adamic covenant of works and the covenant of grace given by Christ in the sermon *The Righteousness of Faith*. Wesley explained that the covenant of law was dependent upon humanity's efforts; "whereas the covenant of grace, in order to man's *recovery* of the favour and life of God, requires only *faith*–living faith in him who through God justifies him that *obeyed not*" (BE), 1:209. For the full discussion see: Wesley, *Righteousness of Faith* (BE), 1:202–16.

38. Wesley, *Farther Thoughts on Christian Perfection* (BE), 13:97.

Wesley declared, "We, secondly, believe, that there is *no such perfection* in this life, as implies an entire deliverance, either from ignorance, or mistake, in things not essential to salvation, or from manifold temptations, or from numberless infirmities, wherewith the corruptible body more or less presses down the soul."[39] Furthermore, such errors in understanding or mistakes in judgment could lead to faulty practices.[40] Thus, one could be made "scripturally perfect" in the sense that the love of God reigned without rival in the heart, but an existence without any sin or error was unrealistic.[41] Wesley advised, "But even these souls dwell in a shattered body, and . . . cannot always exert themselves as they would . . . . They must times think, speak, or act wrong—not indeed through a defect of love, but through a defect of knowledge . . . notwithstanding that defect, and its consequences, they fulfil the law of love."[42] Part of being human meant that a perfected believer could, at times, unintentionally sin; yet, Wesley noted, "Where every word and action springs from love, such a mistake is not properly a sin."[43] That is, entirely sanctified believers always fulfilled the law of love even if their performance was not perfect.

Wesley dismissed Bell's extreme perfectionism because it denied the reality of the human condition. Wesley noted, "I myself believe that such perfection is inconsistent with living in a corruptible body; for this makes it impossible 'always to think right.' While we breathe we shall more or less mistake. If, therefore, Christian perfection implies this, we must not expect

---

39. Wesley, *Plain Account of Christian Perfection* (BE), 13:155.

40. Wesley noted that even one who was entirely sanctified "may believe either past or present actions which were or are evil to be good; and such as were or are good to be evil. Hence, they may judge not according to truth with regard to the characters of men . . . ." Wesley, *Christian Perfection* (BE), 2:102.

41. Wesley defined what he meant by "scripturally perfect" in a letter to Miss March. He wrote, "Thus much is certain: They that love God with all their heart, and all men as themselves, are scripturally perfect . . . [but] you dwell in a poor, shattered house of clay, which presses down the immortal spirit. Hence all your thoughts, words, and actions are so imperfect; so far from coming up to the standard. . . that you may well say, till you go to Him you love, —"Every moment, Lord, I need, The merit of thy death." Wesley, *Letters* "To Miss March" April 7, 1763 (Telford), 4:208.

42. Wesley, *Farther Thoughts upon Christian Perfection* (BE), 13:101.

43. Wesley, *Plain Account of Christian Perfection* (BE), 13:168. Wesley went on to note, "I believe there is no such perfection in this life as excludes these involuntary transgressions which I apprehend to be naturally consequent on the ignorance and mistakes inseparable from mortality" (13:169–70).

it till after death."[44] Unlike Bell, Wesley realized the physical body had suffered the consequences of sin as much as humanity's spiritual nature; therefore, mistakes, corruption, and decay were ever present realities. Death, disease, and physical infirmities were among the many consequences of sin which must be humbly accepted. Furthermore, Wesley did not view the effects of sin on the body to contradict the highest degrees of purity; rather, he believed the tension "to be a natural consequence of the soul's dwelling in flesh and blood."[45] Wesley noted that entirely sanctified believers were, "not free from infirmities, such as weakness or slowness of understanding, irregular quickness or heaviness of imagination.... From such infirmities as these none are perfectly freed till their spirits return to God."[46]

The Body Is Not Sinful

Even though Scripture itself often referred to the corruption of sin as "flesh," Wesley recognized this language to be metaphorical. Wesley did not believe the body itself was sinful just because it suffered the consequences of sin. In his sermon *On Perfection*, Wesley addressed the popular assertion that the sinful nature could not be removed in this lifetime since the body was sinful.

> A sinful body? I pray observe, how deeply ambiguous, how equivocal, this expression is! But there is no authority for it in Scripture: The word sinful body is never found there. And as it is totally unscriptural, so it is palpably absurd. For no body or matter of any kind, can be sinful: Spirits alone are capable of sin. Pray in what part of the body should sin lodge? It cannot lodge in the skin, nor in the muscles, or nerves, or veins, or arteries; it cannot be in the bones, any more than in the hair or nails. Only the soul can be the seat of sin.[47]

In its essence, sin was a breach of humanity's holy relationship with God and the rest of the created order. As embodied beings, the motivations of the human heart can only be recognized through words or actions, but

---

44. Wesley, *Letters* "To Dorothy Furly" September 15, 1762 (Telford), 4:188.
45. Wesley, *Plain Account of Christian Perfection* (BE), 13:168.
46. Wesley, *Plain Account* (BE), 13:147. Elsewhere, Wesley noted that he did "not expect to be freed from actual mistakes, till this mortal puts on immortality." Wesley, *Plain Account of Christian Perfection* (BE), 13:168.
47. Wesley, *On Perfection* (BE), 3:79–80.

Wesley primarily viewed sin as relational. He explained, "But why is this corruption termed flesh? Not because it is confined to the body . . . If 'sin reigns in our mortal bodies,' it is because the sinful soul uses the bodily members as 'instruments of unrighteousness.'"[48] Thus, the body is not only liable to death but is a faulty tool that cannot carry out the intensions of the perfected heart. This did not make the body itself sinful; it was simply a result of the Fall which would not be righted until the Kingdom of God is fulfilled and the faithful receive resurrected bodies.

Physical Death Does Not Sanctify

If only the soul could be the "seat of sin," and the body was an instrument for the soul, then it stood to reason that the death of the body could not affect the condition of the soul for good or ill. Thus, a person's heart must be cleansed from the being of sin *before* death; otherwise, Wesley insisted it would never happen at all. Referring to one of the morning prayers from the Psalter, Wesley exclaimed, "You then said, 'Make me a clean heart, O God, and renew a right spirit within me.' . . . when did you expect God would answer that prayer? when your body was in the grave? Too late! Unless we have clean hearts before we die, it had been good we had never been born.'"[49]

Wesley did not always think along these lines. Early in his career, he subscribed to the common belief that death was the solution to the problem of sin.[50] In his very first sermon, *Death and Deliverance*,[51] Wesley credited

---

48. Wesley, *Doctrine of Original Sin Pt. V* (BE), 12:415.

49. Wesley, *Letters* "Letter to the Rev. Mr. Potter" November 4, 1758 (Telford) 4:44. This prayer is included in the morning prayer for the tenth day of the month.

50. Charles Wesley seemed to ascribe to the view that a person was not freed from the being of sin until the moment before death, and it became a source of tension with John. Ironically, John had previously agreed with Law's position (that true perfection was unattainable in this life though a good goal) until 1738. His sermon *On the Trouble and Rest of Good Men (1735)* is testimony to this. Likewise, Richard Baxter placed the possibility for whole heart purity after death. Speaking of heaven, Baxter wrote, "My will shall there be better than here, as it shall have *nothing in it displeasing to God,* no sinful inclination, no striving against God's Spirit, no grudging at any word or work of God, nor any principle of enmity or rebellion left." Baxter, *Dying Thoughts,* 65.

51. Wesley wrote this sermon directly following his ordination as a deacon in 1725. Outler noted that this sermon is evidence of Wesley's "preoccupation with 'the art of dying' . . . and his view of life as chiefly a preparation for death and eternity." Outler, Wesley, *Death and Deliverance* (BE), 4:203–5.

death with freeing the believer from "the tyranny of sin, a yoke they could never hope to cast off entirely as long as they carried about them those mortal bodies...."[52] Wesley went on to state that "the law of our members" would battle continually with the "law of our mind" until death when "we lay down these infirmities with this veil of flesh."[53] In yet another sermon written in 1735, Wesley asserted, "For in the moment wherein they shake off the flesh, they are delivered, not only from the troubling of the wicked, not only from pain and sickness, from folly and infirmity; but also from all sin"[54] Years later Wesley openly admitted he was mistaken on this matter. In a letter to Elizabeth Hardy, Wesley explained that twenty years prior he believed Christians could not "put off the infection of nature but with our bodies." However, he concluded, "But I believe otherwise now, for many reasons...."[55]

Wesley did not spell out his "many reasons" for changing his opinion in the letter to Elizabeth, but he made his rationale clear elsewhere.[56] First of all, he thought that to make death the element which cleansed the believer from all sin was to limit the efficaciousness of Christ's redemption. Wesley declared, "To say Christ will not reign alone in our hearts in this life, will not enable us to give him all our hearts—this in my judgement, is making Him a half-Saviour. He can be no more, if he does not quite save us from our sins."[57] In other words, if God's creative intent for humanity (to relate to God in true righteousness and holiness) could never be realized, then the divine plan of redemption was not a true solution to the problem of sin.[58] Outler noted that to suggest Christian perfection was not attainable

52. Wesley, *Death and Deliverance* (BE), 4:212.
53. Wesley, *Death and Deliverance* (BE), 4:212.
54. Wesley, *Trouble and Rest of Good Men* (BE), 3:539.
55. Wesley, *Letters* "To Elizabeth Hardy" April 5, 1758 (Telford), 4:11.
56. Wesley likely borrowed the following arguments from Thomas Drayton who also argued it was necessary the sinful nature be removed prior to death. Drayton listed the following reasons why the sinful nature must be eradicated: 1) God's plan to destroy sin through the work of Christ would be frustrated, and the promises of purity would be ineffectual. 2) Death of the body cannot cleanse the sinful actions of the spirit. 3) If death cleansed from all sin, then no one would die in their sins. Furthermore, physical death would be more effective in mortifying sin "then the Spirit of Grace could do all our life long." Drayton, *Proviso or Condition of the Promises*, 23–26.
57. Wesley, *Letters* "To Mr. Alexander Coates" June 17, 1761 (Telford), 4:158.
58. "Thus, it is clear that for Wesley God's original purpose in His creation cannot be nullified by human corruption. Instead, a reversal of the Fall is being accomplished by the operation of divine grace through Jesus Christ, with the help of the purifying means,

"would be to say that man was made to sin and that his sinful disposition is invincible."[59] Such a view made sin a problem too big for God to resolve within the created order and tasked death (an enemy of God) to do the work that the Creator was apparently incapable of doing. Wesley reasoned that if death was indeed the cleansing factor for inbred sin, then it was death, not the blood of Christ, which truly saves from sin. He asserted,

> Does the soul's 'going out of the body' effect its purification from indwelling sin? If so, is it not something else, not 'the blood of Christ' which 'cleanseth it from all sin?' If his blood cleanseth us from all sin, while the soul and body are united, is it not in this life? If when that union ceases, is it not in the next? And is not this too late?[60]

Secondly, Wesley found the logic which proposed that a believer could retain *some* of the sinful nature until death and still be holy enough for heaven to be self-defeating. In a letter defending the reasonableness of entire sanctification Wesley asked, "Now Sammy, dropping the point of contradiction, tell me simply what you would have more. Do you believe evil tempers remain till death? all, or some? if some only, which?"[61] The idea that believers did not need their hearts entirely cleansed from sin

---

that is, the inward virtues culminating in Love." Lee, "Doctrine of the New Creation in the Theology of John Wesley," 23.

59. Outler, *John Wesley*, 32.

60. Wesley, *Plain Account of Christian Perfection* (BE), 13:181–82.

61. Wesley, *Letters* "To Samuel Furly" October 13, 1762 (Telford) 4:191. Wesley's teaching could be viewed as contradictory to his own tradition especially since the ninth Article of Religion clearly declared that inclination to evil always remained. In his revised Articles of Religion for the Methodists of North America, he left out the entire second half of the ninth article which read, "Whereby man is very far gone from original righteousness, and is of his own nature inclined to evil, so that the flesh lusteth always contrary to the Spirit; and therefore in every person born into this world, it deserveth God's wrath and damnation. And this infection of nature doth remain; yea, in them that are regenerated, whereby the lust of the flesh . . . is not subject to the law of God." See *Homilies*, Appendix. In Wesley's revised Articles, it became the 7th article, "Of Original or Birth Sin." Here the Article concluded, "whereby man is very far gone from original righteousness, and of his own nature inclined to evil, and that continually." Wesley, *John Wesley's Prayer Book*, 309. Wesley was not the first person to dispute the claim that there would be perpetual conflict between the Spirit and the sinful nature. Robert Gell had already addressed this issue and concluded, "I answer, This is in every man's mouth almost. But the Psalmist said, *All men are liars*. 1. It is true, that the *flesh lusts against the Spirit, so long as the flesh lives*. But the *lusting flesh is dead* in the obedient and regenerate *souls*." Gell, "Some Saints Not Without Sin for a Season," 795.

created unanswerable questions such as: Which sinful dispositions were "acceptable"? Could lust, or pride, or anger be retained in the heart until the moment a believer stood before God? If so, then how many unholy tempers could be retained? Such uncertainty was not compatible with what Wesley found in Scripture. He noted,

> "True," say some, "we shall thus be saved from our sins; but not till death; not in this world." But how are we to reconcile this with the express words of St. John?—"Herein is our love made perfect, that we may have boldness in the day of judgment. Because as he is, so are we in this world . . . ." For he saith not, the blood of Christ will cleanse at the hour of death, or in the day of judgment, but, it "cleanseth," at the time present, "us," living Christians, "from all sin." And it is equally evident that if any sin remain, we are not cleansed from all sin: If any unrighteousness remain in the soul, it is not cleansed from all unrighteousness.[62]

Furthermore, Wesley understood the deceitfulness of the human heart. To suggest that the unholy tempers would remain until death created the risk of lulling people into a spiritual stupor which masked the true condition of their heart.

Finally, Wesley could no longer sustain the belief that indwelling sin would be removed by physical death because such a claim cast aspersions on the character of God. It would be a cruel act on the part of God to make demands of Christians which they were incapable of fulfilling. Rakestraw expressed Wesley's reasoning in the following terms: "If God's command is to 'love the Lord thy God with all thy heart, and with all thy soul, and with all thy mind,' such a command must be possible of fulfilment by the believer who responds in faith to God's grace. Otherwise God is commanding and promising that which he is not able to perform."[63] Wesley clarified the matter by asking a simple question. "Has Christ anywhere taught us to pray for what he never designs to give? If so, has he not taught us to pray for perfection on earth? Does he not then design to give it?"[64]

What was at stake for Wesley was the efficaciousness of God's grace in the here and now. To say that God would only cleanse believers from all sin after they had been removed from the pressures and inconveniences of a fallen, temporal world was hardly a remarkable feat. However, to make

---

62. Wesley, *Christian Perfection* (BE), 2:119.
63. Rakestraw, "John Wesley as a Theologian of Grace," 201.
64. Wesley, *Plain Account of Christian Perfection* (BE), 13:182.

the promises of Scripture actually available in the temporal realm demonstrated utter confidence in the power of God's grace. Wesley proclaimed, "But how does it appear that this is to be done before the article of death? From the very nature of a command, which is not given to the dead, but to the living. Therefore, 'Thou shalt love God with all thy heart,' cannot mean, Thou shalt do this when thou diest, but while thou livest."[65] While Wesley acknowledged that physical death removed the transient effects of sin (infirmities, etc.), death could never cleanse the sinful dispositions of the heart. That was a miraculous work only the grace of God could accomplish.

Wesley's teaching on Christian perfection and death sometimes met with resistance from surprising corners. Charles Wesley, with his conviction that perfection could only be achieved through sharing in the "sharpest agonies" of Christ, almost exclusively connected entire sanctification with physical death. Charles quietly distinguished his views on death and perfection from his brother's stance relatively early in the Methodist revival.[66] In a 1739 publication of a hymn (republished as Hymn 148 in *A Collection of Hymns for the Use of the People Called Methodists*), Charles had written the following sentiment: "Doubtful and insecure of bliss, Since death alone confirms me his." In his copy of *Hymns and Sacred Poems* (1739), John scrawled a fervent "No!" in the margin and changed the words in later editions to the existent line, "Since faith alone confirms me his."[67] The disagreement was not resolved despite John's editing. Twenty-eight years later, John penned the following message to his younger brother: "I still think to disbelieve *all the professors* amount to a *denial of the thing*. For if there be *no living witness* of what we have preached for twenty years, I cannot, dare not preach it any longer. The whole comes to one point,—Is there or is there not any instantaneous sanctification between justification and death? I say, Yes; you (*often seem to*) say, No."[68]

The debate between the brothers continued in John's correspondence with other Methodists. In a letter to Dorothy Furly, Wesley complained

---

65. Wesley, *Methodist Societies: The Minutes of Conference, 1747* (BE), 10:197.

66. Tyson noted, "These issues (the nature of perfection, the timing of perfection, and the role of suffering) did not reach their flash point for another twenty years; but it is clear from the series 'Hymns For Those That Wait For Full Redemption' that explosive ideas were already in the air. Charles had begun pursuing his own theological concerns in the doctrine of Christian perfection by the mid-1740's." Tyson, *Charles Wesley on Sanctification*, 236.

67. See hymn text and corresponding footnote. Wesley, "Hymn 148" (BE), 7:266.

68. Wesley, *Letters* "To Charles" February 12, 1767 (Telford), 5:40–41.

that teaching entire sanctification did not occur "until the article of death" or setting "perfection too high (so high as no man that we ever heard or read of attained) is the most effectual (because unsuspected) way of driving it out of the world."[69] He concluded the letter with a criticism that could only be aimed at Charles: "Take care that you are not hurt by anything in the Short Hymns contrary to the doctrines you have long received."[70] That Wesley would openly critique his brother only highlighted the seriousness with which he treated this issue. To expect physical death to mortify the carnal nature was, in Wesley's thinking, a detrimental theological error.

Christian Perfection as a Work of Free Grace

The actualization of Christian perfection marked another point along the *ordo salutis* which Wesley attributed to the work of free grace. Just as the new birth was accomplished by the work of God alone, so too, was the miraculous change wrought in the realization of entire sanctification. Wesley declared, "That great truth, 'that we are saved by faith,' will never be worn out; and that sanctifying as well as justifying faith is the free gift of God."[71] The same free grace which initiated the Christian life was at work once again when the believer was entirely sanctified. That is, nothing but "naked faith" was required of the believer to receive the gift of perfection.[72]

Wesley did not consider the condition of faith to be a "work" on the part of the believer; rather, the faith entailed in perfection was recognition that God alone could complete the work of mortifying the sinful nature. Wesley advised,

69. Wesley, *Letters* "To Dorothy Furly" September 15, 1762 (Telford), 4:188.

70. Wesley, *Letters* "To Dorothy Furly" September 15, 1762 (Telford), 4:189.

71. Wesley, *Letters* "To Ann Foard" October 12, 1764 (Telford), 4:268. It is clear that by "sanctifying faith" Wesley meant entirely sanctifying faith since he was discussing the bestowal of Christian perfection. He made the same point elsewhere when he noted, "Sanctification, too, is 'not of works, lest any man should boast.' 'It is the gift of God,' and is to be received by plain, simple faith." Wesley, *On Patience* (BE), 3:178.

72. "You know," Wesley commented to Mrs. Bowman, "whenever [Christian perfection] is given, it is to be received only by naked faith." Wesley, *Letters* March 4, 1786 (Telford), 7:322. William Greathouse observed the centrality of "faith alone" in Wesley's understanding of Christian perfection. "His originality is seen chiefly in the way he put the truth of perfection in the very center of a Protestant understanding of Christian faith. He freed the idea from any notion of merit and presented it as wholly the gift of God's grace. Perfect love or entire sanctification is attainable now, by simple faith." Greathouse and Bassett, *Exploring Christian Holiness*, 2:76.

And by this token may you surely know whether you seek it by faith or by works. If by works, you want something to be done first, before you are sanctified. You think, 'I must first be or do thus or thus.' Then you are seeking it by works unto this day. If you seek it by faith, you may expect it as you are: and if as you are, then expect it *now*.[73]

To be sure, Wesley recognized that a believer must cooperate with the grace given at the point of justification and regeneration whereby the deeds of the flesh would gradually be mortified.[74] However, even the best of human efforts were powerless to actually erase the being of sin; such a radical cleansing required a divine act on the individual's behalf that was completely independent of the believer's abilities. Wesley insisted,

> ... although we may, "by the Spirit, mortify the deeds of the body;" resist and conquer both outward and inward sin; although we may *weaken* our enemies day by day;—yet we cannot *drive them out*. By all the grace which is given at justification we cannot extirpate them.... Most sure we cannot, till it shall please our Lord to speak to our hearts again, to speak the second time, "Be clean:" And then only... the evil root, the carnal mind, is destroyed; and inbred sin subsists no more.[75]

Christian Perfection Instantaneously Given

If, like the new birth, perfection was a work of free grace, then the obvious conclusion for Wesley was that it also occurred instantaneously. The very nature of entire sanctification demanded it. If the being of sin were really dead, it could not at the same time be partially alive and active. There must be a point when it existed and a time when it did not.[76] If the work of grace seemed to be gradual, it was because Wesley surmised that the person did

---

73. Wesley, *Scripture Way of Salvation* (BE), 2:169.

74. Wesley did not promote a form of antinomianism. He believed that repentance and works suitable for repentance were "necessary in order to the continuance of his faith, as well as the increase of it," but works were only remotely necessary for sanctification while faith was "the only condition which is *immediately* and *proximately* necessary to sanctification." Wesley, *Scripture Way of Salvation* (BE), 2:167.

75. Wesley, *Repentance of Believers* (BE), 1:346.

76. Wesley spent years carefully questioning those who claimed to be perfected. He discovered that "every one of these... has declared that his deliverance from sin was *instantaneous*, that the change was wrought in a moment." Wesley, *On Patience* (BE), 3:178.

"not advert to the particular moment wherein sin ceases to be."[77] Once again, Wesley turned to the metaphor of death to help explain the instantaneous work of perfection. He reasoned, "It is often difficult to perceive the instant when a man dies; yet there is an instant in which life ceases. And if ever sin ceases, there must be a last moment of its existence, and a first moment of our deliverance from it."[78] Wesley concluded, "I cannot but believe that sanctification is commonly, if not always, an *instantaneous work*."[79]

Believers Cannot Die Without Christian Perfection

Wesley's insistence on the instantaneousness of Christian perfection was more than a theological abstraction. For Wesley, the eternal destiny of souls was at stake because he believed that without a total cleansing of the sinful nature a person could not enter heaven. Wesley pointed to the Scripture which stated, "No unclean thing shall enter into [glory]." He concluded, "Therefore, whatever degrees of holiness they did or did not attain in the preceding parts of life, neither Jews nor heathens any more than Christians ever did or ever will enter into the New Jerusalem unless they are cleansed from all sin before they enter into eternity."[80] Wesley was heavily criticized on this point since those not familiar his teaching assumed he meant that believers were in a state of damnation unless they were entirely sanctified. This was a gross misrepresentation of what Wesley meant. Wesley denied that a person was "under the curse of God, till he does attain;" rather, the believer was "in a state of grace, and in favour with God, as long as he believes."[81]

Perfection was not a looming threat to a believer's eternal salvation; it was a precious promise. Wesley insisted that entire sanctification should always be placed "in the most amiable light, so that it may excite only hope,

---

77. Wesley, *Scripture Way of Salvation* (BE), 2:168.

78. Wesley, *Plain Account of Christian Perfection* (BE), 13:188.

79. Wesley, *On Patience* (BE), 3:178. For other examples of Wesley's instance on the instantaneousness of perfection see: Wesley, *Letters* "To Thomas Maxfield" November 2, 1762 (Telford), 4:192. Wesley, *Letters* "To Charles Wesley" June 27, 1766 (Telford), 5:16.

80. Wesley, *Letters* "To Elizabeth Hardy" April 5, 1758 (Telford), 4:11. Elsewhere, Wesley makes the statement that it would be better for a person never to be born than to die without perfecting grace. Wesley, *Letters* "To the Rev. Mr. Potter" November 4, 1758 (Telford) 4:44.

81. Wesley, *Letters* "To Elizabeth Hardy" April 5, 1758 (Telford), 4:10.

joy, and desire."[82] In fact, Wesley thought the doctrine of sanctification was further proof of God's omnipotence and grace.[83] God, not death, chance, or fate, was in control of a believer's life. Accordingly, Wesley declared, "But none who seeks it sincerely shall or can die without it; though possibly he may not attain it till the very article of death."[84] Wesley further explained, "I am persuaded none that has faith can die before he is made ripe for glory . . . . True believers are not distressed hereby, either in life or in death; unless in some rare instance wherein the temptation of the devil is joined with a melancholy temper."[85]

The fact remained, however, that death could come at any moment for any person. This was especially true during the eighteenth century when death seemed utterly capricious. In this context, Wesley's logic regarding entire sanctification as an instantaneous work of free grace made a great deal of sense. If a believer could die at any moment and it was necessary to be perfected before death, then Christians could receive entire sanctification any time after the new birth. God could be trusted to bestow the gift of perfection at the proper moment. "Admire, more and more, the free grace of God . . . ." Wesley assured his followers. "[God] cannot be straitened for time, wherein to work whatever remains to be done in your soul. And God's time is always the best time."[86] The Methodists seemed convinced by Wesley's appeal to the sovereignty of God and were attentive to the work of grace in their hearts. A rapid increase in grace was often taken as an omen of impending death since Wesley's followers expected they would be made entirely holy before they met God face-to-face. For example, Mrs. Oddie's friends rightly predicted that she would die soon because they noted that in the three months prior to her death she "grew exceedingly in every grace" and was "visibly ripening for glory."[87]

Wesley's emphasis on perfection as a work of free grace was most meaningful to those who had neither time nor opportunity to undergo the gradual growth in grace which normally led up to entire sanctification. Much like he offered the hope of salvation to condemned malefactors

---

82. Wesley, *Methodist Societies: The Minutes of Conference, 1747* (BE), 10:199.

83. As Outler noted, "For Wesley, the doctrine of perfection was yet another way of celebrating the *sovereignty* of grace!" Outler, *John Wesley*, 253.

84. Wesley, *Methodist Societies: The Minutes of Conference, 1745* (BE), 10:154.

85. Wesley, *Letters* "To Elizabeth Hardy" April 5, 1758 (Telford), 4:13.

86. Wesley, *Satan's Devices* (BE), 2:148.

87. Wesley, "Some Account of Mrs. Oddie" *AM* (July 1783), 357.

under the shadow of the gallows, Wesley held out the gift of perfection to those who had not spent a lifetime practicing the art of holy living and holy dying. Wesley recorded the story of a woman who had lapsed from the faith and was more fearful that God would not forgive her backsliding than she was of the pain of death. She continued this way until two months before her death when God not only spoke peace to her soul but gave her "a clear testimony of the power of God in saving her from all sin."[88]

The Instantaneous Aspect as a Guard Against Complacency

For those who had plenty of time and opportunity to learn the art of dying well, Wesley stressed the instantaneous nature of Christian perfection for an entirely different reason. He feared that those (like Charles Wesley) who emphasized a more gradualistic understanding of sanctification could lead believers into spiritual complacency.[89] It was a dangerous presumption upon the grace of God to expect that the gradual work of sanctification would inevitably be completed on the deathbed. In other words, to delay immersing oneself in the all-consuming holy love of God with the assumption that such grace could be easily attained at the point of death was to run the risk of missing out on this gift of grace altogether. Wesley declared,

> None are or can be saved but those who are by faith made inwardly and outwardly holy. But this holy faith is the gift of God . . . He can as easily give this faith in a moment as in a thousand years. He frequently does give it on a death-bed, in answer to the prayer of believers, but rarely, if ever, to those who had continued unholy, upon the presumption that He would save them at last.[90]

---

88. Wesley, "Account of Jan Ogilby" *AM* (November 1785), 576. This was somewhat of an inconsistency in Wesley's theology. He confidently proclaimed that deathbed conversions were valid (as in the case of condemned malefactors), but he also insisted that believers must be entirely sanctified before they died. Even if he believed that not much time was needed between the new birth and the point of perfection, Wesley rejected the notion that the new birth and entire sanctification occurred simultaneously. It is difficult to believe that Wesley did not consider this matter; however, there is no evidence that he ever directly addressed this issue.

89. The instantaneous verses gradual aspects of sanctification were a continual source of conflict between John and Charles Wesley. John told Charles, "Press the instantaneous blessing; then I shall have more time for my peculiar calling, enforcing the gradual work." Wesley, *Letters* "To Charles" June 27, 1766 (Telford), 5:16.

90. Wesley, *Letters* "To Philothea Briggs." August 31, 1772 (Telford), 5:337–38.

Furthermore, for those who had truly embraced the mortified life, the approach of death should not trigger a sudden change in faith or behavior. The best testimony of a believer's spiritual standing was that they "died as they lived." Reflecting on the death of William Green, a steadfast believer who trusted God through the storms of life, Wesley mused, "He died, as he lived, in the full assurance of faith, praising God with his latest breath."[91] Of Ann Thwayte, Wesley wrote, "I fulfilled the dying request of Ann Thwayte . . . by preaching her funeral sermon. In all the changes of those about her, she stood steadfast, doing and suffering the will of God: She was a woman of faith and prayer; in life and death adorning the doctrine of God her Saviour."[92] If the grace of entire sanctification was to be put into practice (like in the lives of Green and Thwayte), this logically meant that Christian perfection would ideally occur prior to the deathbed. Wesley declared, "There may be some rare cases wherein God has determined not to bestow His perfect love till a little before death; but this I believe is uncommon. He does not usually put off the fulfilling of His promises. Seek, and you shall find; seek earnestly, and you shall find speedily."[93]

Wesley was so concerned about the tendency to put perfection off until death that he often stressed the immediacy of perfection almost to the exclusion of the gradual work. He warned, "Ye ask amiss, namely that you may be renewed before you die. Before you die! Will that content you? Nay, but ask that it may be done now! Today! While it is called to-day do not call this 'setting God a time'. Certainly, today is his time, as well as tomorrow. Make haste, man, make haste!"[94] Wesley had the pastoral insight to realize that delaying entire sanctification was often an unconscious decision; it was simply a by-product of the expectation that perfection was a future work of grace which could not be accomplished in the present moment. Wesley

---

Elsewhere, Wesley noted, "In all my experience, I have not known one who fortified himself in sin by a presumption that God would save him at the last, that was not miserably disappointed, and suffered to die in his sins. To turn the grace of God into an encouragement to sin is the sure way to the nethermost hell!" Wesley, *Call to Backsliders* (BE), 3:225–26.

91. Wesley, *Journal* June 16, 1777 (BE), 23:56.
92. Wesley, *Journal* November 26, 1778 (BE), 23:113.
93. Wesley, *Letters* "To Dorothy Furly" September 6, 1757 (Telford), 3:221.
94. Wesley *Plain Account of Christian Perfection* (BE), 13:175–76. Even though he placed his emphasis on the immediacy of perfection, Wesley clearly understood that the mortification of the sinful nature which led up to entire sanctification was often a slow, gradual process. However, he also thought to delay seeking after the completed work of grace was paramount with rejecting God's grace in the here and now.

observed, "I find by long experience it comes exactly to the same point, to tell men they shall be saved from all sin when they die; or to tell them it may be a year hence, or a week hence, or any time but now. Our word does not profit, either as to justification or sanctification, unless we can bring them to expect the blessing while we speak."[95] Even if the delay was due to ignorance instead of a deliberate presumption upon God's favor, it could result in the same bitter end. Thus, Wesley continued to stress the immediacy of entire sanctification even while he admitted that for most believers Christian perfection might not be realized until just prior to death.

The Instantaneous as a Guard Against Works Righteousness

Another reason Wesley stressed the instantaneous nature of Christian perfection was his belief that the work was a gift of grace through faith alone. The argument that there must be a considerable amount of time between the new birth and entire sanctification was paramount with denying that perfection was a gift of free grace. He suggested that anyone who perpetuated this idea was proposing a type of works righteousness. Wesley maintained that anyone who thought it was an "invariable rule" there must be considerable time between justification and sanctification, "must think we are sanctified by works, or (which comes to the same) by sufferings; for, otherwise, what is time necessary for? It must be either to do or to suffer. Whereas, if nothing be required by simple faith, a moment is as good as an age."[96]

Wesley was so fearful of the potential nullifying effects of a more gradual understanding that, when he did concede Christian perfection often occurred in the context of impending death, he could rarely refrain from making amending remarks. For example, Wesley confessed that entire sanctification generally occurred "the instant of death, the moment before the soul leaves the body," but he immediately followed this admission by asserting that he knew of no conclusive evidence that perfection could not occur almost directly after justification. He went on, "If it must be many years after justification, I would be glad to know how many ... And how many days or months, or even years, can any one allow to be between perfection and death? How far from justification must it be; and how near

---

95. Wesley, *Letters* "To Charles" April 26, 1772 (Telford), 5:316.
96. Wesley, *Letters* "To Ann Foard" October 12, 1764 (Telford), 4:268–69.

to death?"[97] When Wesley admitted elsewhere that for most believers the moment of entire sanctification would be shortly before death, "the moment before the soul leaves the body," he once again followed this statement with the contention that God was under no constraint to wait this long.[98] "I believe it is usually many years after justification," Wesley avowed, "but that it may be within five years or five months after it, I know no conclusive argument to the contrary."[99] Of upmost concern to Wesley was that his followers understood Christian perfection to be a work of free grace which required nothing but faith on the part of the believer. Time, effort, good works, pronounced suffering, and even death itself could never accomplish what the grace of God could do in the blink of an eye.

Suffering Does Not Sanctify

Wesley not only denied that death could purify from sin, but he also insisted that suffering (whether physical or otherwise) neither added to nor detracted from a person's spiritual standing. Suffering during the dying process was an unfortunate reality in the era before modern medicine, and the deathbed accounts that Wesley published did not attempt to hide the fact that believers sometimes died painful deaths. However, the connection Wesley drew between death and entire sanctification had nothing to do with the notion that the physical and emotional agonies leading up to death resulted in purification of the soul. For Wesley, there was only one instance of suffering which merited the purification of the sinful nature, and that was the suffering of Christ. Wesley declared, "No suffering but that of Christ has any power to expiate sin; and no fire but that of love can purify the soul, either in time or in eternity."[100] By rejecting suffering as a causative factor for the attainment of entire sanctification, Wesley made a clear theological distinction between himself and those who taught that the highest levels of grace could only be reached through the darkness of pain and sorrow. Instead, he insisted that the grace of God alone could act as a sanctifying factor; therefore, suffering was only useful as it aided

---

97. Wesley *Brief Thoughts on Christian Perfection* (Jackson), 11:446.
98. Wesley, *Brief Thoughts on Christian Perfection* (Jackson), 11:446.
99. Wesley, *Brief Thoughts on Christian Perfection* (Jackson), 11:446.
100. Wesley, *Dives and Lazarus* (BE), 4:8–9. See also Wesley's notes on John 19:30 where he termed Christ's suffering "the purchase of man's redemption." Wesley, *ENNT*, 383.

the expansion of the love and grace of God in the heart. The true mark of perfection was not how much one suffered at the end of life—it was how much one loved God and neighbor.

Wesley admitted that suffering could have a positive effect on spiritual growth. In his sermon *Heaviness Through Manifold Temptations*, Wesley explored the ramifications of various forms of suffering and concluded that God may use pain to test and refine the Christian's faith and to "try, to purify, to confirm and increase that living hope" which is present in all believers.[101] As faith and hope increased through affliction, so too, the believer's love for God would also grow resulting in what Wesley termed the "advance of holiness, holiness of heart and holiness of conversation."[102] He also acknowledged that suffering was profitable for teaching a person conformity to will of God and was sometimes an unavoidable part of the Christian life. He observed, "Now in 'running the race which is set before us' . . . there is often a cross lying in the way; that is something which is not only not joyous, but grievous, something which is contrary to our will, which is displeasing to our nature. What then is to be done? The choice is plain; either we must 'take up our cross', or we must turn aside from the way of God . . . ."[103] Such a choice placed the believer in a position of utter compliance with God's will and allowed for the development of greater levels of submission. Wesley instructed, "We ought quietly to suffer whatever befals us . . . thoroughly willing that God should treat you in the manner that pleases him. We are his lambs, and therefore ought to be ready to suffer, even to the death, without complaining."[104]

Finally, Wesley realized that enduring great hardship could have a positive effect on the community at large. The example set by believers who persevered under suffering had a valuable impact on believers and nonbelievers alike. Wesley reasoned, "What examples have a stronger influence . . . than that of a soul calm and serene in the midst of storms, sorrowful, yet always rejoicing; meekly accepting whatever is the will of God, however grievous it may be to nature; saying, in sickness or in pain, 'The cup which my Father hath given me, shall I not drink it?'"[105] However, the experience

---

101. Wesley, *Heaviness Through Manifold Temptations* (BE), 2:232.
102. Wesley, *Heaviness Through Manifold Temptations* (BE), 2:232.
103. Wesley, *Self-Denial* (BE), 2:243.
104. Wesley, *Farther Thoughts upon Christian Perfection* (BE), 13:125–26.
105. Wesley, *Heaviness Through Manifold Temptations* (BE), 2:233.

of suffering in and of itself was no guarantee that the individual would be purified.

Wesley's stance on suffering was an on-going source of contention with his brother Charles since the younger Wesley not only associated entire sanctification with the article of death but also with the act of suffering. In 1749, Charles published *Hymns and Sacred Poems* (a two-volume set) without John's approval. Having escaped the editorial pen of his older brother, these hymns directly associated purification from sin with affliction. In his study of Charles's hymns, Tyson suggested that the younger Wesley went as far as making the extent of a person's pain to be the measure of a believer's holiness.[106] In other words, according to Charles, the more a Christian suffered, the closer fellowship the believer had with Christ. Tyson demonstrated the discrepancy between the brothers' theology by raising the following example of Wesley's editorial remarks regarding one of his brother's hymns. Charles had originally written:

> In sorrow, as in grace, we grow,
>   With closer fellowship in pain,
> Our Lord more intimately know,
>   Till coming to a perfect man,
> His sharpest agonies we share,*
>   And all His marks of passion bear.
>
> Partakers of His bitterest cup,
>   And burden'd with His heaviest load,
> We fill His after-sufferings up,
>   Conform'd to an expiring God;
> And only such our Father own,*
>   And seats on our appointed thrones.[107]

After each asterisk inserted above, Wesley penned a forceful "NO!" in the margin.[108] As noted earlier, Wesley emphasized it was love—not pain—which indicated the depth of a believer's holiness. To place the emphasis on suffering as Charles did (even if it was in imitation of Christ) was to displace love as the essential element of heart purity.[109]

---

106. Tyson noted that the second volume contained at least fifteen hymns which connected inner hurts and outward hardship with purification. Tyson, *Charles Wesley on Sanctification*, 235.

107. Tyson, *Charles Wesley on Sanctification*, 266.

108. Tyson, *Charles Wesley on Sanctification*, 266.

109. Cruickshank noted, "For John, the pattern of life is a race, in which 'our cross' must often be taken up in order to faithfully follow the will of God. He does not conclude,

Furthermore, Wesley found Charles's opinion to be doctrinally insufficient because it communicated the message that entire sanctification was not a work of free grace received and maintained by faith alone but rather a work attained through time, affliction, and discipline. In "Short Hymns on Select Passages of the Holy Scriptures (1762)" Charles spoke of Christian perfection as "a state not to be obtained by a present act of faith in the mercy, truth, and power of God; but as rather the result of severe discipline, comprehending affliction, temptation, long-continued labour, and the persevering exercise of faith in seasons of spiritual darkness."[110] Wesley argued that Christ had already obtained sanctification for believers through his own suffering, and the new covenant was "completely ratified, and all the blessings of it secured to us by the one offering of Christ, which renders all other expiatory sacrifices, and any repetition of his own, utterly needless."[111] Personal suffering was not only unnecessary for believers to initially receive faith, but it was also superfluous to remaining and growing in the faith. Wesley proclaimed, "We are 'justified freely by his grace through the redemption that is in Jesus Christ'. And this is not only the means of our *obtaining* the favor of God, but of our continuing therein. It is thus we come to God at first; it is by the same we come unto him ever after."[112]

Wesley believed the path of sanctification was an assent into true happiness. While God could use inward or outward pain to lead a person into Christian perfection, Wesley preferred to place both the process and the instantiation of Christian perfection in the context of happiness, gratitude, and joy.[113] In a critique of Madam Guyon, Wesley exclaimed, "That God never does, never can purify a soul, but by inward and outward suffering. Utterly false! Never was there a more purified soul than the apostle John.

---

however, that the cross of Christ is the pattern for the whole of life, or that Christians must suffer to the extent that Christ suffered." Cruickshank, "Charles Wesley and the Construction of Suffering in Early English Methodism," 142.

110. Ward, Footnote to *Journal* October 29, 1762 (BE), 21:395.
111. Wesley, *ENNT* (Heb 10:10–15), 839.
112. Wesley, *Lord Our Righteousness* (BE), 1:455–56.
113. Wesley preferred a cataphatic approach to spirituality. His early critique of à Kempis was regarding this very matter. In a letter to his mother, Wesley wrote, "I can't think that when God sent us into the world he had irreversibly decreed that we should be perpetually miserable in it . . . . If our taking up the cross implies our bidding adieu to all joy and satisfaction, how is it reconcilable with what Solomon so expressly affirms of religion, that her ways are ways of pleasantness, and all her paths peace?" Wesley, *Letters* "To Susanna" May 28, 1725 (BE), 25:162–63.

And which of the Apostles suffered less?"[114] He openly counseled the early Methodists to avoid being swayed by any interpretation of perfection that portrayed it merely as an ongoing, painful process which was only brought to fruition in death. He admonished society members, "If you walk closely with God, he is able to give any degree of holiness, either by pleasure or pain."[115]

Christian Perfection as Happiness

Death was not the only image Wesley utilized to describe entire sanctification. There was a longstanding link between holiness and happiness in the Anglican tradition, and it was a connection which Wesley capitalized upon in his explanation of perfection.[116] In his sermon, *God's Love to Fallen Man*, Wesley proposed that a believer's happiness increased in direct portion to the exercise of the holy graces (such as patience, meekness, faith, and love).[117] He concluded, "To sum up what has been said under this head. As the more holy we are upon earth the more happy we must be (seeing there is an inseparable connection between holiness and happiness)."[118] In other words, the death of the sinful nature resulted in genuine happiness.[119] It was the loss of holiness which ultimately led to humanity's unhappiness as Wesley noted, "He lost the whole moral image of God,—righteousness and true holiness. He was unholy; he was unhappy; he was full of sin; full of guilt and tormenting fears."[120] The removal of sin, guilt, and fear restored the condition of happiness. Wesley reasoned, "Is it misery to love God? To

---

114. Wesley, *Extract of the Life of Madam Guion"* (Jackson), 14:277.

115. Wesley, *Letters* "To Miss March" July 5, 1768 (Telford), 5:95.

116. Richard Lucas, John Norris, and John Tillotson were among the authors that Wesley read on this topic. Indeed, Wesley reproduced some of their works in the *Christian Library*.

117. Wesley, *God's Love to Fallen Man* (BE), 2:430.

118. Wesley, *God's Love to Fallen Man* (BE), 2:431. This statement echoed Wesley's sentiments which he penned in 1731. He wrote, "I was made to be happy; to be happy I must love God; in proportion to my love of whom my happiness must increase. To love God I must be like him, holy as he is holy...." Wesley, *Letters* "To Mrs. Mary Pendarves" July 19, 1731 (BE), 25:293.

119. Outler noted that happiness and holiness was one of Wesley's most consistent refrains. The theme emerged in thirty of Wesley's sermons. Outler, Footnote to "Introduction," *Sermons* (BE), 1:35.

120. Wesley, *End of Christ's Coming* (BE), 2:477.

give him all my heart who alone is worthy of it? Nay, it is the truest happiness, indeed the only true happiness which is to be found under the sun."[121]

Sarah Lancaster helpfully pointed out that "happiness" in Wesley's era did not carry the same connotations the term has today. Rather, in eighteenth-century England, happiness depicted a sense of rightness or fitness.[122] Wesley, himself, defined happiness along these lines: "By happiness, I mean, not a slight, trifling pleasure, that perhaps begins and ends in the same hour; but such a state of well-being as contents the soul, and gives it a steady, lasting satisfaction."[123] Happiness as a "state of being" was dependent upon a person's spiritual condition not upon a set of circumstances. This was not to say that Wesley thought an entirely sanctified believer must always maintain a sense of bliss in every situation. He noted that, "A will steadily and uniformly devoted to God is essential to a state of sanctification, but not an uniformity of joy or peace or happy communion with God. They may rise and fall in various degrees; nay, and may be affected either by the body or by diabolical agency."[124] Rather, the happiness which accompanied Christian perfection was an underlying sense that despite one's circumstances all was well between the soul and God.

Taken in Wesley's context, happiness had a teleological theme which focused upon finding the fulfilment of one's self in the love of God. This perspective on happiness had a profound impact on Wesley's view of death since such happiness applied not just to this lifetime. Rather, it merely began in this world and spilled over into the realm after death. Samuel Shaw, a seventeenth-century clergyman, noted, "Man hath not two distinct kinds of happiness in the two distinct Worlds that he is made to live in; but one and the same thing is his blessedness in both, which as I said before, must needs be the enjoyment of God."[125] The implication here was that if one did not attain holiness and happiness or that "steady, lasting satisfaction" of the

---

121. Wesley, *Important Question* (BE), 3:189.

122. For a full discussion on this topic see Lancaster, "Happiness," 31–44.

123. Wesley, *On Love* (BE), 4:386.

124. Wesley, *Letters* "To Mrs. Bennis" January 18, 1774 (Telford), 6:68.

125. Shaw, *Immanuel*, 210. Wesley republished an extract of Shaw's work in the Christian Library. William Law also made the claim that the only true happiness was that which was centered in God. He exclaimed, "Was *all* to die with our *bodies*, there might be some pretence for those *different sorts* of happiness . . . but since *our all* begins at the death of our bodies . . . is it not certain that no man can exceed another in joy and happiness, but so far as he exceeds him in those virtues which fit him for a happy death?" Law, *Serious Call*, 132.

soul in this lifetime then a person could not expect to find it in the next world. Wesley said as much in his sermon, *The Wedding Garment;* "Choose holiness, by my grace; which is the way, the only way, to everlasting life. He cries aloud, "Be holy, and be happy; happy in this world, and happy in the world to come."[126] Joseph Cunningham noted, "In [Wesley's] theology, nothing physical could conduce teleological happiness, which humanity was originally fashioned to enjoy. Neither lavish comforts, nor monetary wealth and high social status can substitute for love of God and neighbour through righteousness, peace and joy."[127] The converse was also true; nothing physical—not even the demise of the body—could rob perfected believers of the true happiness which stemmed from having their hearts fully united with their Creator.

Happy Death

The connection between happiness and holiness makes sense of Wesley's conception of a "happy death" since those who were perfected in Christ took genuine pleasure in knowing that they would soon see their Creator face to face. Indeed, Wesley's correlation between happiness and holiness was so strong he seemed to believe a "happy death" was the greatest indication that the believer had attained the work of entire sanctification. There was plenty of experiential evidence to support Wesley's belief on this matter; his journals were filled with the testimonies of believers who declared their happy estate upon the deathbed. In one such entry Wesley recounted the story of Mary Cook who battled both a long illness and doubts over her spiritual state. One day, she suddenly broke out in praise to God, and when her mother asked the cause of such an outburst, Mary replied, "O mother, I am happy, I am happy: I shall soon go to heaven."[128] She further articulated, "I am assured of God's love to my soul. I am not afraid to die. I know the Lord will take me to himself: Lord, hasten the time! I long to be with thee."[129]

---

126. Wesley, *On the Wedding Garment* (BE), 4:148.
127. Cunningham, "John Wesley's Moral Pneumatology," 288.
128. Wesley, *Journal* August 12, 1745 (BE), 20:82.
129. Wesley, *Journal* August 12, 1745 (BE), 20:82. For more examples of "happy deaths" see: an account of condemned malefactors made "happy," *Journal* November 13, 1748 (BE), 20:252–60; two children who died in "triumph of faith" and "happy in Christ," *Journal* March 21, 1770 (BE), 22:219–22; Charles Greenwood, a melancholy man, who

Ann Beauchamp gave a similar testimony while she lay dying. Wesley especially noted her proclamation of both happiness and freedom from all sin. "I am quite happy," she declared. "I know that my Redeemer liveth, and has taken away all my sins. And my heart is comforted with the presence of God: I long to die, that I may be with Him."[130] In his book, *Mrs. Hunter's Happy Death*, John Fanestil observed that Methodists were by no means the only people who died "happy deaths," but they embraced the tradition with particular enthusiasm. Fanestil noted, "That these deaths were considered 'happy' did not refer merely–or even primarily—to the dying person's subjective emotional state . . . . The ritual of the happy death witnessed to the goodness of God, not just in the present, and not just for the person dying, but indeed for all of time and for all of humankind."[131] There was no better evidence one could give of a holy heart then to live a happy life and die a happy death.

Full Assurance

A fruit of Christian perfection was full assurance of faith. As mentioned in the previous chapter, Wesley acknowledged that there were degrees of assurance which accompanied each stage of the Christian journey. Those who had gone on to perfection received "a clear conviction that *I am now in the favour of God as excludes all doubt and fear concerning it*."[132] Simply put, full assurance was the witness of the Spirit that one had been entirely sanctified.[133] Wesley relied heavily upon the categories of faith laid out by

---

was made "unspeakably happy" and triumphed over the fear of death, *Journal* February 21, 1783 (BE), 23:263.

130. Wesley, *Journal* June 12, 1756 (BE), 21:58–59.

131. Fanestil, *Mrs. Hunter's Happy Death*, 73–74.

132. Wesley, *Letters* "To Hester Ann Roe" April 10, 1781 (Telford), 7:57–58. Wesley also acknowledged a further degree of assurance—the full assurance of hope which Wesley defined in a letter Elizabeth Ritchie as "a divine testimony that we shall endure to the end; or, more directly, that we shall enjoy God in glory." Wesley was very clear that this degree of assurance was a special gift that was not "essential to or inseparable from perfect love." Wesley, *Letters* "To Elizabeth Ritchie" October 6, 1778 (Telford), 6:322–23.

133. Wesley's notion of full assurance of faith was criticized by R. Newton Flew. Flew argued that the term "assurance" was not applicable to the work of entire sanctification since a person could never know themself well enough to know that the sinful nature was gone. Flew wrote, "He can be aware that he is in the hands of One who presence floods his heart with the spirit of supernatural love. But he cannot without pride believe that he is now no longer on a permanently lower level, but on a permanently higher level.

the author of 1 John. Those who were "fathers" in the faith not only experienced deliverance from the carnal nature but "a deliverance from doubts and fears."[134] Wesley expounded, "*There is no fear in love*—No slavish fear can be where love reigns. B*ut perfect,* adult *love casteth out* slavish *fear: because* such *fear hath torment*—And so is inconsistent with the happiness of love ... a father in Christ, loves without fear."[135] Elsewhere Wesley declared, "They shall be comforted by the consolations of his Spirit, by a fresh manifestation of his love .... This 'full assurance of faith' swallows up all doubt, as well as all tormenting fear, God now giving them a sure hope of an enduring substance and 'strong consolation through grace.'"[136] Wesley's doctrine of full assurance differed from a Reformed perspective because it did not imply that the believer could never again fall away from grace; rather, it meant that those who enjoyed this degree of assurance had a present sense of their standing with God that was not marked by any doubt or fear. In his sermon *Free Grace,* Wesley elaborated on this point: "'The full assurance of faith,' is the true ground a of Christian's happiness. And it does indeed imply a full assurance that all your past sins are forgiven, and that you are *now* a child of God. But it does not imply a full assurance of our future perseverance."[137]

The first kind of assurance is a conviction about God. The second kind of assurance is a conviction about himself." Flew, *Idea of Perfection,* 337.

134. Wesley, *On the Discoveries of Faith* (BE), 4:37.

135. Wesley, *ENNT* (1 John 4:18), 915.

136. Arvid Gradin, a German Moravian, gave Wesley the following definition of full assurance: "Repose in the blood of Christ; a firm confidence in God, and persuasion of his favour; the highest tranquillity, serenity, and peace of mind, with a deliverance from every fleshly desire, and a cessation of all, even inward sins." Wesley, *Plain Account of Christian Perfection* (BE), 13:141. Wesley concluded that this was the kind of assurance he had been seeking after for so many years. In a letter to Thomas Rutherford, Wesley explained full assurance as "assurance of being now in the favour of God as excludes all doubt and fear." Wesley, *Letters* "To Dr. Rutherforth" March 28, 1768 (Telford), 5:358. For further examples of Wesley's understanding of full assurance, see: Wesley, *Sermon on the Mount I* (BE), 1:485 and *On the Discoveries of Faith* (BE), 4:36.

137. Wesley, *Free Grace* (BE), 3:549. Wesley also made this point in two separate letters. See Wesley, *Letters* "To Elizabeth Ritchie" October 6, 1778 (Telford), 6:322–23 and *Letters* "To Hester Ann Roe" April 10, 1781 (Telford), 7:57–58.

Full Assurance and Fear of Death

Even natural fears such as the fear of a painful death were mitigated by perfect love. As noted in the previous chapter, Wesley did not consider fear of pain or physical suffering to be indicative of wrongdoing on the part of the believer. However, even these acceptable fears need never overwhelm a believer since those born of God would not be abandoned during their time of need. Wesley assured the tremulous soul, "He will sweeten thy pain: The consolations of God shall cause thee to clap thy hands in the flames. And even when this house of earth is well-nigh shaken down, when it is just ready to drop into the dust, he will teach thee to say, 'O death! where is thy sting? O grave! where is thy victory?'"[138]

Wesley noted the example of one elderly Methodist who literally clapped his hands with joy despite the pains of death. The man could hardly speak to those who surrounded his bed because the act of speaking was too painful for him. However, he mustered the strength to communicate the joy he felt at departing to be with Christ. The old man thrust out his feet, held up his hand, and managed the words, "Here is a sign . . . a dying Christian, full of love and joy! . . . He then desired us to sing, and quickly added, 'He is come! He is come! I want to be gone: Farewell to you all!' When he could no longer speak, he continued smiling, clapping his hands, and discovering an ecstasy of joy in every motion."[139] Such was the state of those who were filled with the perfect love of God which cast out all fear. In a letter to Dr. Conyers Middleton, Wesley concluded that the believer who had been fully conformed to the image of Christ,

> . . . cannot fear pain, knowing it will never be sent, unless it be for his real advantage; and that then his strength will be proportioned to it, as it has always been in times past. He cannot fear death; being able to trust Him he loves with his soul as well as his body; yea, glad to leave the corruptible body in the dust, till it is raised incorruptible and immortal. So that, in honour or shame, in abundance or want, in ease or pain, in life or in death, always, and in all things, he has learned to be content, to be easy, thankful, happy.[140]

---

138. Wesley, *Sermon on the Mount, VIII* (BE), 1:626.
139. Wesley, *Journal* September 25, 1767 (BE), 22:105.
140. Wesley, *Letters* "To Dr. Conyers Middleton" January 4, 1749 (Telford), 2:378.

Desire for Death

Wesley so closely associated happiness with death that he assumed Christians perfected in love would desire to die. Wesley penned the following astonishing statement to one of the members of his society: "It has a little surprised me, that several who are, I believe, filled with love, yet do not desire to die. It seems as if God generally does not give this desire till the time of death approaches. Perhaps in many it would be of little use. First let them learn to live."[141] Wesley was not the first to express such sentiments. Richard Baxter contended that if believers did not yearn to be with God in heaven then their love for God was questionable. Baxter wrote,

> And if heaven dwell in my heart, shall I not desire to dwell in heaven? Would divine love more plentifully pour itself upon my heart, how easy would it be to leave this flesh and world? Death and the grave would be but a triumph for victorious love. It would be easier to die in peace and joy, than to go to rest at night after a fatiguing day, or eat when I am hungry.[142]

The apostle Paul also exclaimed in Phil 1:21–24, "For to me, living is Christ and dying is gain. If I am to live in the flesh, that means fruitful labour for me; and I do not know which I prefer . . . my desire is to depart and be with Christ, for that is far better; but to remain in the flesh with you is more necessary for you" (NRSV). In his commentary on these verses, Wesley asserted it was better "*to depart*—Out of bonds, flesh, the world, *and to be with Christ*—in a nearer and fuller union. It is better *to depart*; it is far better *to be with Christ*."[143]

What was it that about perfection that made Wesley believe it was much better to die than to continue living? To begin with, although he had a very positive view of the body and the temporal world, Wesley recognized that until God's kingdom was fully established the physical realm would always be faulty. He considered the frailty of the body and the troubles of life to be cumbersome and vexing. Death freed the believer from the burden of living in a fallen world.[144] This perspective helps make sense of Methodist

---

141. Wesley, *Letters* "To Miss March" August 12, 1769 (Telford), 5:148.

142. Baxter, *Dying Thoughts*, 116.

143. Wesley, *ENNT*, 729.

144. This sentiment was also expressed the *Book of Homilies*, "But true faith in God's promises . . . with consideration of the joy and everlasting life to come in Heaven will . . . never be able to overthrow the *hearty desire and gladness that the Christian Soul hath to be separated from this corrupt body*, that it may come to the gracious presence of

hymns which seemed to celebrate death as a thing of beauty and made the mourners appear more envious than sorrowful over the deceased's departure. For example, one hymn began:

> Ah, lovely appearance of death!
> > What sight upon earth is so fair?
> Not all the gay pageants that breathe
> > Can with a dead body compare.
> With solemn delight I survey
> > The corpse when the spirit is fled,
> In love with the beautiful clay,
> > And longing to be in its stead.[145]

Yet another hymn intoned,

> Rejoice for a brother deceased!
> > Our loss is his infinite gain,
> A soul out of prison released,
> > And freed from its bodily chain.[146]

Because Wesley understood death primarily in a spiritual sense, physical death was not a major threat to Christians. If a person had thwarted spiritual death by being restored to a holy, happy relationship with God, then physical death could do no true harm. Perfected believers could embrace death as the means whereby they were translated from this fallen realm. It was the "last enemy to be conquered" and an unpleasant event to be endured. However, once the threshold of physical death was passed, Wesley believed that true Christians were ushered into the presence of the divine and would remain safely there until they were united with their perfected, resurrected bodies. Death, therefore, held no real threat for them. As Wesley observed, the true believer "desires to be dissolved and to be with Christ; he desires to quit this house of clay, and to be carried by angels into Abraham's bosom . . . to see the Son of Man coming in the clouds of heaven; to stand at his right hand, and hear that word . . . 'Come, ye blessed, receive the kingdom prepared for you from the beginning of the world!'"[147]

---

our Saviour Jesus Christ." Emphasis is mine. "Exhortation Against the Fear of Death" in Wesley, *Homilies*, 61.

145. Wesley, "Hymn 47" (BE), 7:138–39.
146. Wesley, "Hymn 48" (BE), 7:139–40.
147. Wesley, *Word to a Swearer* (Jackson), 11:168.

Christian Perfection and Children

In eighteenth-century England, children faced the same plight as adults: death could occur at any time. It was commonly accepted that children, like their elders, must be equally prepared to face a holy God and were encouraged to contemplate their own mortality. Wesley did not render children incapable of receiving the highest graces of salvation; therefore, he encouraged them to prepare their young souls for eternity.[148] Indeed, the seriousness with which the Methodists prepared their children for death was demonstrated by John and Charles's choice of hymns for their children's collection. No fewer than sixteen hymns from Charles's *Collection of Hymns Describing Death* were chosen for the 1763 publication of *Hymns for Children*.[149] The opening line of one of these hymns asked, "And am I only born to die?" It went on to inquire,

> How then ought I on earth to live,
> While God prolongs the kind reprieve,
> And props the house of clay?
>   My sole concern, my single care,
> To watch, and tremble, and prepare
>   Against that fatal day![150]

Dying children did not have a lifetime to prepare for heart holiness; however, because entire sanctification was an utter gift of grace, it could be bestowed upon the very young as easily as it was upon the old. Although Wesley utilized the categories of "children," "young men" and "fathers" found in 1 John to explain the stages of growth in grace, these stages did not necessarily align with one's chronological age. Wesley asserted that God could "'[cut] short his work.' He does the work of many years in a few weeks; perhaps in a week, a day, an hour. He justifies or sanctifies both those who have done or suffered nothing, and who have not had time for a gradual growth either in light or grace."[151]

---

148. Wesley was not the only person to encourage children to reach for the highest levels of grace in preparation for death. James Janeway wrote *A Token for Children* in the mid-seventeenth century—a book which offered advice on preparing for eternity and described the dying scenes of various children some as young as five years old. Wesley republished Janeway's work in the *Christian Library*.

149. Hildebrandt and Beckerlegge, *Collection of Hymns for the Use of the People Called Methodists* (BE), 7:131. See footnote.

150. Wesley, "Hymn 42" (BE), 7:133.

151. Wesley, *Farther Thoughts upon Christian Perfection* (BE), 13:106.

Despite their youth, children would often approach death with spiritual maturity that was far beyond their years. In one journal entry, Wesley remarked that he saw a child "dying as an hundred years old, in the full triumph of the faith."[152] Another noteworthy child was ten-year-old John B. When illness overtook him, his sister asked why he was so happy. His response was striking for a child of his age: "Why like as if God was in me . . . I am quite happy when I am saying my prayers; and when I think on God, I can almost see into heaven."[153] When asked if he were afraid to die, he replied, "I have seen the time that I was; but now I am not a bit afraid of death, or hell, or judgment; for Christ is mine. I know Christ is my own. He says, 'What would you have?' I would get to heaven: I will get to heaven as soon as I can."[154] Yet another account in Wesley's journal was of "the first Methodist child who went from the Macclesfield Society to the Church in heaven." She was a youth of just twelve years and "was sanctified within nine days after she was convinced of sin . . . Her look struck an awe into all that saw her. She is now in Abraham's bosom."[155] Perhaps the most remarkable account was Wesley's journal entry on September 16, 1744. Wesley documented that he buried a deeply serious girl who spent her time speaking to or about God. She was "one who had soon finished her course, going to God in *full assurance of faith* when she was little more than four years old."[156] Such accounts only added to the validity of Wesley's claim that Christian perfection was a freely given gift of God's grace which was available to all—even to the least of these.

Conclusion

Wesley's view of Christian perfection was central to his theology. Although he refined his beliefs on the matter, the ideal of perfection was the focal point in Wesley's thoughts from as early as 1725.[157] In his estimation, it was

---

152. Wesley, *Journal* March 18, 1746 (BE), 20:116.

153. Wesley *Journal* March 23, 1764 (BE), 21:446.

154. Wesley *Journal* 23 March 1764 (BE), 21:446.

155. Wesley, *Letters* "To Ann Foard." October 12, 1764 (Telford), 4:268.

156. Wesley, *Journal* September 16, 1744 (BE), 20:39. So remarkable was this case that Wesley was compelled to print it nearly 40 years later in the 1781 edition of the *Arminian Magazine*.

157. When asked about the rise of Methodism during the Annual Conference of 1765, Wesley replied that although their understanding of how to attain holiness

the on-going commitment not just to holiness but to his particular view of perfection which set the Methodists apart from other believers. Less than a year before he died, Wesley penned the following sentiment regarding "full sanctification" to Robert Carr Brackenbury: "This doctrine is the grand depositum which God has lodged with the people called Methodists; and for the sake of propagating this chiefly He appeared to have raised us up."[158] In other words, Wesley postulated that the very existence of the Methodists was dependent upon the proclamation of Christian perfection. After all, who could argue with the testimony of such witnesses who, as Wesley noted,

> . . . are always happy in God. Thus they calmly travel on through life, being never weary nor faint in their minds, never repining, murmuring, or dissatisfied, casting all their care upon God, till the hour comes that they should drop this covering of earth, and return unto the great Father of spirits. Then, especially, it is that they "rejoice with joy unspeakable and full of glory." You who credit it not, come and see. See these living and dying Christians.

> Happy while on earth they breathe;
>   Mightier joys ordain'd to know,
> Trampling on sin, hell, and death,
>   To the third heaven they go![159]

---

changed, "*holiness* was our point, inward and outward holiness." Wesley, *Annual Minutes, 1765* (BE), 10:311.

158. Wesley, *Letters* "To Robert Carr Brackenbury" September 15, 1790 (Telford), 8:238.

159. Wesley, *Farther Appeal to Men of Reason and Religion, Part III* (BE), 11:275.

Chapter 6

TRIUMPHANT DEATH
The Culmination of a Sanctified Life

Introduction

WESLEY RELIED HEAVILY UPON the "living and dying" testimonies of the early Methodists to support his theology of Christian perfection; however, he found the most credible proofs of his doctrine in the "happy" death accounts of the early Methodists. In the eighteenth century, dying words carried special authority since the deathbed was considered a place of self-awareness, honesty, and divine reckoning. Therefore, any deathbed confirmation of entire sanctification was especially valuable, and fortunately for Wesley, there was plenty of such evidence to be had. Wesley's journals were laced with records of Methodists whose triumphant deaths he took to be proof of the entirely sanctifying work of God in their lives. For example, Wesley recounted the story of Joseph Norbury who claimed for three years prior to his death that he had been saved from all sin, and "his whole spirit and behaviour, in life and death, made his testimony beyond exception."[1] After the funeral of another Methodist, Wesley wrote,

> I buried the remains of Rebecca Mills . . . Pain and sickness, and various trials, succeeded almost without any intermission: But she was always the same, firm and unmoved, as the rock upon which

---

1. Wesley, *Journal* November 21, 1763 (BE), 21:439. For other dying exemplars of Christian perfection see the account of Mr. Grimshaw and Elizabeth Mann. Wesley, *Journal* April 1, 1762 (BE), 21:357 and *Journal* October 26, 1752 (BE), 20:442.

she was built; in life and in death uniformly praising the God of her salvation. The attainableness of this great salvation is put beyond all reasonable doubt by the testimony of one such (were there but one) living and dying witnesses.[2]

Best of all, were declarations like those of Judith Berresford who proclaimed upon her deathbed, "Tell all from me that perfection is attainable and exhort all to press after it . . . Send to Mr. W. and tell him I am sorry I did not sooner believe the doctrine of perfect holiness. Blessed be God I now know it to be the truth!"[3]

While Wesley's journals were filled with similar reports of holy deaths, the focus of this chapter is on the accounts published in the *Arminian Magazine*. These accounts are of special interest because they were carefully selected by Wesley himself to be widely distributed among his followers. An examination of these accounts reveals how the Methodists were actually dying and how the doctrine of Christian perfection factored into their final moments.

Missional Purpose of the Deathbed Accounts

Wesley's stated purposed for the *Arminian Magazine* was to defend and promote the truth that *"God willeth all men to be saved."*[4] This was, of course, in contrast to the predestinarian doctrine that "Christ did not die for all, but for one in ten, for the Elect only" which was promoted in contemporary Calvinist magazines such as *The Spiritual Magazine* and *The Gospel Magazine*.[5] It was not that Wesley intended to stir up further controversy with the Calvinists; rather, as he stated in a letter to Thomas Taylor, he was resolved "to guard those who are not poisoned [by Calvinism] yet . . . . I fight them at their own weapons."[6] Specifically, Wesley intended to publish the best evidence for "the Universal Love of God, and his willingness to *save all men* from *all sin*."[7] To accomplish this goal, each issue contained four parts: 1) a defense of the universal love of God for all humanity, 2) an example of the life of a holy person, 3) accounts and letters of "pious persons, the greater

2. Wesley, *Journal* November 15, 1767 (BE), 22:109.
3. Wesley, *Journal* May 5, 1757 (BE), 21:96–97.
4. Wesley, "To the Reader," *AM* (January 1778), iii–iv.
5. Wesley, "To the Reader," *AM* (January 1778), iii–iv.
6. Wesley, *Letters* "To Thomas Taylor" January 15, 1778 (Telford), 6:295.
7. Wesley, "To the Reader," *AM* (January 1778), v.

part who are still alive," and 4) verses which confirmed the above stated doctrine.[8] As the magazine developed, Wesley relied more heavily upon the accounts and letters containing deathbed testimonies to make his case.

Wesley was wise enough to realize the use of strict argumentation was not enough to drive home the claim that God could "*save all men* from *all sin.*"[9] Peter Böhler repeatedly tried to convince Wesley that there was no such state as entire sanctification before death. "Sin *will* and *must* always remain in the soul. The *old man* will remain till death," the Moravian argued.[10] As much as he respected his mentor, Wesley could not reconcile Böhler's edict with the dying testimony of Nancy Morris. Despite her pain, she proclaimed, "Oh, I am happy, happy, happy, for my spirit continually rejoices in God *my* Saviour . . . And he hath cleansed me from all sin . . . It is finished. His grace is free for all. I am a witness."[11] When Wesley believed the end was growing nearer for her, he pointedly asked, "Do you *now* believe?"[12] Morris's testimony never wavered, and she remained in joy and happiness to the moment of death. Her exuberant witness against the backdrop of death convinced Wesley that Christian perfection was truly possible despite Böhler's argument to the contrary. Thus, it is no surprise that Wesley highlighted the value of the "Letters and the Lives" (which often contained deathbed accounts) in the magazine because, in his words, they "contained the marrow of experimental and practical religion."[13]

The number of deathbed accounts increased more than any other type of submission during Wesley's editorship. Because Wesley retained strict editorial control over the magazine from its debut in 1778 until his death in March 1791, this proliferation leaves little doubt that these accounts had a missional purpose. One of the reasons for the increase was Wesley's belief that reports of happy deaths were a source of encouragement and edification to his readers and "may incite many to run the race that is set

---

8. Wesley, "To the Reader," *AM* (January 1778), v–vi.

9. Wesley, "To the Reader," *AM* (January 1778), v.

10. Wesley, *Journal* May 16, 1741 (BE), 19:195. See also the entry for May 2, 1741 *Journals* (BE), 19:192 for an earlier discussion on the topic.

11. Wesley, *Journal* May 14–15, 1741 (BE), 19:194–95.

12. Wesley, *Journal* May 15, 1741 (BE), 19:195.

13. Wesley, *Letters* "To Thomas Taylor" January 15, 1778 (Telford), 6:295. In the 1781 preface to the bound volume of the magazine, Wesley once again highlighted the importance of personal accounts by noting that he would insert "part of the Life of some of those real Christians, who having faithfully served God in their generation, have lately finished their course with joy." Wesley, "Preface" *AM* (1781), v. 4:5.

before them with more courage and patience."[14] In 1781, he announced, "As nothing is more animating to serious people, than the dying Words and Behaviour of the Children of God, I purpose inserting, in each of the following Magazines, one (at least) of these Accounts, and the rather, because the Tracts from which most of them are extracted, are not in many hands."[15] However, a careful examination of the deathbed scenes made it obvious that Wesley choose accounts which would animate his followers to take hold of the claim that believers could be saved from *all* sin prior to death.

Analysis of Deathbed Accounts in the Arminian Magazine

The exact number of deathbed accounts published in the magazine has been debated, and it is easy to understand why.[16] First of all, the criteria for inclusion within the numbered scenes evidently varied from scholar to scholar. Some assessments seemed only interested in the deaths of early Methodists and did not include the death accounts of key historical figures. Secondly, if an analysis only relied upon the table of contents to tally the deaths, the number would be grossly underestimated since many of the scenes are not clearly marked as death reports.[17] Finally, there were often multiple deaths reported within a single letter or account. If such a letter were missed because it was not noticeably labeled as a death report, or if the study only counted the number of submissions vs. the actual number of reported deaths, then it is clear why the total varied from one report to the next. For the sake of clarity, the methodology used in this work to tally the number of death accounts must be explained.

Criteria for inclusion: All deaths (historical figures as well as contemporary ones) were counted as long as the account attributed some meaning or significance to the death. There are singular statements which acknowledge a person's demise without giving any other details. For example, in

---

14. Wesley, *Letters* "To Hester Ann Roe" October 1, 1782 (Telford), 7:144.

15. Wesley, Preface to "An Account of Jane Muncy," *AM* (March 1781), 153.

16. There are few published assessments of the deathbed accounts in the *Arminian Magazine*, and the count differs in each one. Richard Bell numbered the accounts at 152 while Barbara Prosser noted 172.

17. For example, many of the death scenes are found within letters or in autobiographical accounts that were finished by another hand to include the person's dying moments.

a life account, the individual might record the death of a parent or child without elaborating on the event. Since these reports gave little to no information about the person or the nature of the death, they were excluded from the tally.

Method of Counting: The deaths were counted by totaling the number of deceased individuals and not by the number of letters or articles submitted. Thus, a letter which contained the description of four deaths would be tallied not as one but as four separate deaths.

Process of Categorization: The following information (if reported) was collected for analysis: name and age of the deceased, date of death, character qualities and/or brief history of the dying person, the questions directed toward the dying person, reported works of grace upon the deathbed, conflicts or temptations, expressions of fear or assurance, specific testimonies of entire sanctification, the use of Christian perfection language, exhortations by the dying, last words, declarations of the desire to die, and supernatural experiences.

Using the criteria described above, there were a total of 280 reported deaths between the first publication in 1778 and the February issue of 1791.[18] A quick overview of these death narratives revealed they were indeed consistent with the magazine's claim that *all* people could be saved from *all* sin. Many of the accounts suggested (if not outright declared) that the person was entirely sanctified before they died. Forty-seven of the accounts included a clear profession that Christian perfection was attained prior to the deathbed; beyond this, there were thirty-three reports of entire sanctification which occurred after the onset of the fatal illness. Entire sanctification was not the only work of grace described upon the deathbed. There were twenty-two reports of individuals who experienced the new birth (initial sanctification) just prior to death. Additionally, there were instances where an obvious work of grace was wrought upon the deathbed, but the language was unclear leaving the reader to wonder if the individual experienced the new birth, entire sanctification, or perhaps both. Thirty-three of the accounts recorded the deaths of historical figures who could be termed "saints and martyrs" since they include the final moments of well-known individuals such as Martin Luther or Dissenters who were killed for their faith. Not all of the deaths in the magazine were meant to be emulated. There were also twenty-seven reports of unfavorable deaths which recorded the last moments of hardened sinners or those who rejected God's grace.

18. See the Appendix for a table which notes each death account.

TRIUMPHANT DEATH

Accounts that were descriptive of a good death but did not include an obvious work of grace or fit within the one of the other categories were counted under a general heading of "Other." The chart below provides a quick point of reference for the deathbed reports:

New Birth	Christian Perfection	New Birth *and* Christian Perfection–Upon Deathbed	Unspecified Work of Grace	Saints and Martyrs	Unfavorable Deaths	Other	Total
Upon Deathbed 22	Prior to Deathbed 47 / Upon Deathbed 26 / Upon Deathbed 7 — Total of Perfection Testimonies: 80	Upon Deathbed 20	33	27	98	280

If the deaths of those who testified to definite experiences of Christian perfection (80), the reports of the historical "saints and martyrs" (33), and the "unfavorable deaths" (27), are subtracted from the total number of accounts (280), the reader is left with 140 eighteenth-century deathbed scenes. Even though these 140 reports did not make specific claims of perfection, 90 of these accounts used language which was generally associated with the experience of entire sanctification.[19] This left a mere 50 eighteenth-century death scenes which did not at least hint at Wesley's notions of holiness.

---

19. The language associated with Christian perfection will be examined later in this chapter.

Deathbed Genre

It was not long before the Methodist death narrative became a genre in its own right.[20] By the time the *Arminian Magazine* emerged, there was a plethora of seventeenth and eighteenth-century biographies of well-known Anglican Evangelicals in circulation; however, these lengthy tomes differed from Wesley's deathbed accounts in key ways. Although, many of the biographies included a brief treatment of the subject's death, the attention was on the life and accomplishments of the individual rather than the conclusion of his or her life. The deathbed scenes in the *Arminian Magazine* sometimes functioned as short biographies, but the emphasis was reversed. The focus was not on the life and accomplishments of the person but on the moments leading up to death. If a person's life was depicted, the concentration was upon significant spiritual moments (such as conversion or entire sanctification) or on the individual's relationship with the Methodists.

Furthermore, Rack observed that Wesley set a new precedence in eighteenth-century publications by lifting up experiences of the common person. According to Rack, there were very few accounts of individuals belonging to the lower social strata among Anglican evangelical narratives.[21] However, Wesley's deathbed publications championed the stories of the poor, the uneducated, and those who, but for his efforts, would have gone unaccounted for in the pages of history.

Methodist Pattern of Death

Bell rightly noted that the Methodist death narratives in the *Arminian Magazine* quickly took on a standardized pattern.[22] That is, the same types of expressions, questions, events, and behaviors generally occurred in each account. English deathbed scenes had been following the basic pattern of the *ars moriendi* tradition from the time it had been published into English as *The Arte & Crafte to knowe Well to Dye* in 1490.[23] There were variations in deathbed rituals especially as an increasing amount of holy dying

---

20. See: Hindmarsh, "'My Chains Fell Off, My Heart Was Free,'" for a careful examination of early Methodist narratives.
21. See Rack, "Evangelical Endings," 47n33.
22. Bell, "Our People Die Well," 216.
23. For an overview of English deathbed rituals see Houlbrooke's chapter, "Last Rites and the Craft of Dying," 147–82.

literature was published in the sixteenth and seventeenth centuries, but most reported deaths included at least some elements of the sixfold arrangement contained within the original *ars moriendi*. The earliest *ars moriendi* literature highlighted the following six elements: 1) a commendation of death which acknowledged that death could be disconcerting but concluded that it should be welcomed as a friend; 2) the struggle against the temptations of disbelief, despair, impatience in pain, pride, and avarice verses the application of the virtues of faith, hope, love, patience, humility, and disinterested love (detachment); 3) questions to be asked of the dying person; 4) helpful instructions which included prayers, the encouragement of confession, reflection upon Christ's suffering, and guidance for committing one's spirit to God; 5) directions for the dying person's friends, and family; and 6) prayers for bystanders to use on behalf of the dying individual.

Even though the eighteenth century saw a decline in *ars moriendi* literature, it did not mean that the patterns of death were erased. The most striking evidence that these structures were still in place during Wesley's era was the number of young children who conformed to a basic code of deathbed behavior.[24] It is likely that the overarching patterns of the *ars moriendi* were still widely communicated through eighteenth-century culture, devotional literature, and religious teachings. Therefore, the notable aspect of Wesley's narratives is not that there were basic structures to each scene but that Wesley and the early Methodists infused each stage with their own meanings. The rest of this chapter will consider how Christian perfection related to each of the following elements typically found in the *Arminian Magazine* accounts: 1) acceptance of the dying role, 2) examination of the dying person, 3) triumph over temptation, and 4) deathbed testimony.

---

24. An unnamed six-year-old child evidenced knowledge of expected patterns of dying behavior. As she lay dying, she delivered all the prescribed responses to the litany of questions posed to her. Wesley, "Account of a Very Remarkable Child" *AM* (April 1782), 183. See also the account of thirteen-year-old Elizabeth Dunting who was noted to have read Janeway's *Token for Children* the year before she died an exemplary death. Wesley, "Account of the Death of Elizabeth Dunting, aged Thirteen" *AM* (February 1783), 76–77. James Janeway's *A Token for Children* was published in two parts in 1671 and 1673. The work contained the exceptionally pious death accounts of children. Wesley was impressed enough with the narratives that he reprinted Janeway's works.

Acceptance of the Dying Role

Eighteenth-century deathbed scenes were akin to a well-staged play where every person had a distinctive role. The dying person took center stage while surrounding friends, family, and neighbors each assumed a part in the closing scene.[25] David Cressy noted,

> Ideally, the deathbed would be attended by ministers and friends, neighbours and kin, who would share godly comfort and bear witness to a satisfactory passing. If blessed by God, the fortunate Christian would be fully articulate to the end . . . [and] were watched for signs of fortitude and grace, and their silences as well as utterances were weighed for spiritual significance . . . Common cultural practice turned each rite of passage into a social and collective event. Like the birthroom where women gathered to witness the entry into life, the sickroom was an arena of action where people watched and waited for a mortal life to expire.[26]

This dynamic was clearly recognized by the early Methodists, and there was a heavy sense of responsibility upon the dying person to perform his or her part well. The dying were expected to confidently address the probing questions of friends and family, provide clear testimonies of their spiritual standing, exhort and pray for the watchful bystanders, and display endless grace and patience in what was often described as "violent pain."

To add to the pressure of their performance, there were often witnesses who sat by the bedside with pen in hand ready to record any special utterances or last words.[27] There was a prevailing sense that a serious of-

---

25. There were several publications in the holy dying genre which were actually scripted like a play—complete with narrations and parts spoken by each character. Wesley edited one of these scripted dialogues by Thomas Mulso and ran it in the 1786 and 1787 issues of the *Arminian Magazine* as a serial publication. See Wesley, "Extract of Three Dialogues" *AM*, (1786), 39–43; 89–94; 166–68; 222–25; 273–76; 318–21; 369–71; 442–45; 504–6; 554–57; 617–19; 666–69 and (1787), 32–35; 89–92; 143–44; 199–202; 251–54; 312–15; 365–67; 424–28; 472–75; 530–33; 587–90; 638–41. Wesley's edited version was adapted from Mulso, *Callistus. In Three Dialogues*. (London: Printed for Benjamin White, 1768). In his sermon, *On Visiting the Sick*, Wesley also recommended Spinckes's *Sick Man Visits* first published in 1712. Spinkes's work was also written in a scripted dialog.

26. Cressy, *Birth, Marriage, and Death*, 390.

27. Sometimes, as in the case of Elizabeth Mather, the dying person attempted to direct attention away from herself. When she noticed a person taking down her words, Elizabeth instructed, "If you want any dying words to be impressed on your mind, remember my dear Lord's dying words were, 'My God, my God, why hast thou forsaken

fense was committed if a believer's final scene was not adequately recorded.[28] After observing Mary Howard's death, one witness believed it was his solemn obligation to publish her death scene. He reasoned, "As her life and death were happy, I think it a duty I owe to God, to you, and to the Methodists, to give a brief account of her."[29] Failure to attend to one's deathbed "duty"—whether on the part of the bystanders or on the part of the dying person—was to rob God of due credit for a safe passage through the valley of death. It also cheated the community of the person's dying testimony and deprived fellow Methodists of a pattern to follow when their own deaths were imminent.[30]

Although a sudden death was often associated with God's judgment and was therefore generally undesirable, the weight of the dying role lay so heavily upon the minds of some Methodists that a hasty and private demise was attractive to believers who were well-prepared to face God. For example, Susannah Strong, a circumspect Methodist, was considered blessed because of her rapid departure. Her husband attempted to send for some of the neighbors to witness her passing, but she had only enough time to proclaim, "I am as full of Jesus as my heart can hold! I am as happy as if I was in heaven!" before turning over and breathing her last.[31] Her biographer noted how "privileged" she was to pass from this world into the next "without the pomp of dying."[32] Wesley himself longed for the fortune of a

---

me." Wesley, "Account of Mrs. Elizabeth Mather" *AM* (December 1790), 647–48. Elizabeth Shacklock did not even want to be mentioned in her funeral sermon. When a bystander suggested that her dying experience be published for the good of others, she did not want to hear of it. She replied, "If Mr. L. preaches at my funeral, I desire he will not say a word about me; for there is nothing in me but unworthiness. It is all Jesus!" Wesley, "Account of Mrs. Elizabeth Shacklock" *AM* (November 1789), 577.

28. Wesley received a letter lamenting the fact that Henry Foster's friends "neglected" to record an account of the life and death of a man who possessed "much good sense and unaffected piety." One was left with a sense that a grave injustice had been done to both Henry and the community of faith. Wesley, "Account of Mr. Henry Foster" *AM* (October 1788), 516.

29. Wesley, "Short Account of the Death of Mrs. Mary Howard" *AM* (April 1789), 182.

30. It is evident the dying relied upon the death accounts of fellow believers to help them through their own transition because they were known to claim the dying expressions of other Methodists for themselves. For example, upon recalling Mrs. Hall's last words, "Precious faith!" Mrs. Crask declared, "Now I prove it precious! It is all in all!" Wesley, "Some Account of Mrs. Crask" *AM* (December 1783), 645.

31. Wesley, "Short Account of Mrs. Susannah Strong" *AM* (August 1789), 418.

32. Wesley, "Short Account of Mrs. Susannah Strong" *AM* (August 1789), 418.

quiet, private death. On one occasion he penned the following sentiment: "such a faintness and weariness seized me that it was with difficulty I got home. I could not but think how happy it would be . . . to sink down and steal away at once, without any of the hurry and pomp of dying! Yet it is happier still to glorify God in our death, as well as our life."[33]

Authority of the Deathbed Role

The dying role may have been burdensome to some Methodists, but it also brought with it an authority that many believers did not typically enjoy during their lifetime.[34] Because the dying hovered between this world and the next, they acted as conduits of spiritual wisdom to the Methodist community. One way they fulfilled this role was to share their glimpses into the world beyond. Sometimes as believers grew nearer to the moment of death the portals of heaven were briefly opened, and they described their vision of the supernatural world to the onlookers. Wesley published over thirty accounts which included heavenly encounters; these narratives described visions of angels, indescribably beautiful music, breath-taking landscapes, visitations from deceased family members, and appearances of Christ. If the surrounding friends and family were fortunate, they might actually experience a taste of heaven themselves. Sarah Brough's husband was one of these privileged few. His vision of the heavenly realms was so powerful that he also wished to die. He exclaimed,

> Yea, my tongue and pen cannot utter the light and power we both possessed together. Every pain was a spring of joy to our souls. I never saw before, (no not the ten thousandth part) so far into the invisible world. I beheld the great Three-One, with all the heavenly quires, smile to see the saints below suffer their various trials with patience! . . . I travelled with her in my very heart and arms through the valley of the shadow of death. I never was, before so far out of the body: I went with her to the very threshold of heaven; as when she expired, she with her arms round me seemed to draw me after her. So my soul conducted her to the very presence of the

---

33. Wesley, *Journal* December 12, 1755 (BE), 21:36–37.

34. Gregory Schneider noted that the early Methodists "offered a community of spiritual equality based both on personal disciplines that led to and sustained the 'new birth' and on the shared sentiments that resulted from it." Schneider, "Ritual of Happy Dying among Early American Methodists," 350–51.

angels, and then fell back again to its poor habitation. Oh how did I long, to keep my hold, and return back no more!³⁵

The impact of these visions cannot be underestimated. Not only did they help reveal God to the rest of the community, but they also made death seem less threatening to the bystanders.

With such a direct connection to the spiritual realm, it is easy to see why dying Methodists held the respect of the entire community. Every dying word and action was examined for its spiritual significance. For many, death was the most significant moment of their lives. Women, children, the poor, and illiterate were suddenly pushed from the fringes of society to the center of attention. It was often the first (and only) time they had an important voice in the community, and even if they did not have a supernatural vision, they could be assured that their words would be taken seriously. For example, one account in the *Arminian Magazine* related the story of a six-year-old child who felt free to rebuke her mother: "O mammy! you must seek Jesus: indeed you must. He says, *Except a man be born again, he cannot enter the kingdom of God.* No mammy! no unclean *thing can enter within the gates of the new Jerusalem.*"³⁶ Likewise, Mrs. Walker had no qualms about exhorting not only her servants but also a Methodist preacher to "abide by the old Methodist Doctrine."³⁷

By publishing the Methodist deathbed accounts, Wesley added to the authority of the dying, and he capitalized on their voice to further his message of holiness. It has already been noted that Wesley championed the stories of individuals typically overlooked by eighteenth-century society. However, by placing the dying accounts of humble Methodists among stories of well-known saints and martyrs, Wesley communicated a subtle, but powerful, message to his readers. First, he implied that the same grace and holiness possessed by the saints of antiquity was freely available to the lowliest believers. Secondly, it raised the status of the dying individual; that is, just as historical believers were exemplars of spiritual bravery and tokens of holiness in their deaths, so too, the dying Methodist could be a beacon of faith for the rest of the community.³⁸ Indeed, some of the accounts Wesley

---

35. Wesley, "Some Account of the Life and Death of Mrs. Sarah Brough" *AM* (November 1780), 598.

36. Wesley, "Account of a Very Remarkable Child" *AM* (April 1782), 183.

37. Wesley, "Some Account of the late Mrs. Walker" *AM* (May 1788), 242.

38. In his introduction to the "Acts and Monuments of the Christian Martyrs," Wesley recorded, "May we all learn from these worthies, to be not almost only, but altogether

published made direct comparisons between dying Methodists and martyrs. It was said of Mrs. Moore, "She often put me in mind of the Martyrs, rejoicing and clapping their hands in the flames; for the God of the Hebrews was evidently with her in her fiery trials! What else could enable her to triumph over all the decays of nature, and in the agonies of death!"[39]

Examination of the Dying Person

It was a matter of great concern to establish a person's spiritual standing at the onset of the dying process. Since Wesley believed God's grace was immediately available, the examination allowed a believer to seek deeper levels of grace if he or she was found wanting. Often the questions were asked at least twice: at the onset of illness and again as death drew near. Anyone around the deathbed could stand in the role of "examiner" and ask questions designed to reveal the state of the person's soul. Even if a person's spiritual condition was well-established, the questions could still be utilized to provide an opportunity for the dying person to proclaim their gratitude for what God had done for them. What was most notable about this examination process was that it revealed what Wesley and the early Methodists believed to be absolutely necessary for a person to die well. It is clear from the questions asked that there were several basic elements for which the Methodists were searching, and it should hardly come as a surprise that the key requirements for a good death aligned with the characteristics of Christian perfection.

The most frequent inquiries recorded in the *Arminian Magazine* can be summarized in the following questions: "How do you find your soul?" "Are you afraid to die?" "Are you happy?" "Are you willing (or do you desire) to die?" From these questions, it is obvious that Wesley believed a "good death" meant the individual possessed a definite testimony of God's work in their soul, freedom from the fear of death (assurance), the characteristics of holiness (happiness, love, and gratitude), and utter resignation to God's will. The answers to these questions varied from person to person, however the general content of the responses retained a remarkable level of consistency.

Christians! To reckon all things but dung and dross for the excellency of the *experimental* knowledge of Jesus Christ! And not to count our lives dear unto ourselves, so we may finish our course with joy!" Wesley, *Christian Library*, 2:4.

39. Wesley, "Short Account of the Death of Mrs. Moore" *AM* (February 1787), 77.

How Do You Find Your Soul?

The first two questions, "How do you find your soul?" and "Are you afraid to die?" measured whether the individual had experienced the salvific grace of God. These two questions cut directly to the heart of the matter and quickly exposed a soul that was not ready to meet its maker. For those who were prepared for death, the query, "How do you find your soul?" was most frequently answered with declarations of being "full of love," "rejoicing in God," and "happy." One young woman proclaimed, "I have nothing but the prospect of happiness before me! I have not power to utter half of what I feel. Mercy! mercy! a sinner saved! I rejoice that I am saved by God alone!"[40] John Morgan's examiner was "pretty well satisfied" with Morgan's answer that he was "wholly resigned to God," but he admitted that he had hoped that Morgan would give a more "experimental confession of the love of Jesus to him."[41] He was not disappointed during his second examination; Morgan confidently proclaimed, "I have been searching my heart for Pride, Anger, and other evil Tempers; but blessed be God I find none! Where are they! They are all gone. I have fought the good fight, I have finished my course, I have kept the faith!"[42] When a friend of Elizabeth Francis asked her how she was, Elizabeth responded, "I am ill in body; but well in my soul!" She then cried out,

> Hallelujah they cry,
> To the King of the sky,
> To the great, everlasting I AM!
> To the Lamb that was slain,
> And liveth again,
> Hallelujah to God and the Lamb![43]

Christopher Peacock responded to this question with confidence: "My soul is kept in peace, and staid upon God. I have no anxiety respecting life or death; no fear of any kind."[44] Such assertions testified to the person's clear standing with God.

---

40. Wesley, "Miss Hatton's Account of Her Sister's Death" *AM* (October 1782), 525.

41. Wesley, "Account of the Death of Mr. John Morgan" *AM* (March 1783), 129–30.

42. Wesley, "Account of the Death of Mr. John Morgan" *AM* (March 1783), 130.

43. Wesley, "Short Account of the Life and Death of Elizabeth Frances, of Birmingham" *AM* (January 1787), 23.

44. Wesley, "Account of the Death of Mr. Christopher Peacock" *AM* (July 1786), 355.

Are You Afraid to Die?

The question, "Are you afraid to die?" was designed to expose not only if a person was born again but also reveal the level of assurance the believer possessed. The ideal was found in believers like Prudence Williams who could fearlessly respond, "Oh! blessed be Jesus, he has destroyed the last enemy in so glorious a manner, that I can triumph over death and hell."[45] Elizabeth Henson's mother also modeled the highest levels of grace in her proclamation, "Perfect love casteth out all fear that hath torment. I have nothing to do now but to fear offending my good and gracious God. He is the good Shepherd, and careth for his sheep. What a good Shepherd have I? But O, how little have I laboured for him! But the precious blood of Christ is all my dependence now."[46]

While Wesley deemed it necessary for all believers to triumph over the fear of death; he did not condemn those who struggled with lapses of assurance during the dying process.[47] Rather, he modeled how such believers should be treated when he was called to the bedside of his dying friend, Mr. Thompson, who had "doubts concerning his final state and rather feared than desired to die." Wesley determined that his "whole business was to comfort him and increase and confirm his confidence in God."[48] Wesley's example was emulated in the pages of the *Arminian Magazine*. When William Burton, a new convert, struggled with lapses of assurance, he was treated with similar care and concern. He was attended by Methodists who prayed, sang hymns, and read Scripture to him until God spoke peace to his soul and erased the fear of death. When the actual moment of death arrived, the fear of death was always vanquished. In the case of Burton, his fear was so completely erased that he welcomed death. "O what shall I do ... to praise him?" Burton cried out. "I thought I was going, and I felt such transporting joy, that I hope I shall die in the next fainting fit."[49]

---

45. Wesley, "Account of the Death of Prudence Williams" *AM* (October 1790), 526.

46. Wesley "Elizabeth Henson's Account of the Death of Her Mother" *AM* (May 1785), 249.

47. It was individuals like William Crips who said he was not afraid to die but could give no sufficient reason for his confidence that were the most worrisome. In the case of Crips, he soon recognized that he was not yet justified and born of God and began seeking those graces immediately. Wesley, "Account of the Behaviour of Three Malefactors" *AM* (August 1786), 428–29.

48. Wesley, *Journal* September 2, 1782 (BE), 23:251.

49. Wesley, "Some Account of the Death of William Burton" *AM* (December 1784), 643–44.

Are You Happy?

The second set of questions, "Are you happy?" and "Are you willing (or do you desire) to die?" measured the degree of holiness a person possessed. One may recall from the previous chapter that Wesley believed "the more holy we are upon earth the more happy we must be (seeing there is an inseparable connection between holiness and happiness)."[50] "Happy deaths," therefore, were equivalent with "holy deaths," and grand displays and declarations of happiness were taken as signs of genuine purity and readiness to meet God. In fact, even in healthy believers a sudden upsurge of happiness could signal impending or sudden death. Wesley related the story of a young woman who experienced a sudden surge of happiness. One morning she "was much happier and had a fuller manifestation of the love of God than ever."[51] The same day she was accidently shot in the chest and died immediately.[52] Likewise, the *Arminian Magazine* reported increasing levels of happiness among dying believers as death approached. One example of this reoccurring phenomenon was Jane Allen. Her husband wrote, "As her Fever increased and her end drew near, she was happier and happier . . . The Tuesday before her death, she seemed to be quite transported with joy . . . There was in her such a spirit of love and gratitude, as I never saw before in any creature."[53] Some of the Methodists were reported to be so happy and animated as death drew near that even though they were dying they were described as being "full of life." Such was the case of one of Wesley's preachers, T. Cappiter. "As Death approached, his joys increased; and he seemed like a celestial inhabitant, full of life, love, joy, and praise . . . . Indeed he was so filled with the divine life, that his very countenance shone; which all who were near him could not but behold!"[54]

---

50. Wesley, *God's Love to Fallen Man* (BE), 2:431.

51. Wesley, *Journal* August 28, 1767 (BE), 22:100.

52. For a similar example see the account of the elderly Vincent Perronet. His granddaughter found him in a sort of ecstasy, "the tears running down his cheeks from a deep sense of the glorious things which were shortly to come to pass." He remained immeasurably happy until he died three days later. Wesley, *Journal* May 7, 1785 (BE), 23:355–56.

53. Wesley, "Some Account of Mr. John Allen" *AM* (December 1779), 638–39.

54. Wesley, "Some Account of the Death of Mr. T. Cappiter" *AM* (April 1785), 200.

Are You Willing (Or Do You Desire) to Die?

The question, "Are you willing (or do you desire) to die?" was a twofold test of holiness. The willingness to die was an indication that one was utterly resigned to the will of God and ensured that no self-will remained. When thirteen-year-old John Woolley was asked if he still chose to die, he replied, "I have no will: my will is resigned to the will of God. But I shall die . . . I shall go away like a lamb."[55] An almost identical answer was provided by William Adams. When asked if he were willing to die, he answered, "I have no will in it: the will of the Lord be done."[56] To be sure, there were some who struggled to resign themselves to death. Often it was mothers with young children who, in their own words, found it "hard to nature" to leave behind their families.[57] Those who lacked this resignation were considered ill-prepared to die. Elizabeth Shacklock, a dying wife and mother, confessed, "when I think of myself in my present state, as not fit to die, and of parting with my husband, and children, whom I love so dear, I think it hard . . . I think we have made idols of one another, and God saith, 'I will take away thy idols.'"[58] For Methodists such as Shacklock, who had not yet completely surrendered herself or her family over to the will of God, a brief but often bitter struggle ensued before self-will was banished. However, God's grace always won out in the end. The author of Mrs. Trimnell's death scene observed, "For the first two or three days, she was at times in great anguish of spirit. The giving up her husband and four children . . . was a

---

55. Wesley, "Short Account of John Woolley, who died in February 1742" *AM* (May 1781), 263.

56. Wesley, "Short Account of the Life and Death of William Adams" *AM* (April 1784), 193.

57. Martha Rogers mourned, ". . .it seemed hard to nature to be parted from Mr. R. after living so happy in each other." Wesley, "Short Account of Mrs. Martha Rogers" *AM* (February 1785), 83. Mary Goffe, a young mother who was dying at a distance from her home and young children, told the minister, "It is my misery that I cannot see my children." Wesley, "Extract from Mr. Baxter's 'Certainty of the World of Spirits'" *AM* (October 1783), 548.

58. Wesley, "Short Account of Mrs. Elizabeth Shacklock" *AM* (September 1789), 468. Shortly before her death, she was so overpowered with the love of God that she was able to resign her children and her husband into God's hands. When her husband expressed sadness at parting with her, she replied, "I can give you all up to God. He has promised to be a father to the fatherless; and a husband to the widow: and I trust, I shall meet you all again in heaven!" Wesley, "Account of Mrs. Elizabeth Shacklock, Continued" *AM* (November 1789), 578.

sore struggle between nature and grace; but grace was predominant, and made her victorious."[59]

The highest degrees of holiness were indicated by those who not only were willing to die but actually *desired* death.[60] It was previously noted that Wesley believed the desire to die was indicative of Christian perfection. Part of holiness was the proper ordering of a person's loves; therefore, the desire for death was not a fatalistic, suicidal, or an escapist impulse. Rather, it demonstrated that the believer wanted to be in the presence of Christ. Thus, women such as Susannah Bridgment were featured in Wesley's deathbed accounts. She had found the grace of Christian perfection before her deathbed and was not at all upset at the onset of her illness because she was "happy", and her soul had been "set at perfect liberty." Even though she had a kind husband and two young children, she never once expressed a desire to live.[61] Indeed, the will or desire to die was so strongly connected to Christian perfection that Sarah Bulgin was thought herself tempted by Satan "to wish to live longer in the world" after she experienced entire sanctification in her final illness.[62] However, true to form, it was not long before

---

59. Wesley, "Account of the Illness and Death of Mrs. Trimnell" *AM* (February 1790), 83.

60. The person was often asked the question, "If life and death were set before you, which would you choose?" The answer that received the most approval was "to die and be with Christ." For example, fourteen-year-old John Woolley was asked, "'If life and death were set before you, what would you chose then?' He answered, 'To die and to be with Christ. I long to be out of this wicked world.'" Wesley, "Short Account of John Woolley" *AM* (May 1781), 262.

61. Wesley, "Short Account of the Life and Death of Susannah Bridgment" *AM* (September 1787), 464. At times, Wesley seemed to lack a basic understanding of the dynamics involved in emotional and relational connections. He may have been so focused on his marks or "proofs" of holiness that he neglected to comprehend the very real pain of separation and grief over the loss of a loved one. This unwavering focus might explain his unfeeling letter to his sister Martha Hall after the loss of her children. Wesley told her that the death of her children was a sign of God's goodness to her. Now that her children were dead, he elaborated, your "time is restored to you, and you have nothing to do but to serve our Lord without carefulness and without distraction, till you are sanctified in body, soul, and spirit." Wesley "To Mrs. Martha Hall" November 17, 1742 *Letters* (BE), 26:90–91. William Briggs accused Wesley of being unfeeling. Briggs wrote to Wesley, "I think you have *knowledge* of all *experience*; but not the *experience* of all you *know*." He went on to reprimand Wesley for "...the want of *sympathy* in your discourses and conversation." There were many who "went on lamenting and weeping, and yet trust in God," said Briggs. He went on to ask, "When do you *feelingly* and with *tears* address yourself unto *such*?" "From William Briggs" April 5, 1750 *Letters* (BE), 26:415.

62. Wesley, "Extract of the Experience, and Happy Death of Mrs. Sarah Bulgin" *AM* (August 1787), 411.

Bulgin proclaimed, "I have lived, and I rejoice to die a Methodist. Come, Lord Jesus! my sweet, dear Jesus!"[63]

Deathbed Examination and Christian Perfection

The correlation between the deathbed questions and Wesley's scrutiny of those who professed entire sanctification should not be overlooked. In 1760, Wesley was keen to examine those who claimed to have been perfected. After questioning two different Methodists who testified to this work of grace, he noted that they felt nothing but love in their hearts, desired nothing but the will of God, had a constant sense of assurance, and were overwhelmed with gratitude and praise for the work God had accomplished in their souls.[64] Over twenty years later, Wesley reiterated these marks of holiness when he published Mrs. C. M.'s letter detailing her experience of Christian perfection in the June 1786 edition of the *Arminian Magazine*. C. M. claimed to possess "peace which passeth all understanding," to be "passive in the hand of God, and willing to be disposed of as seemeth good to him," to have found "heaven on earth" and "such love to souls" that she wept and prayed for everyone.[65] The similarities between the responses to a deathbed examination and the answers provided by those who claimed perfection are so similar they could be easily interchanged. By publishing deathbed accounts which focused upon the four specific questions discussed above,

---

63. Wesley, "Extract of the Experience, and Happy Death of Mrs. Sarah Bulgin" *AM* August 1787), 412. Men were also expected to express a desire for death. Charles Wesley was described by his daughter as "eager to depart," and if anyone spoke to him, his continual cry was "Let me die! Let me die!" Wesley, "Account of the Death of the Late Rev. Charles Wesley" *AM* (August 1788), 408. Likewise, Christopher Middleton's desire for death was so strong that he was tempted to think God dealt harshly with him by not hastening his demise. Wesley, "Short Account of the Life and Death of Mr. Christopher Middleton" *AM* (March 1787), 123.

64. Wesley, *Journal* March 6, 1760 (BE), 21:243 and *Journal* March 6, 1760 (BE), 21:244–45. Days later, after questioning other professors of perfection, Wesley determined that those who had experienced full salvation demonstrated the following characteristics: 1) They felt no inward sin and committed no outward sin. 2) They "saw" and loved God in every moment and prayed, rejoiced, and gave thanks continuously. 3) They had a clear witness or assurance of being perfected. Wesley, *Journal* March 12, 1760 (BE), 21:247.

65. Wesley, "Letter CCCXCVII, From Mrs. C.M. to the Rev. J. Wesley" *AM* (June 1786), 341.

Wesley promoted not only a means to verify one's preparedness to die, but he also teased out declarations consistent with the testimony of Christian perfection even if the dying person did not make explicit claims of that work of grace.

Triumph Over Death and Sin

If Wesley's questions were meant to examine a person's degree of holiness, then the assault brought on by a deathbed temptation was an extremely demanding trial meant to appraise the depths of the soul. One might be able to give a false performance in answering the examiner's questions; however, no amount of acting could withstand the trials suffered by the dying. Judith Beresford confirmed that all disingenuous pretenses would be swept aside in the face of death. She explained, "I experience more upon this bed of my own nothingness and the free grace of God in Christ than ever I did in all my life. The best of my performances would be damnable without Christ."[66] While true believers always triumphed over death, their victories were hard-earned.[67] Only genuine faith and the virtue of patience, born out of a consuming love for God, could successfully bring a person through a deathbed conflict. "Without charity," Wesley proclaimed, "nothing can make death comfortable. By comfortable I do not mean stupid or senseless . . . by a comfortable death I mean a calm passage out of life, full of even, rational peace and joy. And such a death all the acting and all the suffering in the world cannot give, without charity."[68]

Death was the last remaining vestige of sin; therefore, to die triumphantly, that is, to die with filled with assurance and the love of God, was for Wesley on par with triumphing over sin, death, and the devil. To prove that God's grace was greater than sin's curse, many of the Methodists extended the invitation to, "Come see a Christian die, triumphant over Death, Hell and the Grave!"[69] Signs of victory over the "last enemy" were ever-

---

66. Wesley, *Journal* May 5, 1757 (BE), 21:97.

67. Hindmarsh noted, ". . .if conversion was in some sense a response to the eschatological threat it [death] represented, then it should come as no surprise that the final coda to the evangelical conversion narrative was often an account of how the convert was finally enabled to vanquish death by the grace of God." Hindmarsh, *Evangelical Conversion Narrative*, 256. See also Wilson, *Many Waters Cannot Quench* for an examination of the role of suffering and death in Methodist conversion experiences.

68. Wesley, *On Love* (BE), 4:386–87.

69. Wesley, "Words of a Dying Saint" *AM* (April 1783), 191. For more examples of

present in the accounts Wesley published. Elizabeth Flook, for example, soared above death on imaginary wings. "Tell my sisters, tell my friends, it is a great thing to die," she proclaimed. Then she called for her sister, "Nancy, this is dying! This is dying! This is going home!" She spread out her arms and cried, "Wings, wings, wings!" Not long after this display she was "launched into the blaze of endless day."[70] Mrs. Trimmell seemed to mock death when she discovered God's grace buoyed her above its discomforts. "Is this dying?" she asked. "Why there is no misery in this."[71]

The signs of triumph did not need to be dramatic. As the elderly Jonathan Simpson lay dying, he frequently raised his right hand. When asked why he did this, he explained it was a "sign of victory."[72] During his last moments, Simpson gave a final signal that death would not prevail against him: he lifted his right hand, smiled pleasantly and died.[73] Even the manner in which one passed from this world into the next was viewed as a sign of the believer's triumph over death. To approach one's final moments with a sense of calm assurance and peace, was the ideal way to demonstrate that death held no threat. Therefore, an overwhelming majority of the published accounts mention that the person died "without a struggle or groan."[74] No verbalized proclamation of victory was necessary; a radiant countenance or sweet smile was enough to mark a believer fit for heaven and victorious over death.[75] Mrs. Langridge was an example of a silent victor. As she

---

invitations see: John Lancaster in: "Some Account of Sarah Peters" *AM* (March 1782), 133; "Account of a Woman who Died in the Lord" *AM* (May 1784), 249; "Some Account of the Death of Mr. John Tregellas" *AM* (May 1786), 252.

70. Wesley, "Short Account of the Death of Elizabeth Flook" *AM* (November 1790), 584.

71. Wesley, "Account of the Illness and Death of Mrs. Trimmell" *AM* (Feb. 1790), 84.

72. Wesley, "Short Account of Mr. Jonathan Simpson of Horsley upon Tyne" *AM* (September 1789), 474.

73. Wesley, "Short Account of Mr. Jonathan Simpson of Horsley upon Tyne" *AM* (September 1789), 475.

74. The phrases "fell asleep" and "rested in Jesus" were other popular ways to describe death. There were believers whose final moments were nothing less than horrific (see the example of Hugh Pue in the following pages), but these types of death were rarely reported in the magazine. Violent or difficult deaths were reserved almost exclusively for those with broken relationships with God.

75. For example, Miss Cockle's "heavenly smiles shewed the raptures of the place to which she was hastening." Wesley, "Some Account of the Last Sickness and Death of Miss Cockle" *AM* (April 1789), 187. Simon Parsons was so happy before his death that his face shone. Wesley, "Short Account of Mr. Simon Parsons" *AM* (July 1789), 358. After testifying to the grace of Christian perfection, Robert Dennis's countenance was

approached her final moments, a sudden "rapture of joy diffused new life over her dying countenance;—her eyes beamed with unusual vivacity and pleasure;—she strongly attempted to express the sentiment of admiration and bliss, which she appeared to feel; but her exertions were in vain . . . In a moment, the effort was over!"[76] Unable to communicate, she calmly closed her eyes and died triumphant in the faith.

It was difficult for some of Wesley's Anglican contemporaries to accept the victorious death accounts of the early Methodists. To begin with, many Anglicans disproved of what they perceived as an over-dependence upon feelings or "Methodist emotionalism and excessive claims for 'assurance.'"[77] Their skepticism sometimes led to unfortunate misunderstandings. When Charles Dean (a notoriously wicked man) experienced a deathbed conversion through the ministry of the Methodists, he sent for the Curate and requested the sacrament. The Curate, upon hearing Dean proclaim the "blessed change he had found" thought that Dean was delirious and refused to serve him communion "until he was more composed."[78] Furthermore, Wesley's strong association between Christian Perfection and triumphant death was problematic for many of his fellow clergymen.[79] Indeed, the Reverend Charles Simeon (1759–1836), Vicar of Holy Trinity, Cambridge, highly disapproved of "triumphant death-beds" and proclaimed, "If you should see me die, you will not see me die in that manner . . . No, triumph will not suit me till I get to heaven . . . But while I am here, I am a sinner–a redeemed sinner . . . ."[80]

---

so heavenly that his mother proclaimed, "I never saw thee so beautiful before." Wesley, "Some Account of Robert Dennis" *AM* (July 1785), 367.

76. Wesley, "Short Account of the Death of Mrs. Langridge" *AM* (February 1791), 83.

77. Rack, "Evangelical Endings," 49. There are other differences between Anglican death accounts and those of the Methodists. For example, the ideal Methodist approached death with declarations of triumph while the ideal Anglican approached death calmly and cheerfully but lacked such displays of victory and utter certainty. The final scene of Jonas Hanway is an example of a good Anglican death. Pugh, *Remarkable Occurrences in the Life of Jonas Hanway*, 164–66.

78. Wesley, "Letter CCCXCVI, From Miss H.B. to the Rev. J. Wesley" *AM* (June 1786), 340.

79. John Walsh noted that two of the most deeply felt differences between Evangelical Anglicans and Arminian Methodists was Wesley's doctrine of Christian Perfection and his teaching regarding assurance. Walsh, "Methodism at the End of the Eighteenth Century," 290.

80. Cecil, "Holy Dying," 32.

Triumph over Pain

In an era prior to modern medicine, death could bring unspeakable agony, and Wesley did not spare readers the gruesome details of rotting flesh, open wounds, coughing fits, raging fevers, or the excruciating pain brought on by unknown diseases. Hugh Pue's condition caused him to cough up large clots of blood, yet he lay sweetly resigned in the arms of redeeming love. When his worried mother asked him if he still experienced the same salvation that he preached to others, he unswervingly declared, "Glory be to God I do! Jesus is all in all."[81] His death scene was very distressing, but it was over quickly. His weary spirit took flight when a large blood clot lodged in his throat, and he was not able to cough it out. John Morgan was in so much discomfort that he wryly commented, "If I dared to complain, I might say, This is hell."[82] Despite the pain, he consistently maintained his love for God until he "quietly rested in Jesus."[83]

Despite the terrible ways death and disease effected the body, there was a prevailing confidence among the Methodists that God would not allow more suffering than the person was able to withstand. The accounts were evidence in themselves that God took a personal interest in every believer. If one were especially weak, then temptation and extreme suffering would not be allowed. Such was the case for Elizabeth Henson's mother. She proclaimed, "The enemy is constrained to withdraw; for the Lord knows my weakness, and does not suffer me to be tempted."[84] When suffering was permitted, relief was always provided. Sometimes it came in the form of divine aid. Susannah Bridgment realized that when she praised God, she did not feel any pain, and her final days were filled with hymns of praise.[85] At other times, physicians attempted to dispel the pains of death with sleeping draughts and other medicines. On more than one occasion, however, the

---

81. Wesley, "Short Account of the Death of Mr. Hugh Pue" *AM* (December 1789), 637. See also the account of Robert Dennis whose body was so wasted and full of sores that his family was afraid his backbone would come through the skin. Despite his pain, he was able to praise God with joy. Wesley, "Some Account of Robert Dennis" *AM* (July 1785), 366–68.

82. Wesley, "Account of the Death of John Morgan" *AM* (March 1783), 130.

83. Wesley, "Account of the Death of John Morgan" *AM* (March 1783), 131.

84. Wesley, "Elizabeth Henson's Account of the Death of Her Mother" *AM* (May 1785), 249.

85. Wesley, "Short Account of the Life and Death of Susannah Bridgment" *AM* (September 1787), 464.

physician's medical ministrations were rejected. Eighteen-year-old Martha Brewton refused to take any more of the sleeping drops the physician gave her because she did not want to be prevented from praising God during her final hours.[86]

Triumph over Satan

While any serious illness could be debilitating, physical discomfort had the potential to bring with it spiritual conflicts such as the temptation to be angry with God for allowing the believer to suffer. For example, Thomas Legge exclaimed upon his deathbed, "O! . . . today [the enemy] has been tempting me to be angry with, and curse God; but he is gone now."[87] Even more troubling than the temptation toward impatience or anger, however, was the possibility of a direct diabolical assault. In one of its earliest formats, the *ars moriendi* contained eleven woodcut illustrations which vividly depicted demons crouching near the bed waiting to assault the dying person in their weakest moment.[88] However, Houlbrooke observed that by the eighteenth-century references to demonic attacks had all but disappeared.[89] It was Wesley's dramatic deathbed narratives which revived this tradition. While it is difficult to determine exactly why this phenomenon reappeared in Methodist deathbed scenes, it is likely that Wesley's emphasis on triumphant death played a part in it. Cecil observed that the "triumph" was "a triumph over the devil, who was thought to be particularly active at the deathbed, either gloating over the victim who was about to fall into his clutches, or trying at the last moment to snatch a soul in the throes of doubt . . . ."[90]

Satan was certainly active at Methodist deathbeds, but the enemy's appearance at the death scene was always short lived. Every time a diabolic force appeared, it was soundly crushed. In one instance, Satan tempted Caster Garret with the thought that God had departed from him. Terrified

---

86. Hoping to encourage her, the doctor told Martha she might recover. Martha emphatically retorted, "I do not want to live." Wesley, "Short Account of Martha Brewton" *AM* (October 1787), 520.

87. Wesley, "Account of the Death of Thomas Legge" *AM* (March 1790), 136.

88. See Verhey, *Christian Art of Dying,* 110–34, for reproductions and careful descriptions of these woodcut prints.

89. Houlbrooke, *Death, Religion and the Family in England 1480–1750,* 200.

90. Cecil, "Holy Dying," 31.

at the thought, Garret cried out, "I am undone! undone! I have lost my way! The Lord is departed from me!"[91] Garret's biographer quickly reminded him that the issue was not with God, but "the enemy who wants to destroy your confidence . . . ."[92] It was not long before God spoke peace to the troubled man's soul. "God is faithful and just!" Garret declared. "Then giving a stamp with his foot; he said 'Satan! I stamp thee under my feet.'"[93] This scenario was repeated every time Satan appeared upon the scene. When Satan suggested to Martha Cook that he would have her after all, she was pointed to Christ's suffering on the cross, the promises of the Gospel, and the fact that even Christ was tempted. She suddenly looked at one place, as if she saw something invisible, and said, "Satan, I defy thee! Thou ugly monster, thou deceiver of poor souls; who would be thy servant?"[94] The night Nathaniel Norwall died, he confidently declared, "Satan, thou canst not hurt me. Thou knowest I cannot stand against thee of myself: but Christ will make thee fall before me, as Dagon fell before the ark! God is love, I know! I feel! I know that God is love!"[95]

Suffering, pain, death, and the devil were the worst imaginable manifestations of sin; however, Wesley's triumphant death scenes once again proved that God could save all people from *all* sin. Wesley acknowledged that believers exist in "frail, feeble, perishing bodies . . . but the afflictions, yea, death itself are so far from hindering the ministration of the Spirit, that they even further it, sharpen the ministers, and increase the fruit."[96] Physical pain or diabolical assaults were an unwelcome possibility of death; however, if these trials did occur, they were viewed as opportunities for

---

91. Wesley, "Short Account of the Conversion and Death of Caster Garret" *AM* (January 1787), 20.

92. Wesley, "Short Account of the Conversion and Death of Caster Garret" *AM* (January 1787), 20.

93. Wesley, "Short Account of the Conversion and Death of Caster Garret" *AM* (January 1787), 20.

94. Wesley, "Short Account of the Death of Martha Cook" *AM* (January 1791), 19.

95. Wesley, "Short Account of Nathaniel Norwall" *AM* (Feb. 1789), 75. The "great red dragon" attempted to overthrow Martha Brewton on the day she died. At the same time her bodily pain became almost unbearable. However, it was short-lived, and she testified, "Jesus has appeared and sweetened every pain." Wesley, "Short Account of Martha Brewton" *AM* (Nov. 1787), 576–77. Ann Ritson also faced sore temptations. Once, after prayer, she cried, "O pray for me; the enemy tells me that I am not ready," but, after wrestling with God in prayer, the enemy did not make any further attempts to harm her. Wesley, "Short Account of the Death of Miss Ann Ritson" *AM* (December 1788), 633.

96. Wesley, *ENNT* (2 Corinthians 4:7), 653.

greater manifestations of God's Spirit. Thus, the victorious deaths of the early Methodists sent a clear message that neither suffering, nor death, nor Satan himself could outweigh the love and grace of God.

Deathbed Testimony—A Gift to the Community

The period leading up to death was a precious time both for the dying individual and the community of faith. Wesley viewed the time surrounding death as "a season one would wish to improve to the uttermost; for then the windows of heaven are open."[97] One of the ways in which the "windows of heaven" opened was through the testimonies of the dying Methodists. A person's final testament was considered to be a ministry or a parting gift to the rest of the community. In a letter written in 1768, Wesley observed,

> S[ally Ryan] continues with you a little longer to quicken you in the way. Why should not a living Christian be exactly of the same spirit with a dying Christian; seeing the difference between her life and ours is nothing when compared to eternity? The last scene of life in dying believers is of great use to those who are about them. Here we see the reality of religion and of things eternal; and nothing has a greater tendency to solemnize the soul, and make and keep it dead to all below.[98]

Wesley's emphasis on the effectiveness of the "last scene in life" helped the dying remain an essential part of the community of faith. It placed a tremendous amount of worth upon the individual as well as highlighted the ways in which the dying contributed to the Methodist fellowship. Therefore, when an individual became too weak to attend Methodist meetings, the society brought the meeting to the bedside.[99]

The deathbed meetings proved to be especially beneficial because of the dying person's contributions. Jane Nancarrow hosted a weekly prayer meeting as she lay dying. Her biographer recalled that because of her dying witness "these meetings, while such a remarkable instance of God's

---

97. Wesley, *Letters* "To Hannah Ball" May 23, 1773 (Telford), 6:27. This was in response to Ball's account of Charles Dean's death which was published in the *AM* (June 1786), 339–40.

98. Wesley, "To Miss March" July 5, 1768 *Letters* (Telford), 5:95–96.

99. Because of Emmanuel Jowit's illness, he could not attend class meetings. Instead, he hosted public prayer-meetings at his house. Wesley, "Short Account of the Life and Death of Emmanuel Jowit" *AM* (January 1784), 24.

goodness and power was present, proved not a little useful to those who attended them. Several have been convinced, and some found peace with God through the prayers and praises offered up at these times."[100] Sarah Utley's deathbed testimony was so moving that one young man who had long been a seeker of God's grace was converted at her bedside.[101] During his illness, Robert Windsor continued with his Band meetings. He prayed, discussed his struggles, and praised God with them; it was a great source of encouragement to all involved. When the Band members gathered around the bedside for their last meeting, Windsor was too weak to say anything but "Pray, pray."[102] He slipped from this world into the next when, without the least struggle or groan, he fell asleep. Being a part of these final scenes helped fortify fellow society members in their confidence that sin could be fully conquered, and it prepared them for their own deaths. After observing Mrs. Dawson's death, her deathbed reporter asserted, "Her death was a means of strengthening my Faith. I was enabled to believe that sin should not again find a place in my heart; and that my God would be with *me* also in the dark valley."[103]

Furthermore, no one wanted to miss out on the gift of a saint's final words, blessings, or parting prayers. This is partly due to the fact noted earlier that dying believers were thought to be closest to God; however, it was also because eighteenth-century Methodists believed the words and prayers of the dying held special power and had continued ramifications even after their death.[104] In a letter to Mary Savage, Wesley wrote, "Right precious in the sight of the Lord is the death of his saints! And I believe many of the blessings which we receive are in answer to their dying prayers."[105] This belief caused bystanders like those around the saintly Mrs. Norman's bed to beg for her "departing prayers and blessing."[106] It seems that the dying

100. Wesley, "Account of the Death of Jane Nancarrow" *AM* (April 1790), 191.
101. Wesley, "Account of the Death of Sarah Utley" *AM* (October 1784), 531.
102. Wesley, "Short Account of Robert Windsor" *AM* (February 1791), 78.
103. Wesley, "Account of the Death of Mrs. Dawson, of Dublin" *AM* (June 1783), 305.
104. This was a long-held view. Jeremy Taylor admonished that the sick should give good counsel, help family and friends to reconcile, and "charm them into Religion by the authority of a dying Person; because the last words of a dying Man are like the tooth of a wounded Lion, making a deeper impression in the agony than in the most vigorous strength." Taylor, *Rules and Exercises of Holy Dying*, 177.
105. Wesley, *Letters* "To Mrs. Savage" August 31, 1771 (Telford), 5:276.
106. Mrs. Norman had welcomed both Wesley and Whitefield into her home during their early preaching days. Wesley, "An Account of Mrs. Norman" *AM* (May 1789), 245.

graciously accepted their role as intercessors for the community. They selflessly dedicated part of their final season to petition on behalf of others even though they knew they were not likely to see the results of their supplications. Trusting that God would honor their dying requests, Methodists such as Elizabeth Shacklock told her husband, "The prayers I have put up to God for you, will not be forgotten. I trust you will reap the benefit when I am in my grave."[107]

Christopher Middleton's account contained a prime example of a dying prayer. First, Middleton prayed for all those around him that they would be kept from the spirit of the world and that they would be blessed in their work. Next, he called for God's blessing upon those who attended him in his final illness. Then he interceded for his parents, their children, and their children's children; he asked that God use any means to ensure none of them would perish. The Methodists were next in line for Middleton's petitions. He requested that the preachers would be filled with the Spirit and that God would provide "nursing fathers" and "nursing mothers" to guide the Societies. Finally, he shifted his attention to all the church and for the whole world asking that God would hasten his kingdom.[108]

The final words and blessings offered by the dying also had heightened efficiency on those around the bedside. For example, when William Adams spoke at the last quarterly meeting he attended, his "words seemed like fire, that flowed from a heart, glowing with the love and Jesus,"[109] and saints and sinners alike "formed many resolutions to seek God more earnestly than ever" after they witnessed his dying triumphs.[110] After observing Mary Thomas's last scene, her biographer claimed to be blessed with a stronger yearning for God and wrote, "I feel such desires in my soul after God . . . . I feel there is not a moment's time to spare . . . . It is no matter to me, how I was an hour ago. Is my soul now waiting upon God?"[111] Mrs. Walker "preached Jesus" to all who called on her, and never had her observers seen such an instance of God's glory and power.[112] Other dying Methodists humbly offered the gift of heavenly wisdom to their bystanders. Isaac Kilby had little

107. Wesley, "Account of Mrs. Elizabeth Shacklock" *AM* (November 1789), 520.

108. Wesley, "Short Account of the Life and Death of Mr. Christopher Middleton" *AM* (May 1787), 237.

109. Wesley, "Account of William Adams" *AM* (March 1784), 140.

110. Wesley, "Account of William Adams" *AM* (April 1784), 194.

111. Wesley, "Some Account of the Death of Mary Thomas" *AM* (January 1782), 22.

112. Wesley, "Some Account of the Death of Mrs. Walker" *AM* (May 1788), 244.

strength to speak, but when he did "his words were strangely powerful; just as if they came from one, who was now before the throne of glory."[113] His words "were full of divine wisdom, expressing a deep sense of the presence and mercy of God, and of his own unworthiness."[114] Sometimes, a verbalized testimony was not even necessary for the surrounding witnesses to receive a final blessing. The place where Martha Brewton lay was filled with such an extraordinary measure of the divine presence that her uncle claimed he could not go near her bed without feeling the power of God.[115]

Deathbed Testimony—A Final Testament to Christian Perfection

The Methodists were aware that their deaths were their most powerful legacy, and they wanted to leave no doubt among those they left behind about the extent and power of God's grace.[116] Therefore, it is no surprise that eighty of the deathbed accounts published in the *Arminian Magazine* contained clear testimonies to the grace of Christian perfection. Some, like the account of Mary Parkinson, had been entirely sanctified years before her death. She testified that nine years prior to her final illness, "her soul was filled with the pure love of God," and her manner of death fully supported her testimony.[117] In all her illness, she never complained but rather gave thanks in everything and prayed without ceasing. Her final words were: "I see the gate of heaven open to receive me; and hear the Lord say, Come up, my love, my dove, my undefiled! He assures me I shall enter in; seeing my robes are washed, and made white in the blood of the Lamb. I shall soon mount up as on the wings of an eagle, and be where pain and sickness, sorrow and weeping shall be no more!"[118] Saying this, she fell asleep in Jesus.

In contrast to Mary Parkinson, Mr. King did not experience the grace of entire sanctification until he was struck with the illness that led to his death. He admitted that he had "lived below his privileges," yet his

113. Wesley, "Some Account of the Death of Isaac Kilby" *AM* (January 1782), 22.
114. Wesley, "Some Account of the Death of Isaac Kilby" *AM* (January 1782), 23.
115. Wesley, "Short Account of Martha Brewton" *AM* (Nov. 1787), 578.
116. Hannah Wood instructed her son, "If you ever have a family, tell the children they had a grandmother that feared God, and found the comforts of it on her death-bed." Wesley "Some Account of Mrs. Hannah Wood" *AM* (July 1785), 362.
117. Wesley, "Short Account of Mary Parkinson" *AM* (May 1786), 249.
118. Wesley, "Short Account of Mary Parkinson" *AM* (May 1786), 249.

testimony of Christian perfection was just as strong as his counterpart.[119] He gave witness to the "Sun of Righteousness" filling his soul with uninterrupted happiness and triumphed over all temptations.[120] "Can this be dying!" he wondered? "It is like going to sleep . . . My dear friends, it is not for want of matter, but want of breath that I do not continue speaking. I am full and abound! O the love of Christ! O the love of Christ! If anyone had told me, I could not have conceived what I feel."[121] His last words were "Sanctified by faith!"[122] He then departed to be with the one he loved. Whether a believer was perfected years prior to death or just moments before the end of life, the dying testimonies stood as proof that God could indeed save from all sin. After hearing Jan Ogilby bear a strong testimony of the power of God in saving her from all sin, one bystander declared, "This . . . confirms the doctrine I have just now delivered; and it gives me abundant satisfaction to see and hear one just on the verge of eternity, and nothing but skin and bone, witness that God's promises are fulfilled even at this day."[123]

Perhaps most intriguing are the ninety accounts that Wesley published which utilized the language of perfection without a specific claim to this work of grace. To clarify what is meant by the "language of perfection," it is helpful to consider a list of questions Wesley asked Sarah Ryan to test her degree of holiness. In this letter he asked,

> "Do you find no interruption or abatement at any time of your joy in the Lord? Do you continually see God, and that without any cloud or darkness or mist between? Do you pray without ceasing, without ever being diverted from it by anything inward or outward? Are you never hindered by any person or thing? by the power or subtlety of Satan, or by the weakness or disorders of the body pressing down the soul? Can you be thankful for everything without exception? And do you feel all working together for good? Do you do nothing great or small, merely to please yourself? Do you feel no touch of any desire or affection but what springs from the pure love of God? Do you speak no words but from a principle of love and under the guidance of His Spirit? O how I long to find

---

119. Wesley, "Short Account of the Death of Mr. King" *AM* (March 1789), 126.
120. Wesley, "Short Account of the Death of Mr. King" *AM* (March 1789), 126.
121. Wesley, "Short Account of the Death of Mr. King" *AM* (March 1789), 129.
122. Wesley, "Short Account of the Death of Mr. King" *AM* (March 1789), 129.
123. Wesley, "Short Account of the Life and Death of Jan Ogilby" *AM* (November 1785), 576.

you unblameable in all things, and holy as He that hath called you is holy!"[124]

Much like the four questions most commonly utilized at the deathbed, these questions revealed Wesley's criteria for a holy heart. That is, to answer these questions in the affirmative—to enjoy uninterrupted happiness, unclouded communion with God, to pray continually, to triumph over Satan and a broken body, to be grateful in all situations, to trust in God's goodness, to be unselfish and resigned to God in all things, to act and speak only out of a principle of divine love—is what is meant by the language of holiness.

With Wesley's longstanding record of "editing" the work of others to make it compatible with his own ideology, there is little doubt that he would have manipulated these ninety accounts to include at least some utterance of a testimony to perfecting grace if he deemed it necessary. The fact that Wesley did not attempt to make every Methodist narrative conform to this pattern (or publish only the ones which did) heavily implied that by using the language of Christian perfection the reality of this grace was already present. For example, Mary Rounsevill was never credited with a proclamation of perfection, but she never lost her peace, was always happy, and fully resigned to God's will.[125] The elderly Richard Russel's account also contained no proclamation of entire sanctification, but he was described as "an ornament of religion" and "steady and uniform in his Christian conversation." He overcame his enemies with love, sweetly reproved sin, praised God continually, and had complete control over all his passions.[126] The fact that Wesley admonished the reader to "Go and do likewise," at the end of Russel's narrative indicated Wesley's approval of Russel's life and death.

If a person was well-respected and well-known within the community, a reiteration of their spiritual state was not necessary. Such was the case of John Nelson who died too suddenly to give a personal testimony. The author of the account, however, identified Nelson as a "holy" man and noted his key involvement in the spread of religion.[127] The evidence indicated in

---

124. Wesley, *Letters* "To Mrs. Ryan" November 22, 1757 (Telford), 3:241. Also republished in the *Arminian Magazine* "Letter CCXI" (January 1782), 46–47.

125. Wesley, "Short Account of God's Dealings with Mary Rounsevill" *AM* (December 1787), 633.

126. Wesley, "Account of the Death of Mr. Richard Russel" *AM* (December 1788), 630–31.

127. Others must have agreed with the author's assessment; Nelson was mourned so

the ninety accounts revealed that Wesley accepted a witness to Christian perfection given by dying deportment just as readily as he accepted verbal testimonies to this work of grace. After all, when the final moments closed in, the radiance of a purified soul was at its zenith. Words were not necessary to describe what was blatantly obvious to those surrounding the bedside; for, nothing could hide the unmistakable beauty of a purified soul as it took flight.

John Wesley's Death—A Testimony to Holiness

Much ado has been made over the happy deaths of the early Methodists. A physician once made the observation to Charles Wesley, "Most people die for the fear of dying; but I never met with such people as yours. They are none of them afraid of death, but calm, and patient, and resigned to the last."[128] Wesley highlighted the deathbed scenes of his people because he believed that they supported his doctrine of Christian perfection and his claim that none would die without first being made "ripe for glory." In the years preceding Wesley's death, his doctrine of perfection was placed under scrutiny because Wesley never clearly testified to experiencing this work of grace himself. However, the recognition that Wesley utilized the deathbed accounts to tease out evidence of entire sanctification without requiring a direct testimony of its attainment may shed some new light on his own life and death. It is clear from the questions posed to dying Methodists that Wesley believed the following signs upon the deathbed were indicative of a perfected heart—even if a clear declaration of full salvation was not made: 1) acceptance of death or the dying role, 2) a peaceful, happy soul, 3) freedom from the fear of death, 4) the desire or willingness to die, 5) triumph over deathbed temptations, and 6) the marks of holiness such as love, gratitude, uninterrupted happiness, resignation to God's will, victory over sin, and a heart overflowing with praise. Since Wesley applied this criterion to his followers to determine the state of their souls; it is only fair to examine Wesley's own dying experience with the same benchmarks.

Wesley appeared to accept the reality of his impending demise even before his final illness. On his eighty-sixth birthday, he wondered if his slow

---

deeply, that his remains were attended through the street by thousands of singing and weeping people. Wesley, "Another Account of the Death of John Nelson" *AM* (November 1788), 574.

128. Wesley, *Manuscript Journal*, May 4, 1741.

decline signaled an imminent death, but declared it made little difference to him. "Whether or not this [the pains of old age] is sent to me warning that I am shortly to quit this tabernacle, I do not know. But be it one way or the other, I have only to say,

> My remnant of Days
> I spend to his praise
> Who died the whole world to redeem:
> Be they many or few,
> My days are his due,
> And they all are devoted to Him!"[129]

The aging patriarch conveyed the same type of acceptance in a letter to Ezekiel Cooper written a month before Wesley's death. "My Dear Brother," Wesley wrote, "Those that desire to write or say anything to me have no time to lose; for time has shaken me by the hand and death is not far behind. But I have reason to be thankful for the time that is past...."[130] When it became evident that he was gravely ill, Wesley quietly assumed the dying role even while those attending him attempted to bid for more time by sending for medical help. When Dr. Whitehead arrived, Wesley made light of their concerns. "Doctor," he said, "they are more afraid than hurt."[131] As his condition worsened, Wesley's attendants wanted to call for a second opinion in hopes of prolonging the inevitable, but Wesley waived off the suggestion. "I am perfectly satisfied, and will not have any one else," he resolved.[132] He was resigned and willing to die even if his followers were not yet ready to relinquish him.

It appeared at first that Wesley would not be able to leave a final testimony. He was so lethargic in the beginning of his decline that Elizabeth Ritchie pleaded with God—not to spare his life—but to allow Wesley's followers to "at least receive his dying charges, and enjoy the comfort . . . of hearing him seal, with his latest breath, the blessed truths we had long been accustomed to receive from God through him."[133] She was not disappointed. Three days prior to his death, Wesley's health rallied, and he had strength enough to examine his niece Sally about her spiritual condition,

---

129. Wesley, *Journal* June 28, 1788 (BE), 24:97.

130. Wesley, *Letters* "To Ezekiel Cooper, of Philadelphia" February 1, 1791 (Telford), 8:259.

131. Ritchie, "Handwritten Account of John Wesley's Last Days and Death," 6.

132. Ritchie, "Handwritten Account of John Wesley's Last Days and Death," 12.

133. Ritchie, "Handwritten Account of John Wesley's Last Days and Death," 7–8.

speak parting words to those around the bedside, and periodically break out in hymns of praise. His repertoire included hymns from the Methodist collection such as "Till glad I lay this body down, Thy servant, Lord, attend," "And can it be," "All glory to God in the sky," and "I the chief of sinners am, but Jesus died for me."[134] He returned consistently to Isaac Watts's hymn,

> I'll praise my Maker while I've breath,
> And when my voice is lost in death,
> Praise shall employ my nobler powers;
> My days of praise shall ne'er be past,
> While life or thought or being last,
> Or immortality endures.[135]

When Wesley's strength failed him, he called others to the bedside to "pray and praise" in his stead.[136]

Wesley had long been free from the fear of death. In 1753, he became so ill that he believed he might die. Unshaken, he calmly sat down and penned his own epitaph to "prevent vile panegyric."[137] Wesley faced death again after falling ill at the Bristol Conference in 1783 but passed through the threat with remarkable ease. As Wesley lay dying of his final illness, he was too weak to speak for any length of time. Therefore, to communicate the state of his soul, he referred to the brush with death he encountered in 1783. "There is no need for more," he murmured. "When at Bristol, my words were: I the chief of sinners am, But Jesus died for me." "Is this the present language of your heart, and do you now feel as you then did?" he was asked. Wesley replied with a simple, "Yes."[138]

The day before he died Wesley desired to give a final testimony of his faith; however, he was so weak the bystanders could not understand his attempts to communicate. Ritchie recorded Wesley's struggle:

> Finding we could not understand what he said, he paused a little, and then, with all the remaining strength he had, he cried out, 'The best of all is, God is with us.' Then, as if to assert the faithfulness of our promise keeping Jehovah, and comfort the hearts of his weeping friends, lifting up his dying arm in token of victory and raising

---

134. Ritchie, "Handwritten Account of John Wesley's Last Days and Death," 8–9, 10, 12–13, 14–15.

135. Ritchie, "Handwritten Account of John Wesley's Last Days and Death," 14.

136. Ritchie, "Handwritten Account of John Wesley's Last Days and Death," 16.

137. Wesley, *Journal* November 26, 1753 (BE), 20:482.

138. Ritchie, "Handwritten Account of John Wesley's Last Days and Death," 9–10.

TRIUMPHANT DEATH

his feeble voice with a holy triumph not to be expressed again repeated the heart reviving words, 'The best of all God is with us!'[139]

After this point, Wesley only spoke short phrases, but they were filled with gratitude for God's grace and for the kindness of those who attended him.[140] While his spirit continued to glorify God, his weak flesh failed him. He attempted to sing Watts's hymn of praise, but could only manage the words, "I'll praise—I'll praise—!"[141] On Wednesday morning, March 2, 1791, Wesley uttered his final word: "Farewell!"[142] It was a fitting end for the Father of Methodism; he did not need to say more. His witness had been sealed by the testimony of his holy life and triumphant death. He had found the "one thing" he had sought—"the way to heaven—how to land safe on that happy shore."[143]

---

139. Ritchie, "Handwritten Account of John Wesley's Last Days and Death," 19–20.

140. For instance, when someone wet his lips he declared, "We thank Thee, O Lord, for these and all Thy mercies; bless the Church and King: grant us truth and peace, through Jesus Christ our Lord now and for ever." Ritchie, "Handwritten Account of John Wesley's Last Days and Death," 21.

141. Ritchie, "Handwritten Account of John Wesley's Last Days and Death," 22.

142. Ritchie, "Handwritten Account of John Wesley's Last Days and Death," 24.

143. Wesley, *Preface to Sermons* (BE), 1:104–5.

CONCLUSION

UNTIL THE RISE OF modern medicine, death was an ever-present part of everyday life. This was especially true of eighteenth-century England; mortality rates were high and infectious diseases seemed to strike without warning. The unpredictability of death was often a source of profound anxiety, and John Wesley, himself, grappled with the fear of death. Wesley was convinced "the cause of [his] uneasiness was unbelief," and he spent years searching for a solution to his spiritual angst. Wesley finally found the answer to his problem when he met Peter Böhler in 1738, and Wesley experienced "a true, living faith" that set him free from his fear of death.[1] Although the "sin of fear" no longer plagued him, the motif of death continued to play a significant role in Wesley's theology.[2] He discovered the value of the *ars moriendi* tradition through Jeremy Taylor's work, *The Rule and Exercises of Holy Dying*. The holy dying tradition taught that, no matter how long one lives, life is short, and holy living is best encouraged by keeping the end of life in view. Wesley embraced the notion that the secret to dying well was living well, and he set out to craft a theology which addressed the realities of spiritual, physical, and eternal death.

The practical emphasis of the holy living, holy dying tradition fit well within the whole of Wesley's theology. However, he distinguished himself from his theological predecessors when he exchanged a more gradual understanding of justification and regeneration with his newly discovered conception of free grace. The reinterpretation of justifying and regenerating grace had profound ramifications on Wesley's ministry to the dying—especially to those who had fallen out of favor with the Anglican Church or who were looked upon by Calvinists as unworthy reprobates. Unlike those

---

1. Wesley, *Journal* May 24, 1738 (BE), 18:247.
2. Wesley, *Journal* January 24, 1738 (BE), 18:211.

in the holy dying tradition who were reluctant to promise God's love and acceptance to dying sinners, Wesley offered real hope of salvation and assurance to the worst offenders. He championed the doctrine of free grace, and therefore, bypassed the extended process of conversion called for by Jeremy Taylor and others within the tradition. Wesley viewed the instance of death as an opportunity to proclaim the free grace of God, and he utilized the deathbed and gallows as the proving ground for his claim that God's grace was free *for all* and *in all*.

The issue of death brought to light the nuances within Wesley's theology of holiness and grace. On the one hand, he affirmed that the transformation of the human soul from a state of sinfulness to holiness required an endowment of God's free grace. On the other hand, like those in the holy living, holy dying tradition, Wesley affirmed the cooperant nature of grace. The path of holiness was marked by a gradual death to sin and growth in grace. However, just as the moment of death inevitability ended the dying process, so too, must the process of dying to the sinful nature be brought to a close. Wesley reasoned that if the process of sanctification was like the process of dying, then the reception of sanctifying graces could be granted in an instant by the free grace of God—much like the sudden release of the soul from the disease ridden body. Thus, the process of dying and death itself was emblematic of Wesley's conjunctive theology of grace (both free and cooperant) especially as it informed his understanding of the temporal dimensions of sanctification.

Wesley utilized the deathbed narratives of his followers to further his theological presuppositions. Unsurprisingly, the accounts he published in the *Arminian Magazine* overwhelmingly emphasized his theology of entire sanctification. Through the careful selection of deathbed accounts, Wesley not only provided a pattern for the Methodists to follow, but he also utilized dying testimonies to confirm the validity of his followers' spiritual experiences. Death, therefore, was not only an important theme in Wesley's writings but was the final seal to the entirety of his theology of grace and holiness.

APPENDIX

Death Accounts in the *Arminian Magazine*
1778 to Feb. 1791

	Name of Deceased	Age	Date of Death	Publication Date
1	Arminius	49	Oct. 19, 1609	Jan. 1778
2	Martin Luther	62	Feb. 18, 1546	June 1778
3	Bernard Gilpin	66	Mar. 4, 1583	Sept. 1778
4	"Old Gentleman"		1747–1748?	Nov. 1778
5	William Holmes	--	1747?	Nov. 1778
6	John Jane	--	1750?	May 1779
7	Bishop Bedell	--	1642	July 1779
8	John Donne	--	Mar. 31, 1631	Sept. 1779
9	Archbishop Usher	--	--	Nov. 1779
10	Jane (Westfal) Allen	--	1778?	Dec. 1779
11	Preacher Seccombe	--	Oct. 10, 1759	May 1780
12	Robert Brewer		Dec. 1760	Aug. 1780
13	Sarah Brough	--	--	Nov. 1780
14	Gregory Lopez	54	July 20, 1596	Concluded Dec. 1780
15	Sr. Gervase Ellwis	--	Nov. 1615	Dec. 1780
16	Jane Muncy	--	1741	Mar. 1781
17	Sarah Whiskin	--	Jan. 25, 1742	Apr. 1781
18	John Woolley	14	Feb. 1742	May 1781
19	Susannah Wesley	--	July 30, 1742	June 1781

APPENDIX

	Name of Deceased	Age	Date of Death	Publication Date
20	Alice Benden	--	Sixteenth-century excerpt from Foxe's Martyrs	Aug. 1781
21	Charles Perronet	--	Aug. 12, 1776	Oct. 1781
22	Julius Palmer	24	July 16, 1556	Nov. 1781
23	Thomas Eden	60	Apr. 27, 1781	Dec. 1781
24	Elizabeth Marsh	--	1744	Dec. 1781
25	"Young Man"	--	1744	Dec. 1781
26	Child	4	1744	Dec. 1781
27	Mary Cook	--	1745	Jan. 1782
28	Mary Thomas	--	1745	Jan. 1782
29	Isaac Kilby	--	1745	Jan. 1782
30	Monsieur Isaac Lefevre	--	--	Jan. 1782
31	Child of Mrs. Nowers	4 or 5	1746?	Feb. 1782
32	Mr. Clayton - Rector of Wensley	"Old"	1746	Feb. 1782
33	Francis Coxon	--	1747	Feb. 1782
34	Peter Mauru	--	Seventeenth Century	Feb. 1782
35	Patrick Hamilton	--	1527	Feb. 1782
36	Sarah Peters	--	Nov. 13, 1748	Mar. 1782
37	Account of Sarah Peters: John Lancaster	--	Oct. 28, 1748	Mar. 1782
38	Account of Sarah Peters: Thomas Atkins	19	1748	Mar. 1782
39	Account of Sarah Peters: Thomas Thompson	--	1748	Mar. 1782
40	Account of Sarah Peters: John Roberts	--	1748	Mar. 1782
41	Account of Sarah Peters: William Gardiner	--	1748	Mar. 1782
42	Account of Sarah Peters: Sarah Cunningham	--	1748	Mar. 1782
43	Account of Sarah Peters: Samuel Chapman	--	1748	Mar. 1782
44	Remarkable Deaths, Cont.: Francis Butts	--	1748	Mar. 1782

APPENDIX

	Name of Deceased	Age	Date of Death	Publication Date
45	Remarkable Deaths, Cont.: William Turner	--	1748	Mar. 1782
46	Remarkable Deaths, Cont.: Mr. Glanvile	--	1748	Mar. 1782
47	Mr. Wishart	--	1546	Mar. 1782
48	Unnamed Child	6	--	Apr. 1782
49	Victims of the Plague	--	--	Apr. 1782
50	Robert Wilkinson	--	Dec. 8, 1780	May 1782
51	Joseph Taylor	"Very old man"	--	May 1782
52	Ann Hall	--	Letter written Feb. 12, 1782	May 1782
53	Samuel Massey	--	Oct. 31, 1761	June 1782
54	John Warrick	10	--	Sept. 1782
55	Mr. Marshal's daughter	11	--	Sept. 1782
56	A Buss, a Gardiner, of Rochester	--	Dec. 19, 1777	Sept. 1782
57	Miss Hatton's Sister	--	1767	October 1782
58	Joseph Lee	--	1768	November 1782
59	Two sudden deaths: A notorious sinner	--	1782	November 1782
60	The second sudden death: Gentleman's gardener	--	1782	November 1782
61	John Furz's Wife	--	--	December 1782
62	Richard Blackwell	--	1767	December 1782
63	Mrs. Doyle	--	1767	December 1782
64	J. Burley's Son	7	1767	December 1782
65	Richard Boardman	--	--	Jan. 1783
66	Hon. Fr. N--t, Son to the late ---	--	1692	Jan. 1783, Feb. 1783, Mar. 1783
67	Ugolino's Children - A Florentine Count	--	Thirteenth century	Jan. 1783
68	Sister Smith - not yet deceased but on her deathbed	--	1767	Jan. 1783
69	"Sister" Yarner	--	1758	Feb. 1783
70	Elizabeth Dunting	13	1767	Feb. 1783

APPENDIX

	Name of Deceased	Age	Date of Death	Publication Date
71	Ann Belton	18	--	Feb. 1783
72	Ann Dunn	--	1767	Mar. 1783
73	John Morgan	--	1782	Mar. 1783
74	John Morgan	--	1782	Mar. 1783
75	John P.	--	1767	Apr. 1783
76	Jonathan Handy	--	July 25, 1759	Apr. 1783
77	Elizabeth King	13	100 years ago	Apr. 1783
78	William Stafford	--	1765	May 1738
79	Two Sisters: Agnes & Johan Payne	--	1560	May 1783
80	Mr. B. - a dissenting minister	--	176?-?	June 1783
81	Mrs. Dawson of Dublin	--	--	June 1783
82	Charles Greenwood	--	Feb. 20, 1783	June, July 1783
83	Mrs. Oddie	--	--	July 1783
84	Dr Dodd	--	1777	July 1783
85	A Drunkard	--	--	Aug. 1783
86	Elizabeth Booth	--	1783	Aug. 1783
87	Benjamin Wood	--	1783	Aug. 1783
88	R. Boardman's Wife	--	1769	Sept. 1783
89	Cyrus	--	--	Sept. 1783
90	Martha Thompson	--	--	Sept., Oct. 1783
91	Mary Goffe	--	June 4, 1691	Oct. 1783
92	William Blake's Wife	--	1780	Nov. 1783
93	Rev. Mr. Mompesson	--	1666	Nov. 1783
94	Mrs. Crask	--	1783	Dec. 1783
95	Voltaire	--	1778	Dec. 1783
96	Mr. J. Guildford	--	1777	Jan. 1784
97	Emmanuel Jowit	--	--	Jan. 1784
98	John Hatton	8	Dec. 31, 1773	--
99	J.V.	--	--	Feb. 1784
100	Thomas Payne	--	Jan. 6, 1783	Feb. 1784
101	William Adams	20	Dec. 3, 1779	Feb., Mar., Apr. 1784
102	Woman from Whitchurch, Hampshire		Nov. 7, 1783	May 1784

APPENDIX

	Name of Deceased	Age	Date of Death	Publication Date
103	John Duncalf - a man who hands and legs rotten off.	22	--	Apr., May 1784
104	Victims of the Plague at Eyam, in Derbyshire	--	--	May 1784
105	Unknown man	--	--	June 1784
106	Atheist	--	--	July 1784
107	Sarah Utley	--	1784	Oct. 1784
108	Andrees Zekerman - His dying speech at his execution	24	--	Oct. 1784
109	Two Children	Son age 2 1/2 and Daughter age 6	--	Nov. 1784
110	Beautiful Lady from France	--	1599	Nov. 1784
111	R. Roe	--	Sept. 15, 1782	Dec. 1784
112	Mrs. Margaret Baxter	--	June 14, 1681	Dec. 1784
113	William Burton	--	1783	Dec. 1784
114	John Haim; preached	78	Aug. 18, 1784	Jan. 1785
115	Martha Rogers	29	--	Jan., Feb., Mar., Apr., May, June, July 1785
116	Mrs. S. Standering	--	Oct. 1784	Feb. 1785
117	Unnamed mid-wife to the parish	67–68	?	Feb. 1785
118	"Poor Negroes"	--	1771	Feb. 1785
119	Unnamed "sister"	--	1780	Mar. 1785
120	John Ellis	--	1772	Mar. 1785
121	Mr. D. Jenkins	"Old"	Jan. 1772	Mar. 1785
122	Thomas Slater	--	August 15, 1783	Apr. 1785
123	T. Cappiter; preacher	--	Feb. 16, 1772	Apr. 1785
124	James Ashton and his companions	--	1778	Apr. 1785
125	Ann Roylands	19	1784	May, June 1785

APPENDIX

	Name of Deceased	Age	Date of Death	Publication Date
126	Elizabeth Henson's Mother	--	Nov. 26, 1784	May 1785
127	Hannah Wood	48	1784	June, July 1785
128	Robert Dennis	19	1784(?)	June, July 1785
129	Sarah Powell	28	May 21, 1784	Aug., Sept. 1785
130	Mr. Robinson, Chairman of the Spiritual Court	--	--	Aug. 1785
131	John Syms	--	--	Aug. 1785
132	Thomas Wadsworth	46	Oct. 29, 1676	Sept. 1785
133	Richard Wavel	72	Dec. 19, 1705	Sept. 1785
134	Michael Onions	16	1785	Oct. 1785
135	Samuel Lee	64	--	Nov. 1785
136	George Fawnes	--	Dec. 1685	Nov. 1785
137	Jan Ogilby	39	Jan. 11, 1772	Nov. 1785
138	Jedidiah Buxton	"Old Man"	1778?	Nov. 1785
139	Alderman Parker	80	1785	Dec. 1785
140	Mary Crosdall	25	1785	Dec. 1785
141	Three Men	--	1779?	Dec. 1785
142	Ferdinand, 4th King of Spain	--	Sept. 7, 1312	Dec. 1785
143	John Henry	--	1785	Jan. 1786
144	John Nelson's grand daughter	16	--	Jan. 1786
145	Sir Philip Sidney	--	1586?	Jan. 1786
146	Callistus	Fictional Account	(From *Callistus; or, The Man of Fashion. And Sophronius; or The Country Gentleman. In Three Dialogues. By Thomas Mulso.*)	Jan., Feb., Mar., Apr., May, June, July, August, Sept., Oct., Nov., Dec. 1786; Jan., Feb, Mar., Apr., May, June, July, Aug., Sept., Oct., Nov. Dec. 1787

APPENDIX

	Name of Deceased	Age	Date of Death	Publication Date
147	Sophronius	Fictional Account	(From *Callistus; or, The Man of Fashion. And Sophronius; or The Country Gentleman. In Three Dialogues. By Thomas Mulso.*)	Jan., Feb., Mar., Apr., May, June, July, August, Sept., Oct., Nov., Dec. 1786; Jan., Feb, Mar., Apr., May, June, July, Aug., Sept., Oct., Nov. Dec. 1787
148	Howell Harris	--	July 21, 1773	Feb. 1786
149	Mr. Pigot	--	1773	Feb. 1786
150	Thomas Wright	12	--	Feb. 1786
151	Mrs. S. Bumsted	--	1773	Mar. 1786
152	Catherine Lions	--	1773	Mar. 1786
153	Mary Queen of Scotts	--	Feb. 1587	Mar., Apr. 1786
154	M. D.	--	1784	Apr. 1786
155	Lord---	--	--	Apr. 1786
156	Sarah Scools	--	--	Apr. 1786
157	Henry Haddick, Captain of a Custom -House Shallop	--	1783	Mar., Apr. 1786
158	Mary Parkinson	50	1785	May 1786
159	John Tregellas	21	1785	May 1786
160	Mrs. Crowder	--	--	June 1786
161	Charles Dean	--	Letter written 1773	June 1786
162	Christopher Peacock	33	Feb. 15, 1786	July, Oct., Nov. Dec. 1786
163	J.B. Kirkheaton	--	--	July 1786
164	Elizabeth Murlin	75	Jan. 18, 1786	Aug. 1786
165	Three Malefactors: John Steptoe; Richard Hemmings; William Crisps -Executed at Reading	--	Mar. 25, 1786	Aug. 1786
166	S. Chaster	--	--	Aug. 1786
167	Richard the First	--	--	Aug. 1786
168	Thomas Ramsey	--	Nov. 20, 1784	Sept. 1786

APPENDIX

	Name of Deceased	Age	Date of Death	Publication Date
169	H. Booth	--	--	Sept. 1786
170	King Alfred	--	--	Oct. 1786
171	Miss Barham	26	Apr. 7, 1784?	Nov., Dec. 1786
172	Thomas Firmin	66	Dec. 20, 1697	May, Jun., Jul., Aug., Sept., Oct., Nov., Dec. 1786
173	Christopher Middleton	--	--	Jan., Feb., Mar., Apr., May 1787
174	Caster Garret	--	Nov. 27, 1785	Jan. 1787
175	Elizabeth Frances of Birmingham	--	July 17, 1785	Jan. 1787
176	A Daring Sinner	--	1786?	Jan. 1787
177	Yorkshireman	--	1786?	Jan. 1787
178	Thomas Lee	--	1786	Feb. 1787
179	Mr. Hadden, Innkeeper	--	1773	Feb. 1787
180	Mrs. Moore	--	1774	Feb. 1787
181	Rev. Mr. Rochette and 3 Noblemen executed at Thoulouse	--	Feb. 19, 1762	Feb. 1787
182	Mrs. Vaughan	55	Oct. 1, 1772	Mar. 1787
183	Thomas Thompson	70	Nov. 29, 1785	Mar. 1787
184	Ann Nichols	31	Dec. 15, 1786	Mar. 1787
185	Ann Wright	--	Apr. 27, 1786	Apr. 1787
186	Mrs. Peck	--	1786	Apr. 1787
187	Sarah Butler	17	May 10, 1786	May 1787
188	Mrs. Spencer	--	Jan. 16, 1787	June 1787
189	Sarah Bulgin	29	--	June, July, Aug. 1787
190	Samuel Tapper	73	Mar. 3, 1708	June 1787
191	Francis Spira	--	--	July, Aug., Sept., Oct., Nov., Dec. 1787
192	Susannah Bridgment	--	June 15, 1786	Sept. 1787
193	Martha Brewton	18	Jan. 30, 1787	Oct., Nov. 1787
194	Robert Calverley	--	1787	Dec. 1787
195	Mary Rounsevill	87	May 3, 1887	Dec. 1787

APPENDIX

	Name of Deceased	Age	Date of Death	Publication Date
196	Edward Avison - Organist of St. Nicholas	--	1776	Jan. 1788
197	Jane Cumberland	--	Mar. 7, 1787	Jan. 1788
198	Thomas Spear	7	Jan. 15, 1785	Jan. 1788
199	John Lancaster Atkins - 19yrs Gardner - 50yrs Thompson	--	--	Feb. 1788
200	Andrew Dunlap	--	1787	Feb. 1788
201	John Wynn	24	Apr. 4, 1785	Feb., Mar. 1788
202	E.R. (Who appeared to be dying)	--	Letter written June 24, 1777	Mar. 1788
203	Mrs. Walker; late Mrs. Clapham	--	1787	Apr., May 1788
204	Mary Edmonson	--	--	June 1788
205	Joseph Symes	39	Nov. 17, 1787	June 1788
206	Mr. Anderson	--	--	July 1788
207	Hannah Kay	--	--	July 1788
208	Account of Silas Told - Mr. Gibson	--	--	Aug. 1788
209	Account of Silas Told - Mr. Slocomb	--	--	Aug. 1788
210	Account of Silas Told - Silas Told	68	Dec. 1779	Aug. 1788
211	Charles Wesley	81	Mar. 29, 1788	Aug. 1788
212	Mrs. M'Donald - Servant at the Foundry	--	1778	Aug. 1788
213	William Quayle	9	Sept. 24, 1787	Aug. 1788
214	John's Cousin	--	--	Sept. 1788
215	Phebe Moses	--	Feb. 12, 1787	Sept. 1788
216	Rebecca Thornton	15	Mar. 1, 1787	Sept. 1788
217	Mr. Seward	--	1787	Oct. 1788
218	Miss Griffiths	--	--	Oct. 1788
219	John Nelson	--	1774	Nov. 1788
220	Jeremiah Robertshaw	--	Feb. 1788	Nov. 1788
221	Harry Tarboton	--	Feb. 5, 1787	Nov. 1788

APPENDIX

	Name of Deceased	Age	Date of Death	Publication Date
222	Howel Harris & Mr. Watkins	--	--	Dec. 1788
223	Henry Foster	--	Apr. 12, 1787	Sept, Oct., Nov., Dec. 1788
224	Richard Russel	80	June 13, 1787	Dec. 1788
225	Ann Ritson	--	Mar. 23, 1788	Dec. 1788
226	Charles Spear	--	1786	Jan. 1789
227	Charles Steward	18	June 9, 1787	Jan. 1789
228	Matthew Errington	--	Feb. 5, 1788	Jan. 1789
229	Mary Beaumont	--	--	Feb. 1789
230	Nathaniel Norwall	--	1788	Feb. 1789
231	Bishop Gardiner	--	1555	Feb. 1789
232	Mr. King	--	1779	Mar. 1789
233	Rebecca Smith	--	1787	Mar. 1789
234	Mary Howard	--	1778	Apr. 1789
235	Miss Cockle	20	Sept. 26, 1788	Apr. 1789
236	Sarah Cadman	40	Aug. 30, 1788	Apr. 1789
237	John Harvey	--	--	May 1789
238	Mrs. Norman	--	1779	May 1789
239	Issac Shearing	21 Jan. 1778	--	June 1789
240	W.F. Esq.	--	Oct. 31, 1768	June 1789
241	Sarah Spirit	--	1788	June 1789
242	Ruth Hall	--	--	June 1789
243	Mrs. D. B.	60	Sept. 26, 1781	July, August 1789
244	Charles Spear	--	Dec. 25, 1786	July 1789
245	Simon Parsons	--	1789	July 1789
246	Miss C.B.	18	--	July 1789
247	Susannah Strong	--	--	Aug. 1789
248	Elizabeth Shacklock	32	Apr. 14, 1786	Sept., Oct., Nov. 1789
249	Jonathan Simpson	74	May 26, 1787	Sept. 1789
250	Mrs. C. Bretterg	22	May 31, 1601	Sept., Oct., Nov. 1789
251	Abishua Mayo	18	Oct. 30, 1784	Oct. 1789
252	John Stephens	21–22	June 10, 1789	Dec. 1789

APPENDIX

	Name of Deceased	Age	Date of Death	Publication Date
253	Hugh Pue	--	Sept. 7, 1788	Dec. 1789
254	Joseph Stones	3yrs. 5 mon.	May 14, 1789	Dec. 1789
255	William McCornock	--	1789	Jan. 1790
256	Matthew Lamplough	--	Mar. 31, 1789	Jan. 1790
257	Mr. D - an Apothecary	--	Apr. 1789	Jan. 1790
258	Dorothy Wright	--	May 14, 1789	Feb. 1790
259	M.W. - a backslider	--	--	Feb. 1790
260	Mrs. Trimnell	--	May 12, 1789	Feb. 1790
261	John Penrith	--	Nov. 4, 1786	Mar. 1790
262	Thomas Legge	71	Jan. 1787	Mar. 1790
263	Elizabeth Waller	19	June 1, 1787	Mar. 1790
264	Jane Nancarrow	--	June 29, 1788	Apr., May 1790
265	Eliza Bradburn's Son	3	1782	Apr. 1790
266	Elizabeth Richardson	--	Apr. 9, 1786	June 1790
267	Mary Mahony	--	Feb. 11, 1789	July 1790
268	Mrs. Mather	--	1789	July 1790
269	Thomas Plummer's Wife	--	1784	Aug. 1790
270	Villiers Duke of Buckingham	--	--	Aug. 1790
271	Samuel Newman	28	Jan. 25, 1789	Sept. 1790
272	Prudence Williams	--	1782	Oct. 1790
273	Elizabeth Flook	--	--	Nov. 1790
274	Cyrillus Lucaris	--	--	Oct., Nov. 1790
275	John Appleton	--	May 1, 1784	Dec. 1790
276	Elizabeth Mather	--	--	Dec. 1790
277	Martha Cook	--	1786	Jan. 1791
278	Hester Wells	29	Mar. 1789	Jan. 1791
279	Robert Windsor	86	Jan. 29, 1790	Feb. 1791
280	Mrs. Langridge	--	--	Feb. 1791

BIBLIOGRAPHY

Works of John Wesley

The Bicentennial Edition of the Works of John Wesley. Editor in chief, Frank Baker. Nashville: Abingdon, 1984.
———. Vol. 1: *Sermons I.* Edited by Albert Cook Outler. Nashville: Abingdon, 1984.
———. Vol. 2: *Sermons II.* Edited by Abert Cook Outler. Nashville: Abingdon, 1985.
———. Vol. 3: *Sermons III.* Edited by Albert Cook Outler. Nashville: Abingdon, 1986.
———. Vol. 4: *Sermons IV.* Edited by Albert Cook Outler. Nashville: Abingdon, 1987.
———. Vol. 7: *A Collection of Hymns for the Use of the People Called Methodists.* Edited by Franz Hildebrandt and Oliver Beckerlegge. Nashville: Abingdon, 1983.
———. Vol. 9: *The Methodist Societies I: History, Nature and Design.* Edited by Rupert E. Davies. Nashville: Abingdon, 1989.
———. Vol. 10: *The Methodist Societies: The Minutes of Conference.* Edited by Henry D. Rack. Nashville: Abingdon, 2011.
———. Vol. 11: *The Appeals to Men of Reason and Religion and Certain Open Letters.* Edited by Gerald R. Cragg. Nashville: Abingdon, 1989.
———. Vol. 12: *Doctrinal and Controversial Treatises I.* Edited by Randy L. Maddox. 2012.
———. Vol. 13: *Doctrinal and Controversial Treatises II.* Edited by Paul Wesley Chilcote and Kenneth J. Collins. Nashville: Abingdon, 2013.
———. Vol. 18: *Journals and Diaries I, 1735-38.* Edited by W. Reginald Ward and Richard P. Heitzenrater. Nashville: Abingdon, 1988.
———. Vol. 19: *Journals and Diaries II, 1738-43.* Edited by W. Reginald Ward and Richard P. Heitzenrater. Nashville: Abingdon, 1990.
———. Vol. 20: *Journals and Diaries III, 1743-53.* Edited by W. Reginald Ward and Richard P. Heitzenrater. Nashville: Abingdon, 1991.
———. Vol. 21: *Journals and Diaries IV, 1755-65.* Edited by W. Reginald Ward and Richard P. Heitzenrater. Nashville: Abingdon, 1992.
———. Vol. 22: *Journals and Diaries V, 1765-75.* Edited by W. Reginald Ward and Richard P. Heitzenrater. Nashville: Abingdon, 1993.
———. Vol. 23: *Journals and Diaries VI, 1776-1786.* Edited by W. Reginald Ward and Richard P. Heitzenrater. Nashville: Abingdon, 1995.

―――. Vol. 24: *Journals and Diaries VII, 1787-1791*. Edited by W. Reginald Ward and Richard P. Heitzenrater. Nashville: Abingdon, 2003.

―――. Vol. 25: *Letters I, 1721-39*. Edited by Frank Baker. Nashville: Abingdon, 1980.

―――. Vol. 26: *Letters II, 1740-55*. Edited by Frank Baker. Nashville: Abingdon, 1982.

Wesley, John. *The Arminian Magazine*. vols. 1-14. London: Printed for the Editor, January 1778-February 1791.

―――. *Cautions and Directions, Given to the Greatest Professors in the Methodist Societies*. London: n.d., 1762.

―――. *Explanatory Notes Upon the New Testament*. Repr. London: Epworth, 1954.

―――. *Explanatory Notes Upon the Old Testament* 3 vols. Repr. Salem: Schmul, 1975.

―――. *John Wesley's Prayer Book: The Sunday Service of the Methodists in North America*. Edited by James White. Repr. Akron: OSL Publications, 1991.

―――. *The Letters of the Rev. John Wesley, A.M.* Edited by John Telford. 8 vols. London: Epworth, 1931.

―――. *Primitive Physick: Or, an Easy and Natural Method of Curing Most Diseases*. Repr. Nashville: The United Methodist Publishing House, 1992.

―――. *Some Account of the Life and Death of Matthew Lee, Executed at Tyburn, October 11, 1752, in the 20th Year of His Age*. 2nd ed. London: n.d., 1752.

―――. *The Works of John Wesley*. Edited by Thomas Jackson. 14 vols. Repr. Grand Rapids: Baker, 2007.

Wesley, John, and Charles Wesley. *Hymns and Sacred Poems*. London: printed by W. Strahan and sold by James Hutton, Bookseller, 1740.

Works Originally Published before John Wesley's Death (1791)

à Kempis, Thomas. *The Imitation of Christ*. Edited by Paul Bechtel. Chicago: Moody, 1980.

Arndt, Johann. *Of True Christianity Four Books*. 2 vols. London: printed for D. Brown at the Black Swan and Bible without Temple-Bar; and J. Downing in Bartholomew-Close, near West-Smithfield, 1712-1714.

Augustine. "On the Trinity." In *Nicene and Post-Nicene Fathers*, edited by Philip Schaff, 3:17-228. Peabody, MA: Hendrickson, 1994.

Baxter, Richard. *The Dying Thoughts of the Reverend, Learned and Holy Mr. Richard Baxter*, edited by Benjamin Fawcett. Burslem: W. Joynson, 1815.

―――. *The Saints' Everlasting Rest*. Philadelphia: John Highlands, 1885.

Blackburne, Francis. *No Proof in the Scriptures of an Intermediate State of Happiness or Misery between Death and the Resurrection*. London: printed for S. Bladon in Pater-Noster-Row, 1756.

Bull, George. *Harmonia Apostolica: Or, Two Dissertations*. Repr. Oxford: John Henry Parker, 1842.

Butts, Thomas. "Letter to Charles Wesley." April 14, 1743. EMV Box 1 Letter 30. Methodist Archives and Research Centre. John Rylands Library.

Calvin, John. *Calvin: Institutes of the Christian Religion*, edited by John McNeill. 2 vols. Philadelphia: Westminster, 1960.

Caxton, William. "The Art and Craft to Know Well to Die." In *The English ars moriendi,*, edited by David Atkinson, 21-35. New York: Peter Lang, 1992.

BIBLIOGRAPHY

Certain Sermons or Homilies Appointed to Be Read in Churches in the Time of Queen Elizabeth of Famous Memory. Together with the Thirty-Nine Articles of Religion. Published by Authority, for the Use of Churches and Private Families London: printed for C. Hitch, and L. Hawes, 1757.

Cheyne, George. *An Essay of Health and Long Life*. London: Printed for George Strahan, 1724.

Coles, Elisha. *A Practical Discourse of God's Soveraignty*. 6th ed. London: printed for Nath. Hillier, at the Princes-Arms in Leaden-Hall-Street, over against St. Mary Axe, 1708.

Crooke, B. *Two Sermons Preach'd before the Condemn'd Criminals at Newgate, 1695*. London: Printed for Benj. Tooke, 1695.

Drayton, Thomas. *The Proviso or Condition of the Promises, the Strait, but the Straight-Way That Leadeth Unto Happiness Being the Substance of Two Sermons Preached at Wilton, March the First, 1656, Upon 2 Cor. 7.1*. London: Printed by Tho. Newcomb, 1657.

Gell, Robert. "Some Saints Not Without Sin for a Season, Sermon 20." In *An Essay toward the Amendment of the Last English Translation of the Bible*. London: Printed by R. Norton for Andrew Crook, 1659.

Hall, Joseph. *Meditations and Vows, Divine and Moral*. Repr. Berkeley: University of California Libraries, 1863.

Henry, Matthew. *Matthew Henry's Commentary on the Whole Bible*. Vol. 1. New York: Fleming H. Revell Company, n.d.

Hitchens, James. *A Short Account of the Death of Thomas Hitchens*. Bristol: Printed by Farley, 1747.

Law, Edmund. *Considerations on the Theory of Religion* Cambridge: J. Bentham, printer to the University, 1755.

Law, William. *A Practical Treatise upon Christian Perfection*. Repr. Whitefish, MT: Kessinger, 2006.

———. *A Serious Call to a Devout and Holy Life*. Repr. N.d.: Readaclassic, 2010.

"Letter (possibly to Charles Wesley)." November 11, 1738. EMV Box 3 Letter 142. Methodist Archives and Research Centre (John Rylands Library).

Lucas, Richard. *An Enquiry after Happiness*. London: Printed for W. Innys, 1717.

Malham, J. *Infant Salvation: An Essay to Prove the Salvation of All Who Die in Infancy with Answers to Objections*. London: Printed for W. Button, Newington Causey, 1793.

Mather, Cotton. *Victorina. A Sermon Preach'd, on the Decease and at the Desire, of Mrs. Katharin Mather, by Her Father. Whereunto There Is Added, a Further Account of That Young Gentlewoman, by Another Hand*. Boston: Printed by B. Green, for Daniel Henchman, 1717.

Mulso, Thomas *Callistus; or, The Man of Fashion. And Sophronius; or, The Country Gentleman. In Three Dialogues*. London: Printed for Benjamin White, 1768.

Ordinary of Newgate's Account, Old Bailey Proceedings Online. www.oldbaileyonline.org, version 8.0.

Perkins, William *A Salve for a Sicke Man*. In *The English ars moriendi*, edited by David Atkinson, 127–63. New York: Peter Lang, 1992.

Pugh, John. *Remarkable Occurrences in the Life of Jonas Hanway*. London: T. Cadell, Jun. and W. Davies in the Strand, 1798.

Ritchie, Elizabeth. "Handwritten Account of John Wesley's Last Days and Death." May 8, 1791. Lamplough Collection, Methodist Archives and Research Centre. John Rylands University Library.

Rossell, Samuel. *The Prisoner's Director: Compiled for the Instruction and Comfort of Persons under Confinement*. London: printed by J. Applebee, 1742.

Scougal, Henry. *The Life of God in the Soul of Man: Or, the Nature and Excellency of the Christian Religion*. London: printed for Thomas Bever, at the Hand and Star within Temple-Bar, 1702.

Shaw, Samuel. *Immanuel: Or, a Discovery of True Religion*. Repr. Boston: Printed by Rogers and Fowle, for J. Edwards in Cornhill, 1741.

Spinckes, Nathaniel. *The Sick Man Visited and Furnished with Instructions, Meditations and Prayers*. London: C. Rivington, 1731.

Taylor, Jeremy. "*Fides Formata* or, Faith Working by Love." In *The Whole Works of Jeremy Taylor*, 8: 284–302. London: Longman, Brown, Green, and Longmans, 1850.

———. *The Rule and Exercises of Holy Dying*. Repr. Whitefish, MT: Kessinger, 2007.

———. *The Rule and Exercises of Holy Living*. Repr. Whitefish, MT: Kessinger, 2007.

Taylor, John. *A Reply to the Reverend Mr. John Wesley's Remarks on the Scripture-Doctrine of Original Sin*. London: Printed and Sold by M. Waugh, 1767.

———. *The Scripture-Doctrine of Original Sin Proposed to Free and Candid Examination*. London: Printed for the author by J. Wilson at the Turk's-Head in Gracechurch-street, 1740.

Tillotson, John. *Fifteen Sermons on Several Subjects*. London: printed for Ri. Chiswell, 1702.

Told, Silas. "The Life of Silas Told." Repr. London: Epworth, 1954.

Watts, Isaac. "The Ruin and Recovery of Mankind." In *The Works of Isaac Watts*, 6: 47–185. London: John Barfield, 1811.

Wesley, Charles. *Manuscript Journal*. May 4, 1741. https://divinity.duke.edu/sites/default/files/documents/CW%20Manuscript%20Journal.pdf.

Wesley, Sally. "Sally Wesley to Charles Wesley." July 6, 1768. Wesley Family Papers 1/50, Methodist Archives and Research Centre. John Rylands University Library.

Wesley, Susanna. *Susanna Wesley: The Complete Writings*. Edited by Charles Wallace. New York: Oxford University Press, 1997.

Westminster Confession of Faith. Repr. Glasgow: Bell and Bain Ltd., 1990.

Whitefield, George. *A Letter from the Reverend Mr. George Whitefield, to the Reverend Mr. John Wesley, in Answer to His Sermon, Entitled Free-Grace*. Boston: printed by G. Rogers, for S. Kneeland and T. Green in Queen-street, J. Edwards and S. Eliot in Cornhill, 1740.

Willard, Samuel. *The Mourners Cordial against Excessive Sorrow*. Boston: printed by Benjamin Harris, and John Allen, 1691.

Woolnor, Henry. *The True Originall of the Soule Proving Both by Divine and Naturall Reason, That the Production of Mans Soule Is Neither by Creation nor Propagation, but a Certain Meane Way between Both*. London: Printed by T. Paine and M. Symmons, 1641.

Works Published after 1791

Allison, C. FitzSimons. "The Pastoral Cruelty of Jeremy Taylor's Theology." *Modern Churchman* 15 (1972) 123–131.

Anderson, E. Byron. "A Day of New Beginnings: Wesleyan Theologies of the New Birth, 1780 and 1989." *Wesleyan Theological Journal* 38 (2003) 230–50.

BIBLIOGRAPHY

Aries, Philippe. *Western Attitudes toward Death: From the Middle Ages to the Present.* Baltimore: The John Hopkins University Press, 1974.

Ashley, Matthew Paul. "Theology of Death and Resurrection in the Methodist Tradition." Thesis, Duke Divinity School, 2006.

Atkinson, David William. *The English ars moriendi.* Edited by Eckhard Bernstein. Renaissance and Baroque Studies and Texts 5. New York: Peter Lang, 1992.

Beaty, Nancy Lee. *The Craft of Dying: A Study in the Literary Tradition of the Ars Moriendi in England.* New Haven, CT: Yale University Press, 1970.

Beier, Lucinda McCray. "The Good Deaths in Seventeenth-Century England." In *Death, Ritual, and Bereavement,* edited by Ralph Houlbrooke, 43–61. London: Routledge, 1989.

Bell, Richard J. "Our People Die Well: Deathbed Scenes in John Wesley's Arminian Magazine." *Mortality* 10 (2005) 210–33.

Bowmer, John. "John Wesley's Philosophy of Suffering." *The London Quarterly and Holborn Review* (1959) 60–66.

Bryant, Barry E. "Original Sin." In *The Oxford Handbook of Methodist Studies,* edited by James E. Kirby, William J. Abraham, 522–39. Oxford: Oxford University Press, 2009.

Cannon, William Ragsdale. *The Theology of John Wesley.* New York: Abingdon-Cokesbury, 1946.

Carrier, E. Theodore. "Wesley's Views on Prayers for the Dead." *The Proceedings of the Wesley Historical Society* 1 (1898) 123–125.

Cecil, Robert. "Holy Dying: Evangelical Attitudes to Death." *History Today* 32 (1982) 30–34.

Chambers, Wesley A. "John Wesley and Death." In *John Wesley: Contemporary Perspectives,* edited by John Stacey, 150–61. London: Epworth, 1988.

Collins, Kenneth J. "Assurance." In *The Oxford Handbook of Methodist Studies,* edited by James E. Kirby and William J. Abraham, 602–17. Oxford: Oxford University Press, 2009.

———. "John Wesley and the Fear of Death as a Standard of Conversion." In *Conversion in the Wesleyan Tradition,* 56–68. Nashville: Abingdon, 2001.

———. *The Theology of John Wesley: Holy Love and the Shape of Grace.* Nashville: Abingdon, 2007.

Comper, Frances M. M., ed. *The Book of the Craft of Dying and Other Early English Tracts Concerning Death.* New York: Arno, 1977.

Cox, Leo G. "John Wesley's Concept of Sin." *Bulletin of the Evangelical Theological Society* 5 (1962) 8–24.

Cressy, David. *Birth, Marriage, and Death: Ritual, Religion, and the Life-Cycle in Tudor and Stuart England.* Oxford: Oxford University Press, 1997.

Cruickshank, Joanna. "Charles Wesley and the Construction of Suffering in Early English Methodism." Thesis, University of Melbourne, 2006.

Cunningham, Joseph. "John Wesley's Moral Pneumatology: The Fruits of the Spirit as Theological Virtues." *Studies in Christian Ethics* 24 (2011) 275–93.

Davies, Douglas. *The Theology of Death.* London: T. & T. Clark, 2008.

Dobson, Mary J. *Contours of Death and Disease in Early Modern England.* Cambridge: Cambridge University Press, 1997.

Dray, John. "Church and Chapel in a Cornish Mining Parish." *Evangel* 26 (2008) 48–61.

Duclow, Donald F. "'Ars Moriendi.'" In *Macmillan Encyclopedia of Death and Dying,* edited by Robert Kastenbaum, 36–41. New York: Thomson Gale, 2003.

Ebner, Dean. *Autobiography in Seventeenth-Century England*. The Hague: Mouton, 1971.
Fanestil, John. *Mrs. Hunter's Happy Death: Lessons on Living from People Preparing to Die*. New York: Doubleday, 2006.
Flew, R. Newton. *The Idea of Perfection*. London: Oxford University Press, 1934.
Ganske, Karl. "The Religion of the Heart and Growth in Grace." Thesis, University of Manchester, 2009.
Goodwin, Charles H. "Setting Perfection Too High: John Wesley's Changing Attitudes toward the 'London Blessing.'" *Methodist History* 36 (1998) 86–96.
———. "The Terrors of the Thunderstorm: Medieval Popular Cosmology and Methodist Revivalism." *Methodist History* 39 (2001) 99–107.
Greathouse, William M., and Paul M. Bassett. *Exploring Christian Holiness: The Historical Development*. Vol. 2. Kansas City: Beacon Hill, 1985.
Headley, Anthony J. *Family Crucible*. Eugene, OR: Wipf & Stock, 2010.
Heitzenrater, Richard. *The Elusive Mr. Wesley*. Vol. 1. Nashville: Abington, 1984.
Hindmarsh, D. Bruce. *The Evangelical Conversion Narrative*. Oxford: Oxford University Press, 2005.
———. "'My Chains Fell Off, My Heart Was Free': Early Methodist Conversion Narrative in England." *Church History* 68 (1999) 910–29.
Holifield, E. Brooks. *Health and Medicine in the Methodist Tradition*. New York: Crossroad, 1986.
Houlbrooke, Ralph, ed. *Death, Religion and the Family in England 1480 -1750*. Oxford: Clarendon, 1998.
———. *Death, Ritual, and Bereavement*. London: Routledge, 1989.
Johnson, W. Stanley. "Christian Perfection as Love for God." *Wesleyan Theological Journal* 18 (1983) 50–60.
Joling-van der Sar, Gerda J. "The Controversy between William Law and John Wesley." *English Studies* 87 (2006) 442–65.
Kliever, Lonnie D. "Claiming a Death of Our Own: Perspectives from the Wesleyan Tradition." In *Must We Suffer Our Way to Death*, 266–302. Dallas: Southern Methodist University Press, 1996.
Henry H. Knight, "Love and Freedom 'By Grace Alone' in Wesley's Soteriology: A Proposal for Evangelicals." In *Pneuma: The Journal of the Society for Pentecostal Studies* 24 (2002) 57–67.
Krymanski, Bernd. "We See a Ghost: Hogarth's Satire on Methodists and Connoisseurs." *Art Bulletin* 80 (1998) 292–310.
Lancaster, Sarah. "Happiness: A Word for Our Time." *Journal of Theology* 109 (2005) 31–44.
Lee, Hoo-Jung. "The Doctrine of the New Creation in the Theology of John Wesley." Thesis, Emory University, 1991.
Lindstrom, Harald. *Wesley and Sanctification*. Nappanee: Francis Asbury,1980.
Maddox, Randy L. "John Wesley on Holistic Health and Healing." *Methodist History* 46 (2007) 4–33.
———. *Responsible Grace: John Wesley's Practical Theology*. Nashville: Kingswood, 1994.
McGonigle, Herbert. "Arminius and Wesley on Original Sin." *European Explorations in Christian Holiness* no. 2 (2001) 96–108.
———. *Sufficient Saving Grace*. Cumbria: Paternoster, 2001.
McKenzie, Andrea. *Tyburn's Martyrs*. London: Hambledon Continuum, 2007.
McManners, John. *Death and the Enlightenment*. Oxford: Oxford University Press, 1985.

McPherson, Joseph D. *Our People Die Well: Glorious Accounts of Early Methodists at Death's Door*. Bloomington, IN: AuthorHouse, 2008.

Mesimore, Gregory Scott. "The Way of Salvation: A Comparative Analysis of John Wesley's and Jeremy Taylor's Doctrine of Sanctification." Thesis, Trinity Evangelical Divinity School, 1984.

Morgan, Jim. "The Burial Question in Leeds in the Eighteenth and Nineteenth Centuries." In *Death, Ritual, and Bereavement*, edited by Ralph Houlbrooke, 95–104. London: Routledge, 1989.

Naglee, David Ingersoll. *From Font to Faith: John Wesley on Infant Baptism and the Nurture of Children*. New York: Peter Lang, 1987.

Neff, Blake J. "John Wesley and John Fletcher on Entire Sanctification: A Metaphoric Cluster Analysis,. Thesis, Bowling Green State University, 1982.

Newport, Kenneth G. C. "George Bell, Prophet and Enthusiast." *Methodist History* 35 (1997) 95–105.

Newport, Kenneth G. C., and Gareth Lloyd. "George Bell and Early Methodist Enthusiasm: A New Manuscript Source from the Manchester Archives." *Bulletin of the John Rylands University Library of Manchester* 80 (1998) 89–101.

Noble, Thomas A. "John Wesley as a Theologian: An Introduction." *Evangelical Review of Theology* 34 (2010) 238–57.

Oden, Thomas. *John Wesley's Scriptural Christianity*. Grand Rapids: Zondervan, 1994.

Ott, Philip W. "Medicine as Metaphor: John Wesley on Therapy of the Soul." *Methodist History* 33 (1995) 178–91.

Porter, Roy. "Death and the Doctors in Georgian England." In *Death, Ritual, and Bereavement*, edited by Ralph Houlbrooke, 77–94. London: Routledge, 1989.

Prosser, Barbara. "'An Arrow from a Quiver' Written Instruction for a Reading People: John Wesley's *Arminian Magazine* (January 1778—February 1791)." Thesis, University of Manchester, 2008.

Rack, Henry. "Evangelical Endings: Deathbeds in Evangelical Biography." *Bulletin of the John Rylands University Library of Manchester* 74 (1992) 39–56.

———. *Reasonable Enthusiast*. 3rd ed. London: Epworth, 2002.

Rainey, David. "John Wesley's Doctrine of Salvation in Relation to His Doctrine of God." Thesis, King's College, University of London, 2006.

Rakestraw, Robert. "John Wesley as a Theologian of Grace." *Journal of Evangelical Theological Society* 27 (1984) 193–203.

Rawnsley, Willingham Franklin. *Highways and Byways in Lincolnshire*. London: Macmillan and Company, 1914.

Reasoner, Victor P. "Assurance or Presumption? Early Attempts to Reconstruct Methodist Doctrine: 1803–1809." *Wesleyan Theological Journal* 44 (2009) 103–19.

Reed, Rodney L. "Calvin, Calvinism, and Wesley: The Doctrine of Assurance in Historical Perspective." *Methodist History* 32 (1993) 31–43.

Rivers, Isabel. "John Wesley and Religious Biography" In *Bulletin of the John Rylands University Library of Manchester* 85 (2003) 209–26.

Runyon, Theodore. *The New Creation*. Nashville: Abington, 1998.

Ruth, Lester. *Early Methodist Life and Spirituality*. Nashville: Kingswood, 2005.

Schmidt, Martin. *John Wesley: A Theological Biography*. 2 vols. Nashville: Abingdon, 1973.

Schneider, A. Gregory. "The Ritual of Happy Dying among Early American Methodists." *Church History* 56 (1987) 348–63.

BIBLIOGRAPHY

Smith, Timothy L. *Whitefield and Wesley on the New Birth*. Grand Rapids: Francis Asbury Press of Zondervan, 1986.

Southey, Robert. *The Life of Wesley and the Rise and Progress of Methodism*. 2 vols. Edited by Maurice H. Fitzgerald.Oxford: Oxford University Press, 1925.

Stannard, David E. *The Puritan Way of Death: A Study in Religion, Culture and Social Change*. New York: Oxford University Press, 1977.

Stark, David. "The Peculiar Doctrine Committed to Our Trust: Ideal and Identity in the First Wesleyan Holiness Revival, 1758–1763." Thesis, The University of Manchester, 2011.

Thomas, Keith. "Fame and the Afterlife." In *The Ends of Life: Roads to Fulfilment in Early Modern England*, 226–67. Oxford: Oxford University Press, 2009.

Tyerman, Luke. *The Life and Times of the Rev. John Wesley, M.A.* 3 vols. London: Hodder and Stoughton, 1880.

Tyson, John R. *Charles Wesley on Sanctification*. Grand Rapids: Francis Asbury, 1986.

———. "Sin, Self and Society: John Wesley's Hamartiology Reconsidered." *Asbury Theological Journal* 44 (1989) 77–90.

Van Reyk, William George Anthony. "Christian Ideals of Manliness During the Period of the Evangelical Revival, C. 1730 to C. 1840." Thesis, University of Oxford, Wadham College, 2007.

Verhey, Allen. *The Christian Art of Dying: Learning from Jesus*. Grand Rapids: Eerdmans, 2011.

Vogt, Christopher. *Patience, Compassion, Hope and the Christian Art of Dying Well*. Lanham: Rowman & Littlefield, 2004.

Walsh, John. "Methodism at the End of the Eighteenth Century." In *A History of the Methodist Church in Great Britain*, edited by Rupert E. Davies and Gordon Rupp, 276–315. London: Epworth, 1965.

Weber, Theodore R. "Recovering the Political Image of God." In *Politics in the Order of Salvation*, 391–420. Nashville: Kingswood, 2001.

Williams, Colin W. *John Wesley's Theology Today*. Nashville: Abingdon, 1960.

Wilson, D. Dunn. *Many Waters Cannot Quench: A Study of the Sufferings of Eighteenth-Century Methodism and Their Significance for John Wesley and the First Methodists*. London: Epworth, 1969.

Wind, Barry. "Hogarth's *Industry and Idleness* Reconsidered." *Print Quarterly* 14 (1997) 235–51.

Wiseman, Luke. *Charles Wesley: Evangelist and Poet*. London: Epworth, 1932.

Wood, Arthur Skevington. "Love Excluding Sin: Wesley's Doctrine of Sanctification." In *Wesley Fellowship, 'Occasional Paper' No 1*, 1–24. Moorleys, Ilkeston, 1986.

Yrigoyen, Charles. "'I Was in Prison and You Visited Me': The Prison Ministry of John and Charles Wesley and the Early Methodists." *Evangelical Journal* 29 (2011) 11–23.

www.ingramcontent.com/pod-product-compliance
Lightning Source LLC
Chambersburg PA
CBHW031359230426
43670CB00006B/592